IMAGES
of America

THE MAD RIVER VALLEY

IMAGES
of America

THE MAD RIVER VALLEY

John and Ellie Hilferty

ARCADIA
PUBLISHING

ISBN 978-0-7385-3728-3

Published by Arcadia Publishing,
Charleston, South Carolina

Printed in the United States of America

Library of Congress Catalog Card Number: 2004113781

For all general information, contact Arcadia Publishing:
Telephone 843-853-2070
Fax 843-853-0044
E-mail sales@arcadiapublishing.com
For customer service and orders:
Toll-free 1-888-313-2665

Visit us on the Internet at www.arcadiapublishing.com

Contents

ACKNOWLEDGMENTS

Every history of a community of neighbors has a thousand authors—from the local collector who patiently chronicles events and genealogies since the first day of settlement, to each and every resident who kept a family tree or deposited old photographs in a shoebox. It is from all these sources that these fine photographic records of the Mad River Valley are delivered. The historical societies of Warren, Waitsfield, Fayston, Duxbury, and Moretown are to be thanked for the major supply, along with the Warren Library.

The following individuals and associations not only contributed material, but many of them, possessing vast knowledge of their environs, also helped to pinpoint and identify those sometimes-mysterious pieces of evidence where names, dates, and places were incompletely or haphazardly recorded: Ethan Bisbee, Anne Wallis-Bull, Lester Cameron, Mark A. Case, Frena Cutler, Alice DeLong, Howard Ferris, Sally Fisher, Eric Friedman, Hadley Gaylord, Green Mountain Valley School, Rick Haynes, Al Hobart, Jane Hobart, Jennifer Howard, Denise Gabaree, Evelyn Goss, Ozzie Goss, Katherine Hartshorn, Fletcher Joslin, Stephen Joslin, Joslin Memorial Library, Zelda Lavanway, Mad River Glen, Fred Messer, Josette Messer, Cindy Mumford, Patricia Moulton, Stanley Orr, Dwight Palmer, Cedric Reagan, Dolly Reagan, Mary Reagan, Sandy Reagan, Sandra Reilly, Annette Schultz, Michael Sherman, Gary Simpson, Jack Smith, Sugarbush Resort, J. J. Toland, Helen Utton, the Valley Players, the *Valley Reporter*, and Vermont Historical Society.

Special thanks go to Waitsfield and Champlain Valley Telecom, and to the several authors who over several years have been responsible for the ongoing publication of a splendid series of local histories.

BIBLIOGRAPHY

Snapshots, Waitsfield, Vermont 1789–1989. Waitsfield, Vermont: Iota Press, July 1989.

Bushnell Jones, Matt. *History of Waitsfield, 1782–1908*. Lowell, Massachusetts: Courier-Citizen Company, 1909.

Coolidge, A. J. and J. B. Mansfield. *History and Description of New England*. Boston, Massachusetts: Austin J. Coolidge, 1860.

Goss Billings, Lydia. "Brief History of Moretown 1963." Compilation, 1963.

Reagan, Mary. "Brief History of Moretown, Vermont for the Celebration of Moretown's Heritage and St. Patrick's Church Centennial 1982." Compilation, 1982.

Hartshorn, Katherine. *Commemoration of Warren's Bicentennial, 1789–1989*. Waterbury, Vermont: Buy Monthly Publishing, 1989.

Atwood, R. E. "The Vermont Flood, November 1927." Vermont Historical Society Compilation, 1927.

INTRODUCTION

Their names were Holy Writ, assigned from Biblical Scripture: Rachel, Keziah, Abigail, Benjamin, Ebenezer, Seth, Ira, Gabriel, Alonzo, and Lydia.

However, they were mill workers, students, farmers, shopkeepers, loggers, cooks, ministers, doctors, and parents with dawn-to-dusk workdays and straight-ahead goals in a promised land, a sweet little valley they called Mad River. The valley was 20 miles long, half of that wide, and in its cup held a narrow stream that began in V-shaped Granville Gulf.

This was apparently all the expanse that Gen. Benjamin Wait, Seth Munson, the Hazeltines, and others needed to settle down in. They could say in the 1790s, as we say today, "With each twist in a dirt road, few places on earth can offer so many different gratifying scenes on so many different days." Western prairies, skyscraper cities, cookie-cutter suburbs, and even mountain peaks can stretch for monotonous miles.

In the Mad River Valley, settlers saw, as we do, heavy morning fog clearing, sweeping itself broom-like over the river, vanishing in a warmed-up field; the sun's horizontal beam stabbing the wall of an old barn, stretching the shadow of a maple tree, or sending up diamonds from a snow-filled pasture. They saw, as we still do, twilight's purple cast, the tiny prick of a lamp glowing from a window on a mountainside, and a night so black the stars appear as millions.

It is amazing that what the first farmers found in this valley has been so gently handed down and commended to all who followed. They gave us a river and fields protected and unsullied, villages that remain quiet and unhurried. Between the time of the settlers and the present, this was not always so. People yielded to man's natural instinct to mess things up in order to make a living, before finding the means to restore the valley to its perfection.

This book is divided into five chapters: "The Lay of the Land," "Learning," "Making a Living," "People and Places," and the last chapter, a hopefully happy receptacle for everything else, "Good Times." These are photographs that trace from the history of cameras to the present. So, what occurred before 1850 is not recorded, but still seen vividly in the unchanged architecture of many buildings, mostly homes. Of the structures that are gone, the camera left a record. The structures are the mills, numbering close to 50, employing hundreds of men, lining what then was a hardworking river with dams, ponds, and channels, forcing hydro-blasts upon huge wooden paddle wheels, turning gears and machinery, making a living.

"The Lay of the Land" takes advantage of Vermont's unique topography, rugged cliffs, and hillsides that peer down on towns and pastures. The old camera obscura views are mostly wide open and reflective of the forest removal, the clear-cutting of lumber in the 19th century, particularly when 70 percent of the woodland in Vermont was laid bare. This chapter also contains some photographs showing the consequences of living or working too close to a river that often becomes *really* Mad.

"Learning" defies our perception of the connotations of the word rural, where things are considered to be less, not more. Today, the five towns that comprise the valley (Warren, Waitsfield, Fayston, Moretown, and Duxbury) are served by six public schools, including Harwood Union, the private Green Mountain Valley School, and a smattering of preschools, held mostly in homes.

We must stretch our thoughts to envision a valley in the 1800s with about 50 schools operating at various times. For example, there were 15 school districts in Moretown, 8 in Duxbury, 10 in Fayston, 7 in Waitsfield, and 12 in Warren. These were cheaply built one- and two-room wooden structures that had a wood stove, an outhouse, and as many as eight grades and one or two underpaid teachers in each.

Population shifts within the districts caused some of these buildings to be moved by oxen down the road or around a bend; proving that the ancestral stories of kids walking several miles each day to "get learned" are basically true.

"Making a Living" deals with commerce, what economists today call our gross domestic product. Included in this chapter are photographs of the logging industry, road building, stone quarries, mills, farms, and stores. The lumbermills, gristmills, cider mills, clapboard mills, box mills, and sawmills proliferated on the Mad River and its tributaries, but most likely, not a single one of these workshops could pass the zoning and environmental tests we impose today.

Farming in the Mad River Valley also went through a couple of major phases. In the early 19th century, sheep dominated the agricultural scene. In 1826, sheep outnumbered cows by nearly six to one; by 1908 only 113 sheep remained, and 1,843 cows ruled the pastures.

The demise of the sheep industry due to market shifts caused many farms to move from their upland sites down to the valleys and hollows. Today, hikers stumble over old stone fences and cellar holes in the reborn groves of trees. The emphasis on milk, cheese, and dairy cows that followed continues to this day, though the numbers of farms have shrunk in the valley to only a few.

This brings us to a 25-year period encompassing four far-reaching events that produced the most profound changes in the valley. The first was the cataclysmic flood of 1927, which destroyed most of the water-powered mills and many roads, bridges, and lives. That was followed by the stock market crash of 1929 and the ensuing Great Depression. Subsequently, World War II arrived and half of the valley's young men went off to see the world in a uniform; when they returned they brought with them new ideas, including plans to develop ski resorts locally. That development resulted in an economic boom the likes of which their progenitors would never quite believe.

First came Mad River Glen in 1948, followed by Sugarbush and Glen Ellen. The latter two became one, and attracted to the once-sleepy, laid-back valley a glittering array of entertainment superstars and an assortment of urban-dwelling flatlanders. People took to the slopes, and other tourists began visiting the area's many old farmhouses, which were repaired and kept in good condition by the people who loved them. Combined with their beautiful surroundings, the farmhouses became so attractive they spun off another industry: weddings.

Few other tourist areas have held so fast to tradition like this valley. Old general stores still peddle oil lamps, quilts, candles, pickles and preserves, udder balm, needles and thread, sleds and toboggans, flannel shirts, and cumbersome snow boots.

Most of all and best of all, the scenery comes free, and it all connects in the string of time with the people and places whose photographs are in this book.

One

The Lay of the Land

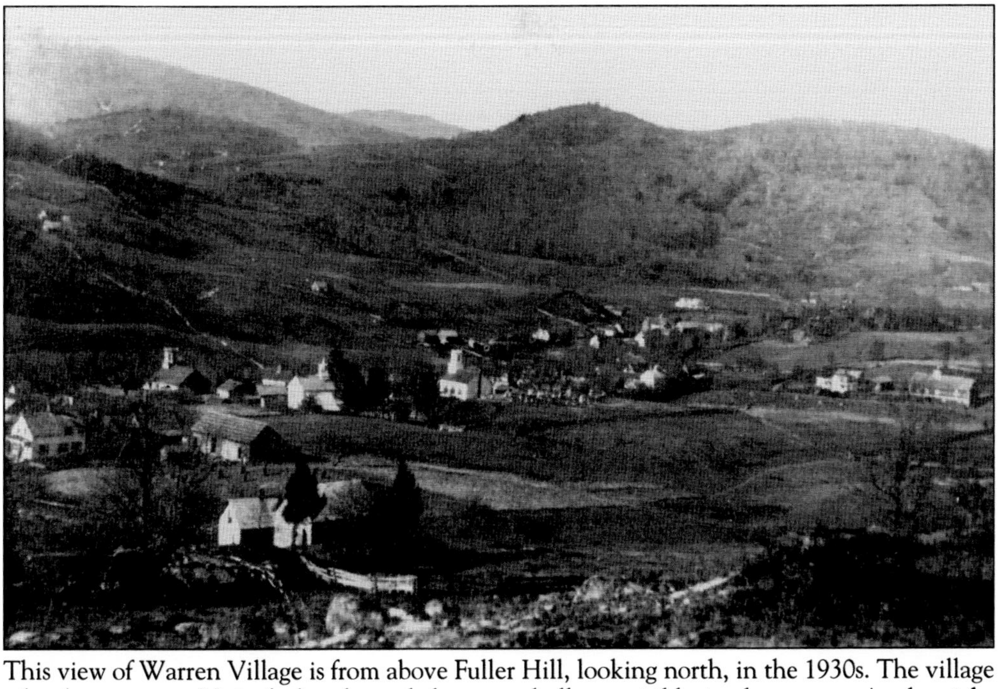

This view of Warren Village is from above Fuller Hill, looking north, in the 1930s. The village school, cemetery, United church, and the town hall are visible in the center. At the right center is the George Long-Martin Farm on the Fuller Hill Road. The farms and other acreage over the years were derived from an original land grant on November 9, 1780. (Courtesy of Katherine Hartshorn.)

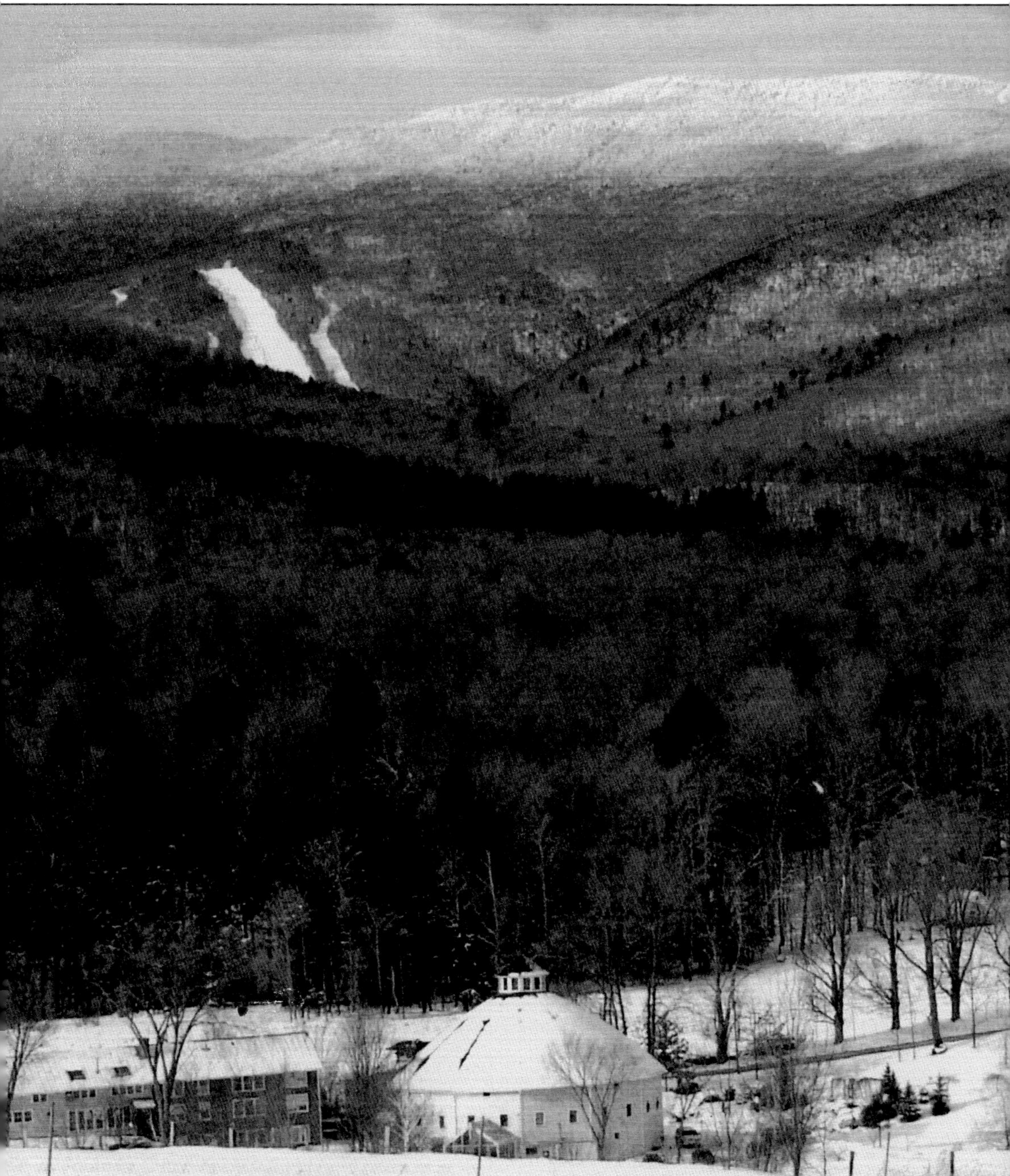

The 19th-century Joslin Farm, in the foreground, and the ski resorts of Sugarbush and Mad River Glen, in the far background, are a photographic abstract of two centuries of settlement of the Mad River Valley. Farms and their well-tended landscapes were and still remain at the heart of what the area represents. Skiing and its attendant tourism are what rejuvenated and kept alive the valley's vibrancy, including the many farms that became tourist attractions.

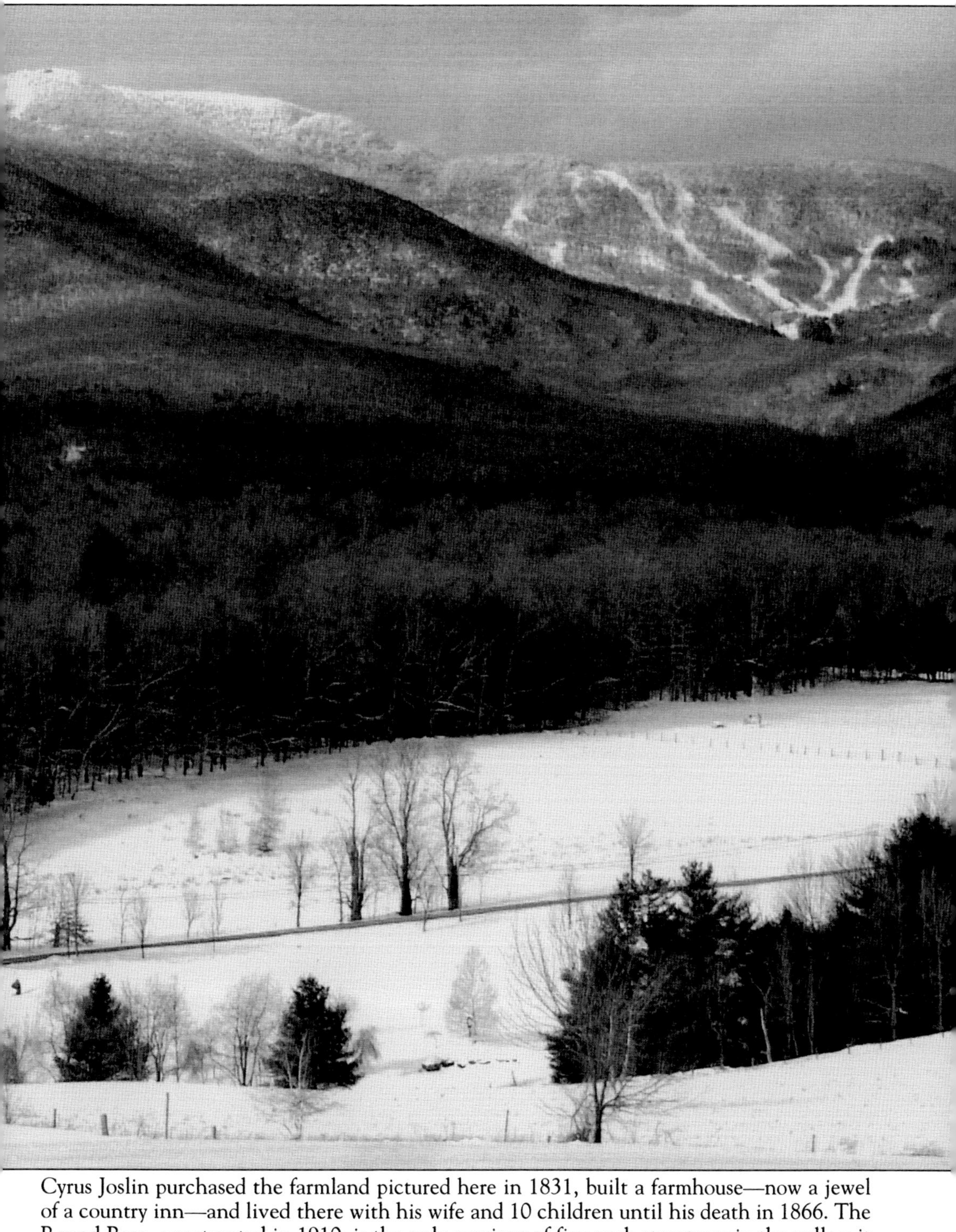

Cyrus Joslin purchased the farmland pictured here in 1831, built a farmhouse—now a jewel of a country inn—and lived there with his wife and 10 children until his death in 1866. The Round Barn, constructed in 1910, is the only survivor of five such structures in the valley; it is maintained now for weddings and several cultural events. (Photograph by Ellie Hilferty.)

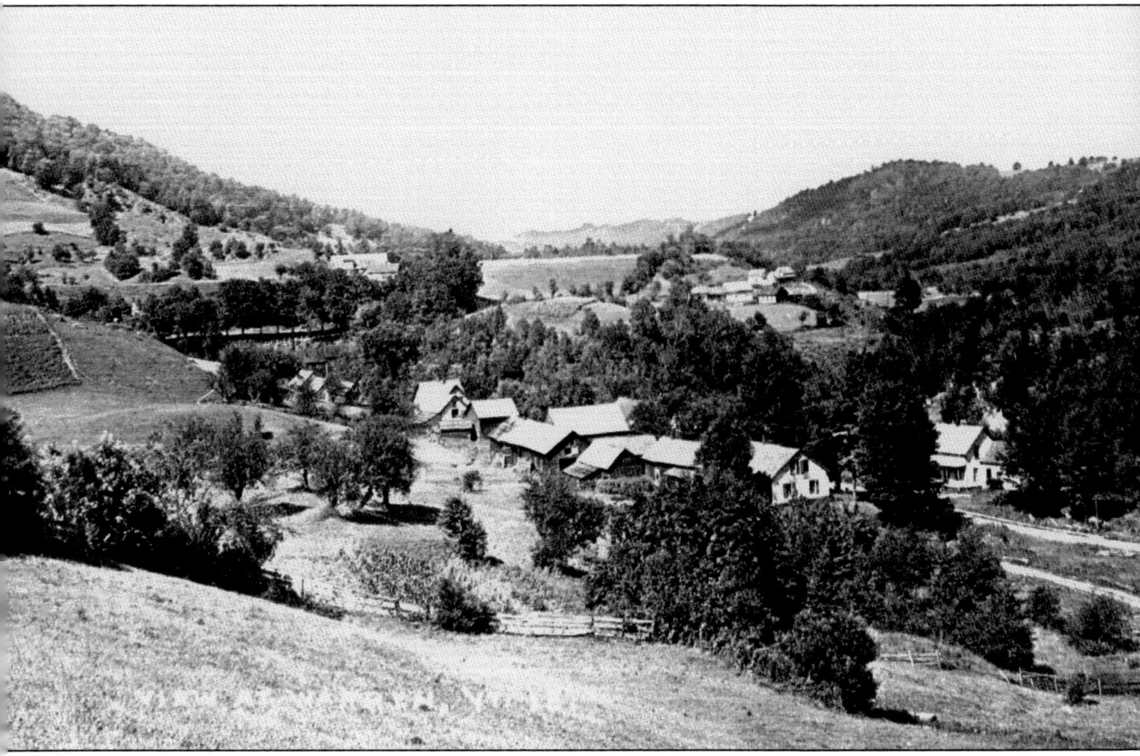

This landscape of Warren Village shows the Ulie Austin Farm, viewed from a field above what is now Trout Hollow, a development of houses at the site of an old mill yard. The buildings in the foreground are the Austin Homestead house and barns, next to the home of Emma Ford, who was the town clerk in Warren for many years. Like Waitsfield and Moretown, Warren was originally settled uphill in East Warren, at the intersection of Roxbury Mountain Road and East Warren Road. Not until the many mills began operating on the Mad River and its tributaries did settlement occur in the village. The pace of building today may not have increased from that of 100 or 200 years ago. In 2003, for instance, only nine buildings were constructed in Warren. (Courtesy of Katherine Hartshorn.)

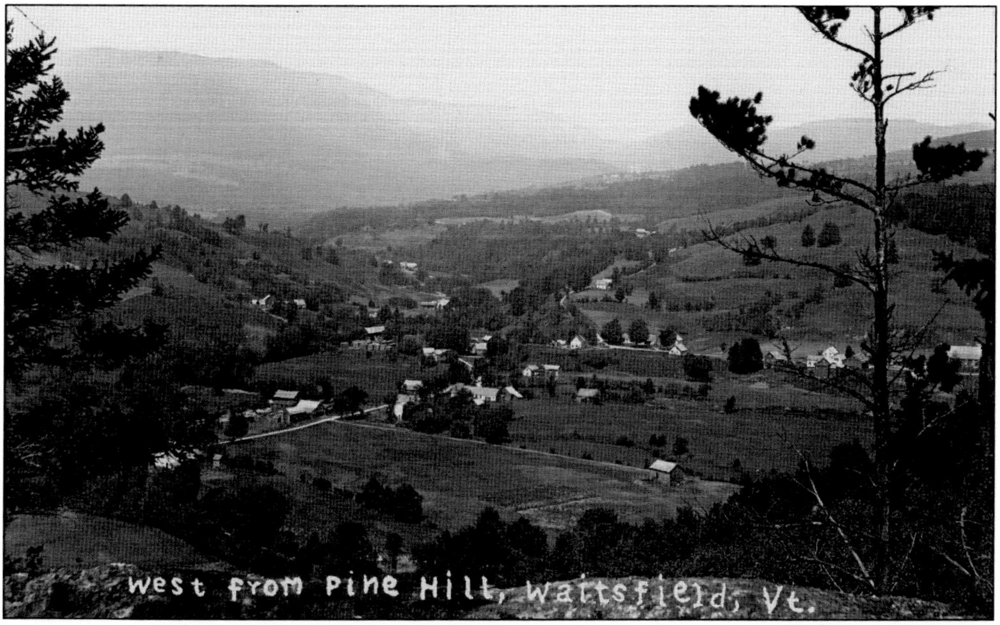

This is a view of Waitsfield from Pine Hill, looking west. Note the many bare spots on the hills. Vermont in 1900 was estimated to be only 30 percent forested and 70 percent open land. This was the result of logging, uphill farming, and the mining of potash, an early commercial ore used to make soap. Sheep farming was paramount in the valley until 1846, when the wool tariff was lifted, drastically lowering prices for wool. (Courtesy of Waitsfield Historical Society.)

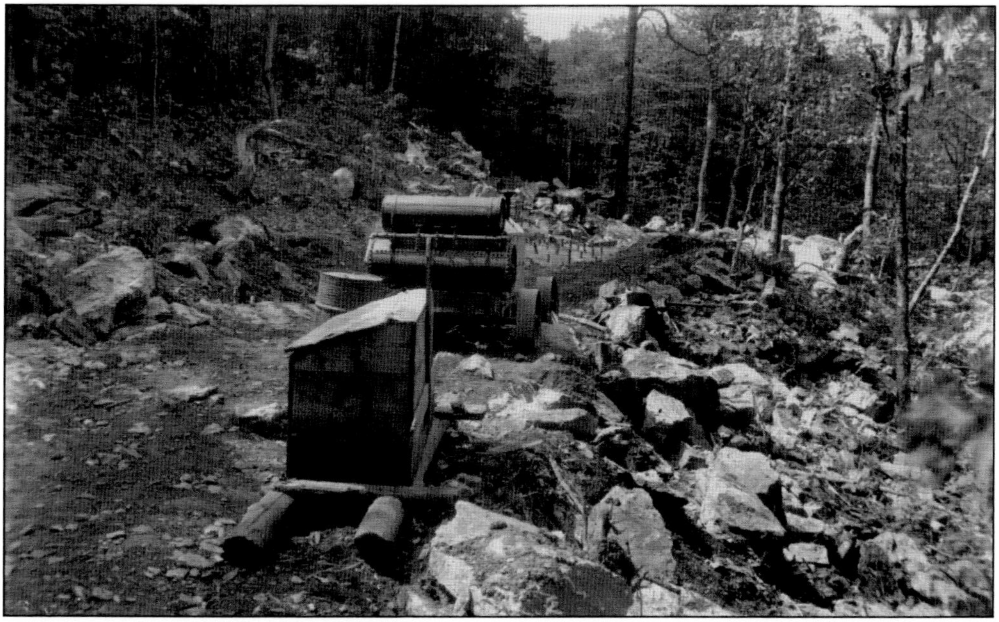
The construction of the McCullough Turnpike (Route 17), which opened in 1957, enabled skiers to more easily get to Mad River Glen, and also provided a road through the heights of the Appalachian Gap. The building of the road, up steep hills, was understandably difficult. Fayston is said to have the highest average elevation of any town in Vermont. (Courtesy of Fayston Historical Society.)

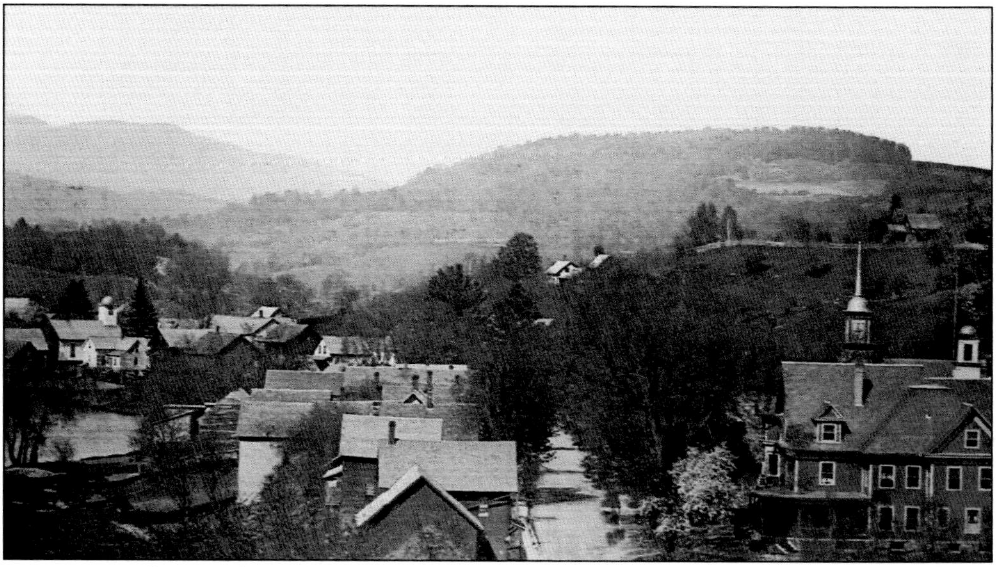

Moretown Village in the early 1900s had many homes and shops on Main Street, but several were destroyed in the 1927 flood, including the three buildings in the center foreground, which stood just a few hundred feet from the Mad River. On the right is the Ward family mansion, constructed in the early 1900s and referred to as the Big House. In the mid-1920s, the population of Moretown had been reduced to a little more than 900 persons, and dropped even more in the two decades following, reaching a low of 375 in 1940. (Courtesy of Moretown Historical Society.)

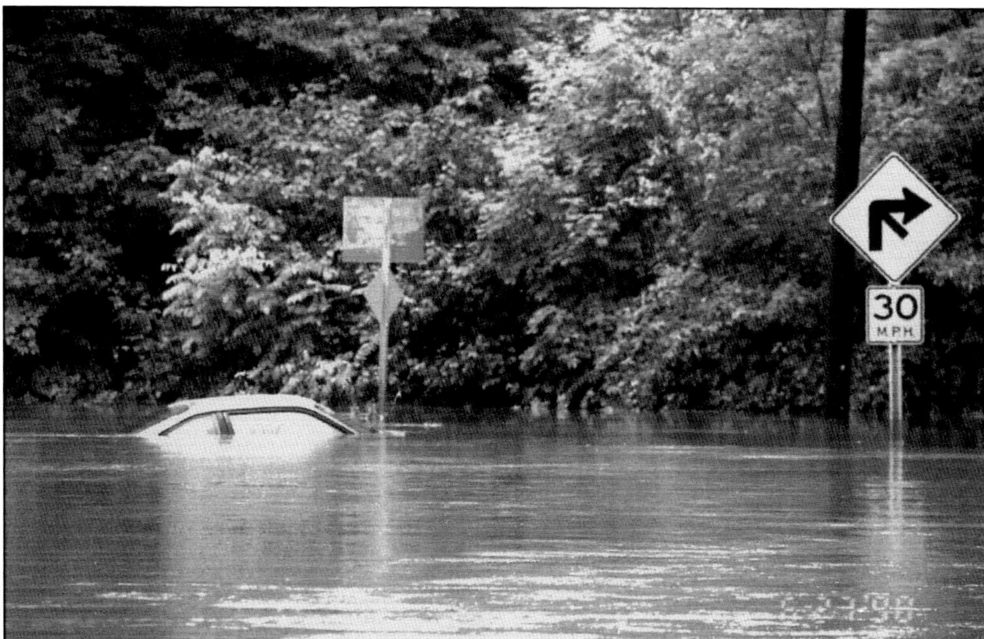

After weeks of heavy spring rain, a deluge of up to five inches fell on the Mad River Valley on June 27, 1998. This flood was exceeded in the 20th century only by the 1927 and 1938 floods. Pictured is the roof of a Volkswagen at the bend in Route 100B just north of the Moretown Village Cemetery. (Photograph by Ellie Hilferty.)

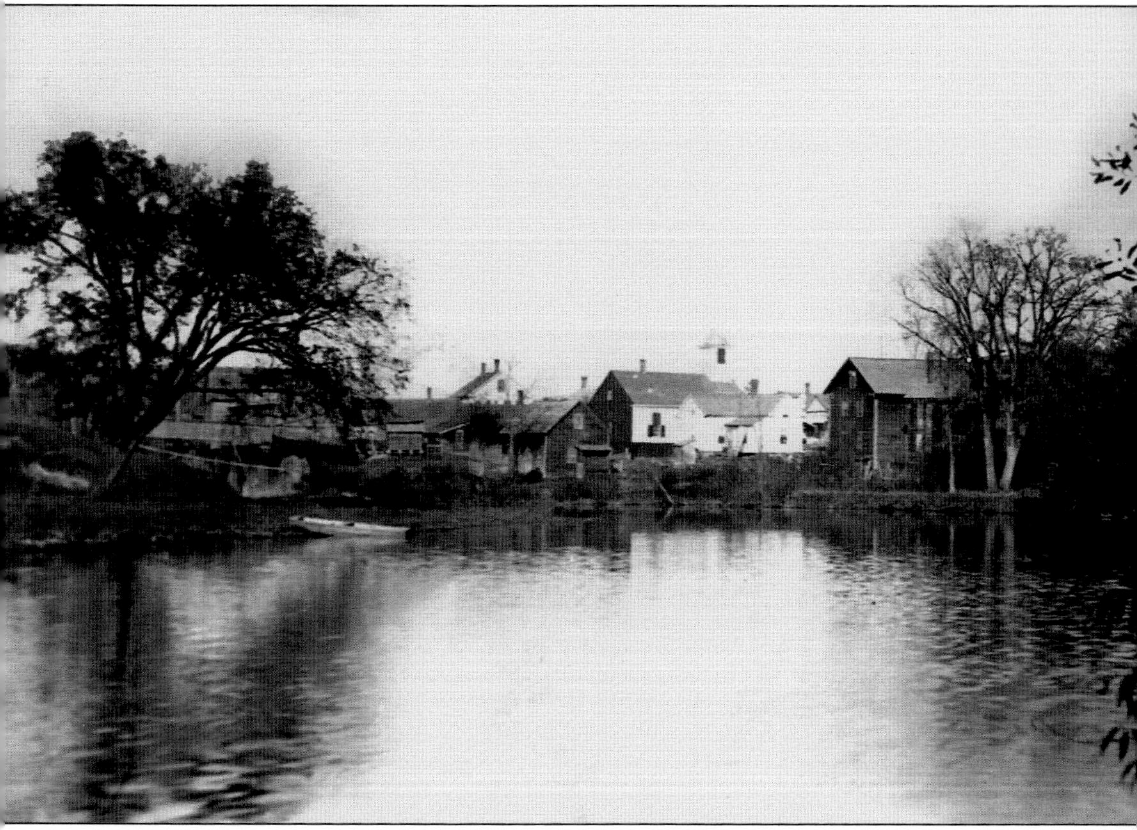

In the early 20th century, a large pond developed in the middle of Moretown Village; it was created by the dam at the Ward Clapboard Mill downstream. When the dam broke at the water-powered mill, the pond disappeared. In the late 1800s, there were many of these ponds created by mill dams along the Mad River. The ponds became recreation areas used for ice skating in winter and boating and swimming in the summer, and also served as water storage areas for the mills. The major recreational pastimes in the area today are fishing and kayaking, the latter being popular in the rapids area north of the town cemetery and continuing to the village swimming hole adjacent to the site of the old creamery on Main Street. This part of the river is also a favorite for photographers, because of the rapids and large boulders. (Courtesy of Moretown Historical Society.)

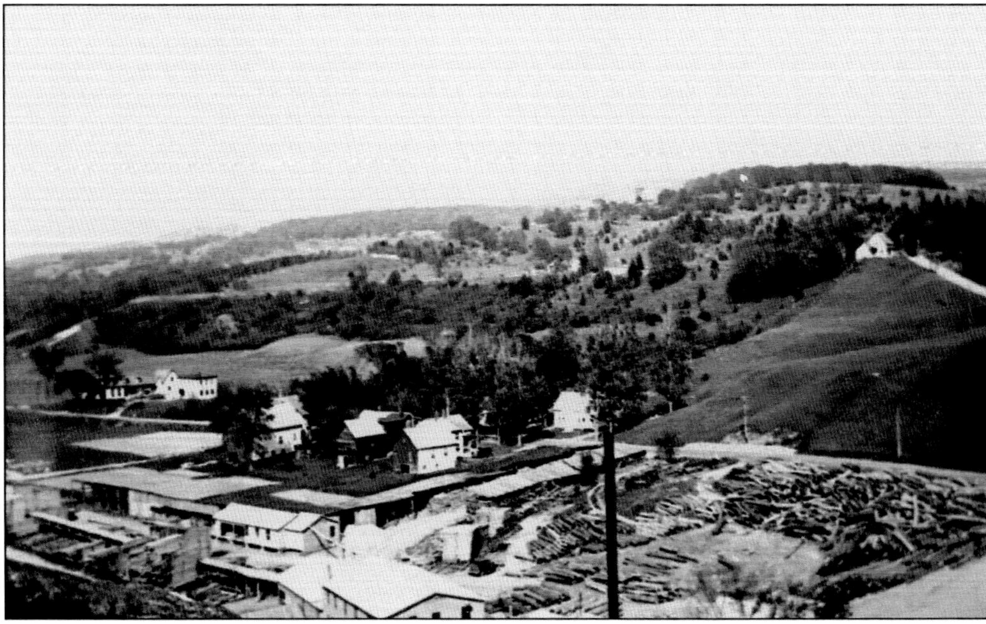

This scene and the next two views of Moretown Village were photographed from the ledges on the west side of the Mad River, a view which today is obscured by trees. Looking toward the northeast, one can see the lumberyard and what is now Route 100B (or Main Street) in Moretown. (Courtesy of Moretown Historical Society.)

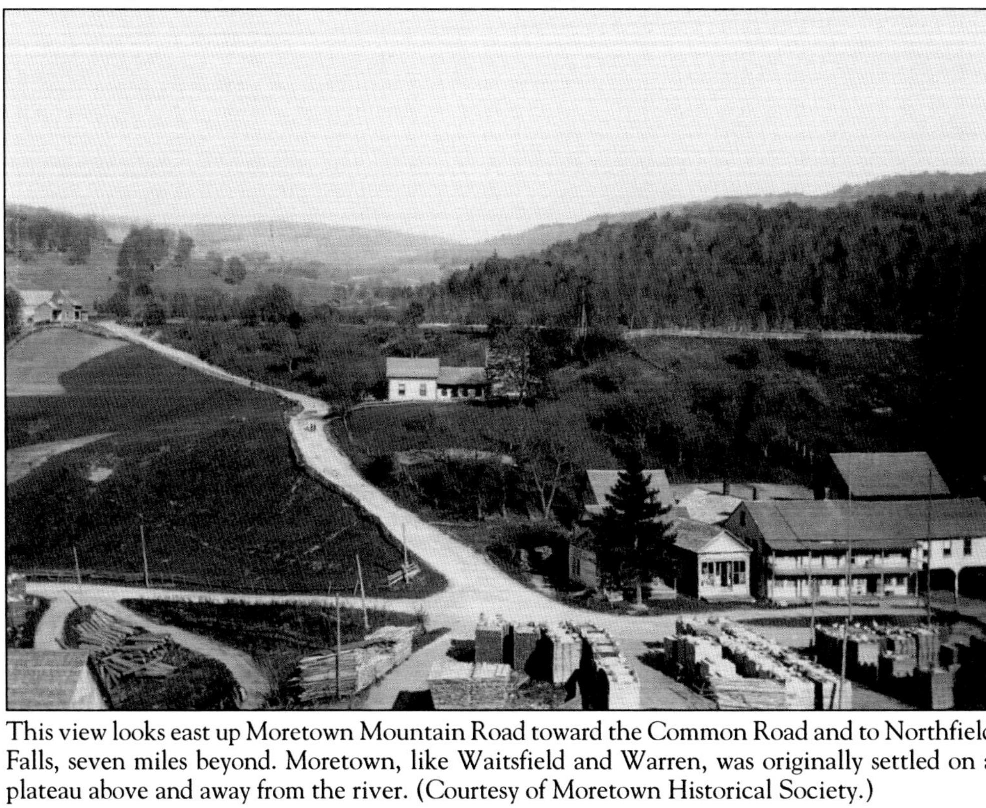

This view looks east up Moretown Mountain Road toward the Common Road and to Northfield Falls, seven miles beyond. Moretown, like Waitsfield and Warren, was originally settled on a plateau above and away from the river. (Courtesy of Moretown Historical Society.)

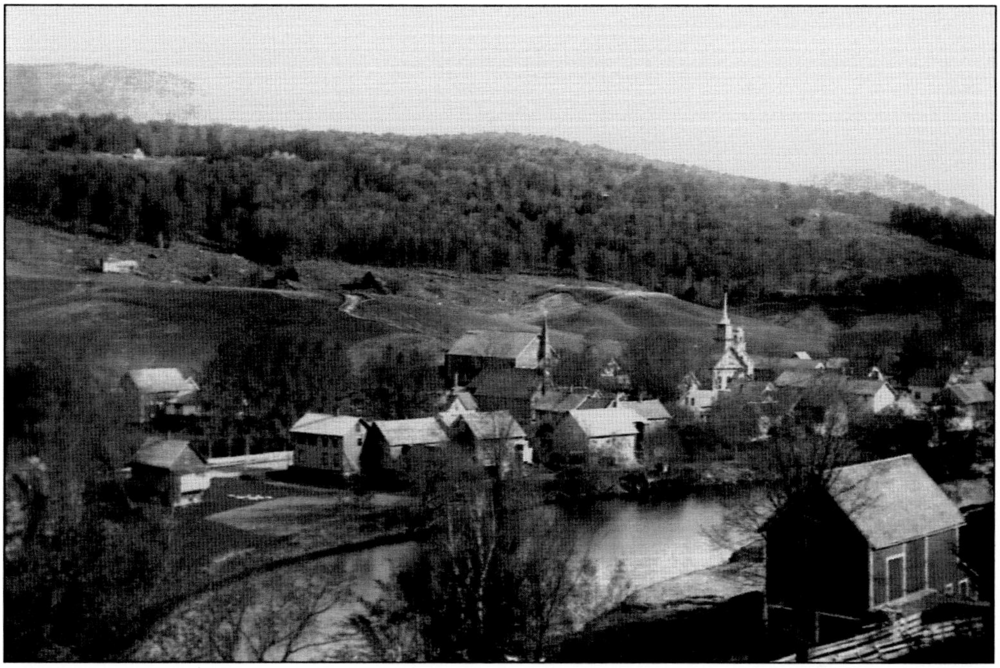

This is a view toward the southeast. Note the barren hillsides where trees had been clear cut for lumbering. Much of Vermont's forests were denuded in the late 1800s. Logging was the first industry in the state, and though Vermont was basically an agriculturally based economy, it was augmented by the many mill industries lying along the river. (Courtesy of Moretown Historical Society.)

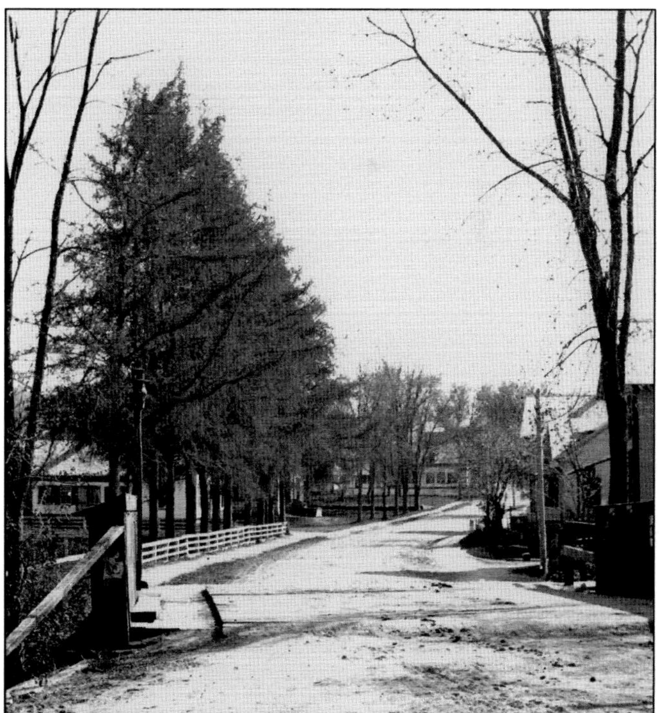

This image was taken facing south down Main Street (Route 100B) in Moretown from the small bridge over Doctors' Brook, just south of the post office. Taking away the grove of tamarack trees on the left and paving the road with asphalt would give you much the same scene as exists today. Route 100B is the only north–south thoroughfare connecting the Mad River Valley with Montpelier, the state capital. (Courtesy of Moretown Historical Society.)

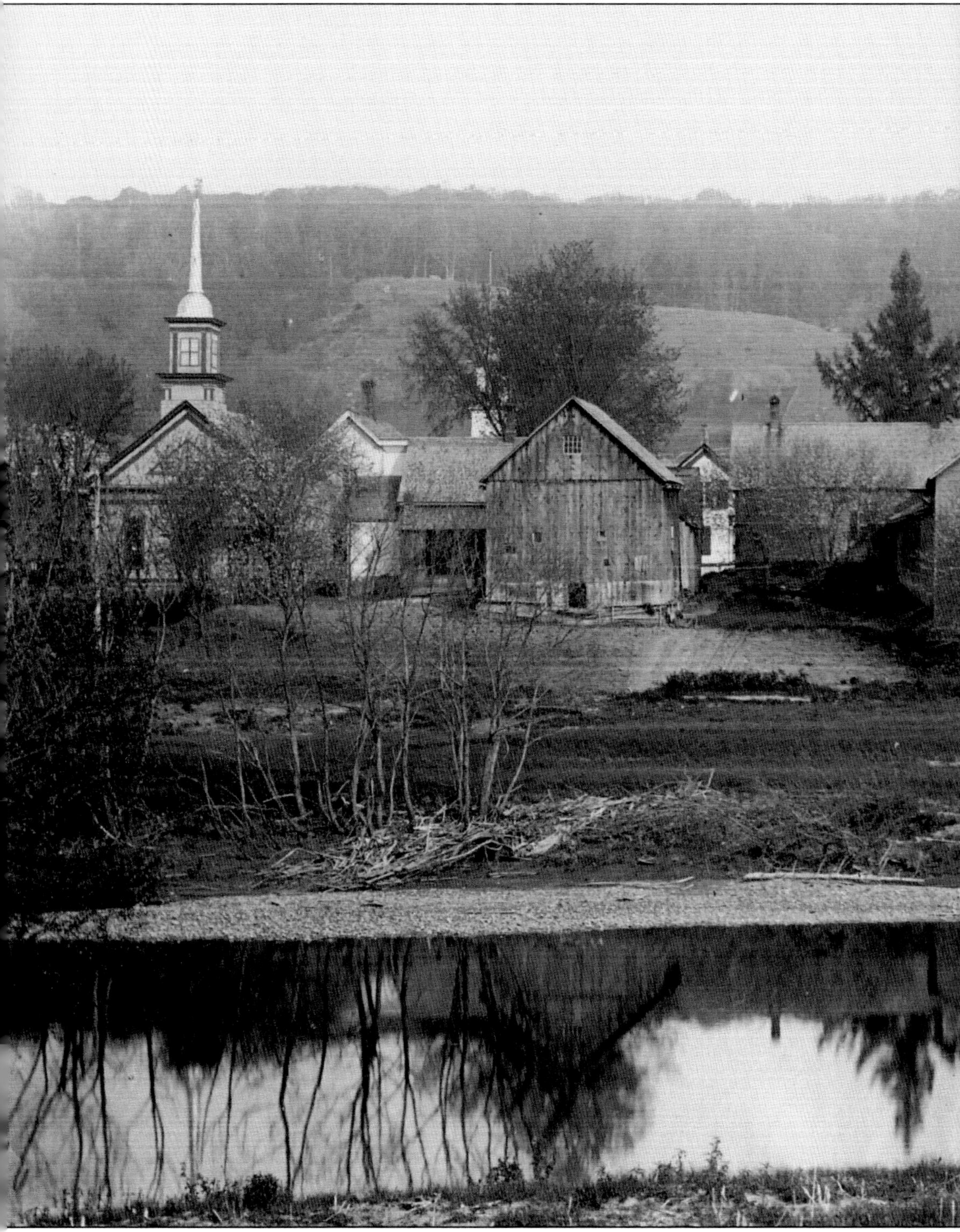

This photograph from the west bank of the Mad River shows the rear yards and backs of houses on Main Street in Moretown and the Methodist church at the left. When the many mills were operating full tilt, the houses on Main Street were occupied by mill workers. Often, rear-yard

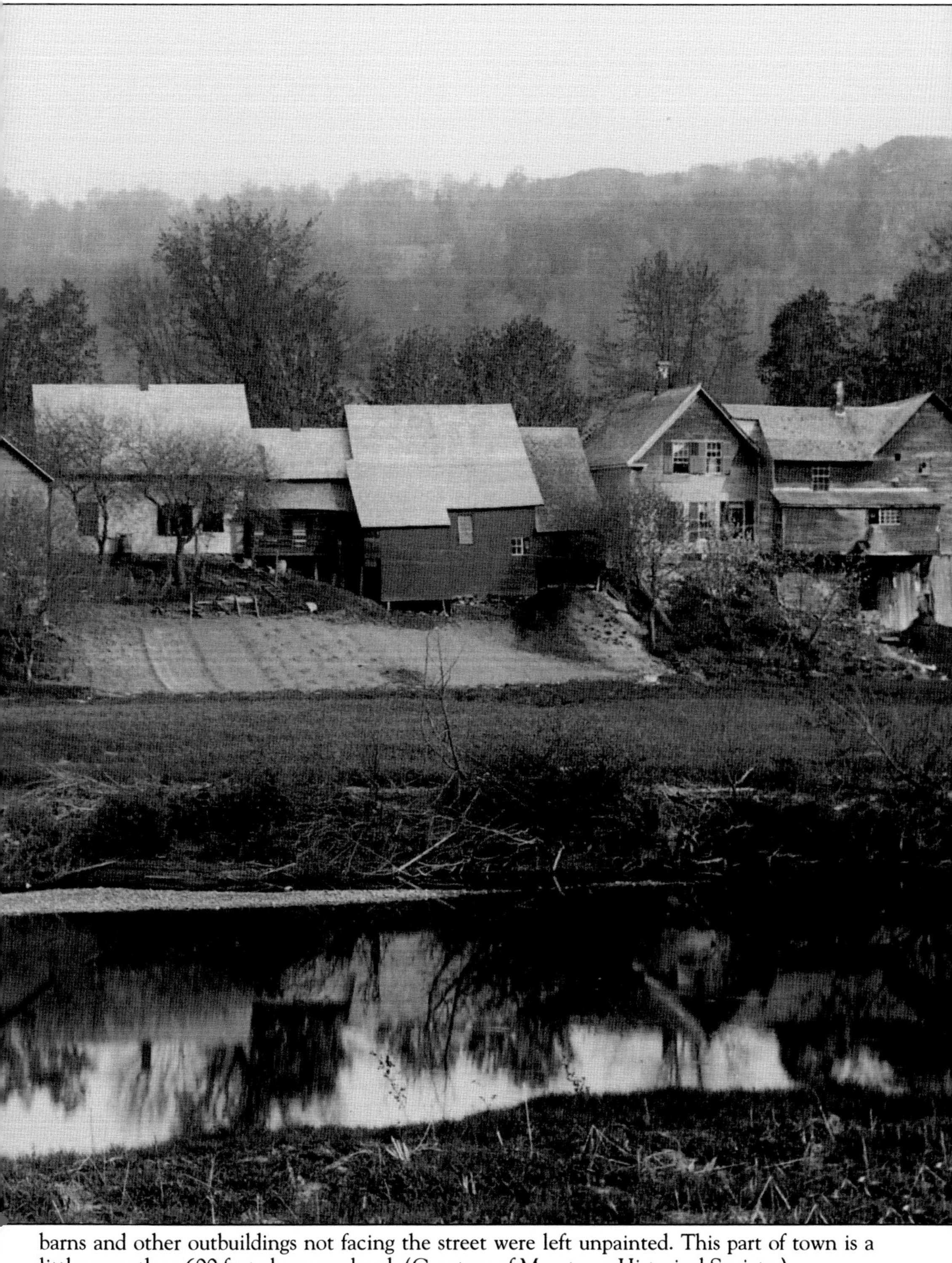

barns and other outbuildings not facing the street were left unpainted. This part of town is a little more than 600 feet above sea level. (Courtesy of Moretown Historical Society.)

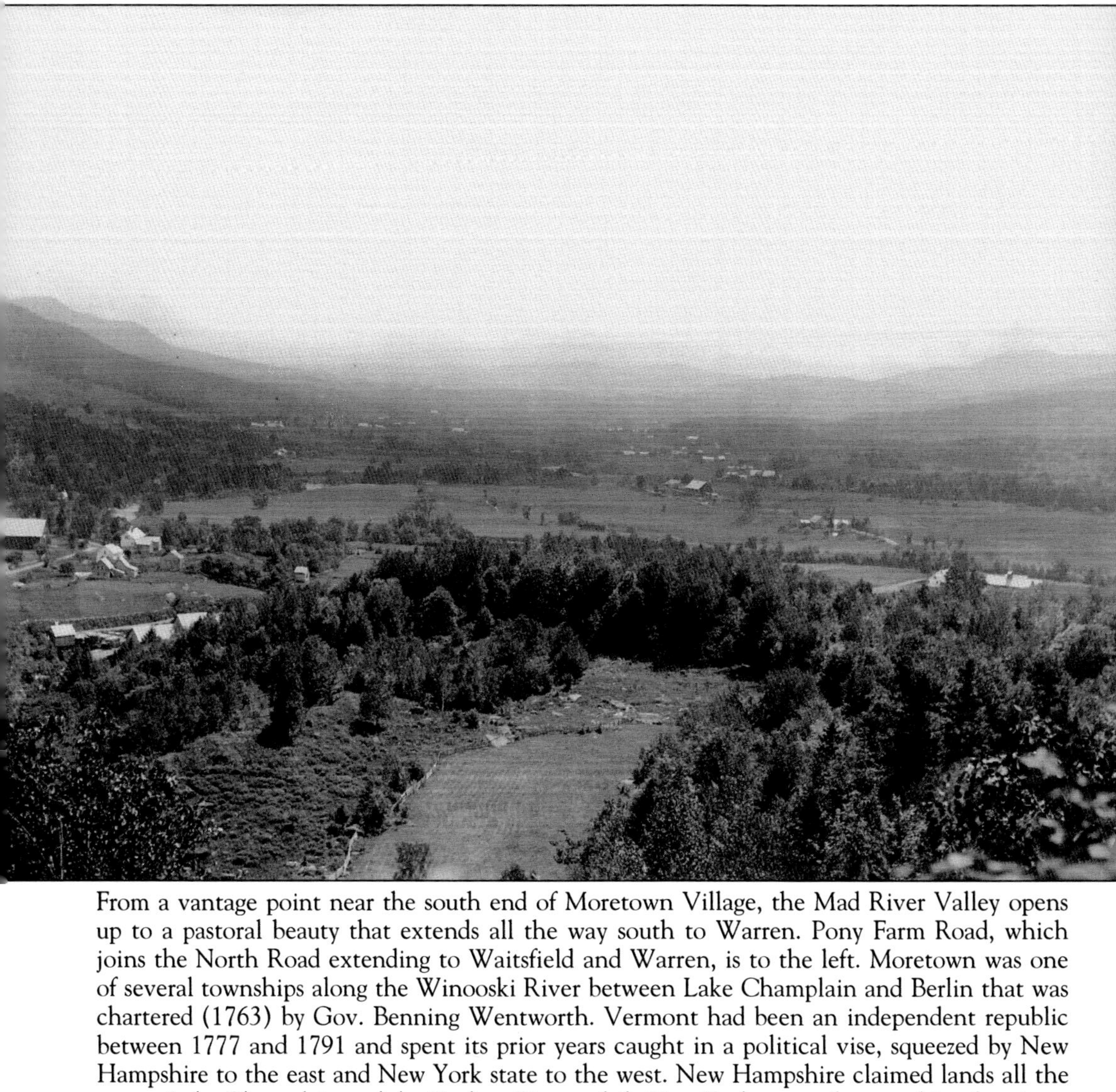

From a vantage point near the south end of Moretown Village, the Mad River Valley opens up to a pastoral beauty that extends all the way south to Warren. Pony Farm Road, which joins the North Road extending to Waitsfield and Warren, is to the left. Moretown was one of several townships along the Winooski River between Lake Champlain and Berlin that was chartered (1763) by Gov. Benning Wentworth. Vermont had been an independent republic between 1777 and 1791 and spent its prior years caught in a political vise, squeezed by New Hampshire to the east and New York state to the west. New Hampshire claimed lands all the way to Lake Champlain and the Hudson River, while New York asserted ownership of territory to the Connecticut River. As an independent entity, prior to being accepted as the 14th state, Vermont encouraged settlement. In a move that recorded the earliest zoning and planning regulations, holders of early land grants were required to cultivate a certain number of acres and build a house of a size not less than 18 square feet. (Courtesy of Moretown Historical Society.)

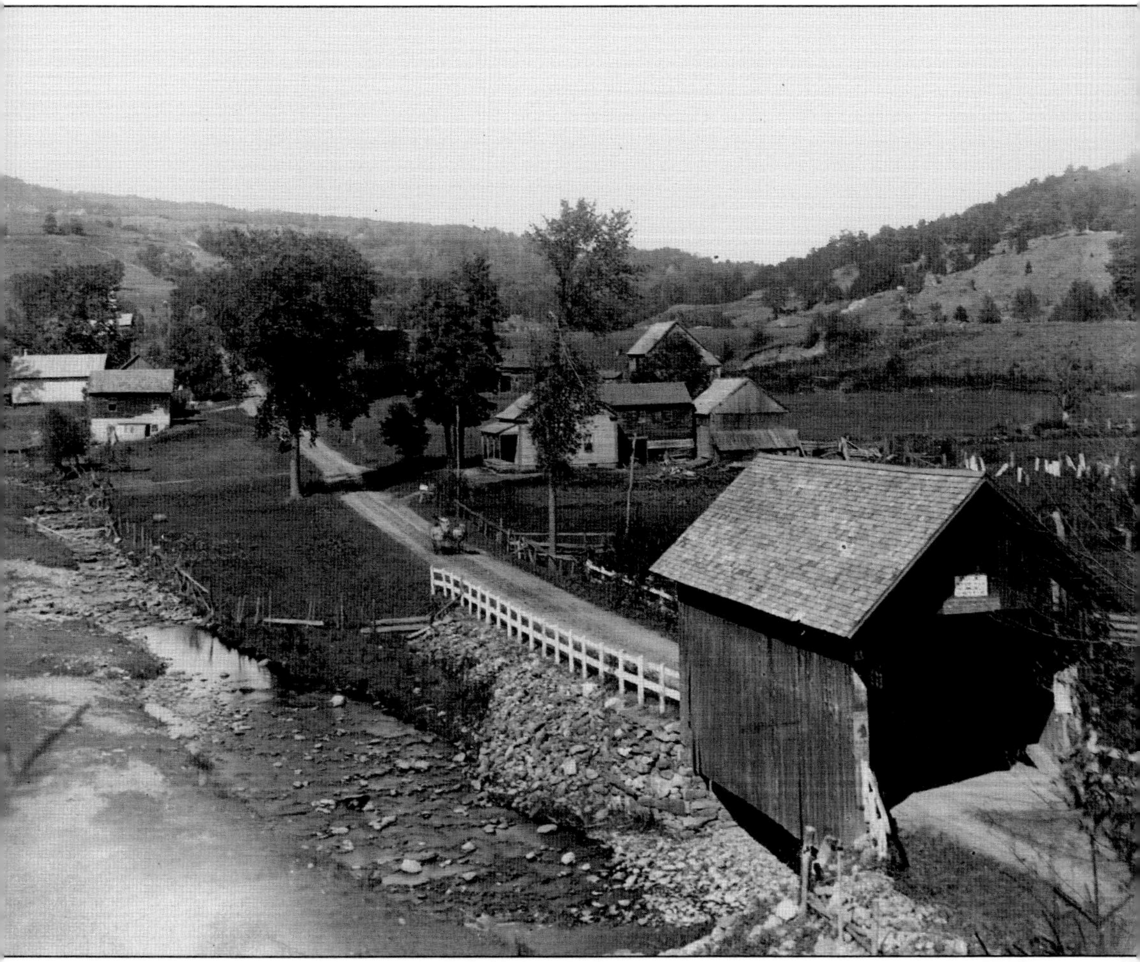

The Dowsville covered bridge in Duxbury, on what is presently Route 100, spanned the Dowsville Brook just over the line separating Duxbury from Moretown. Harwood Union High School was built in 1965 across from the Duxbury Congregational Church, visible here in the upper left. This photograph was taken about 100 years after the town was settled. The first census in 1790, which was just one year before Vermont became the 14th state, listed 39 persons in Duxbury, a number that was nearly quadrupled only 10 years later. Of the 153 residents living in Duxbury in 1800, 77 were younger than 16 years old, an indication that these were young pioneering families with children. Such families were eager to carve a new way of life out of the relative wilderness. Most of these early settlers came from the lower colonies of Massachusetts and Connecticut, as well as New Hampshire. (Courtesy of Alice DeLong.)

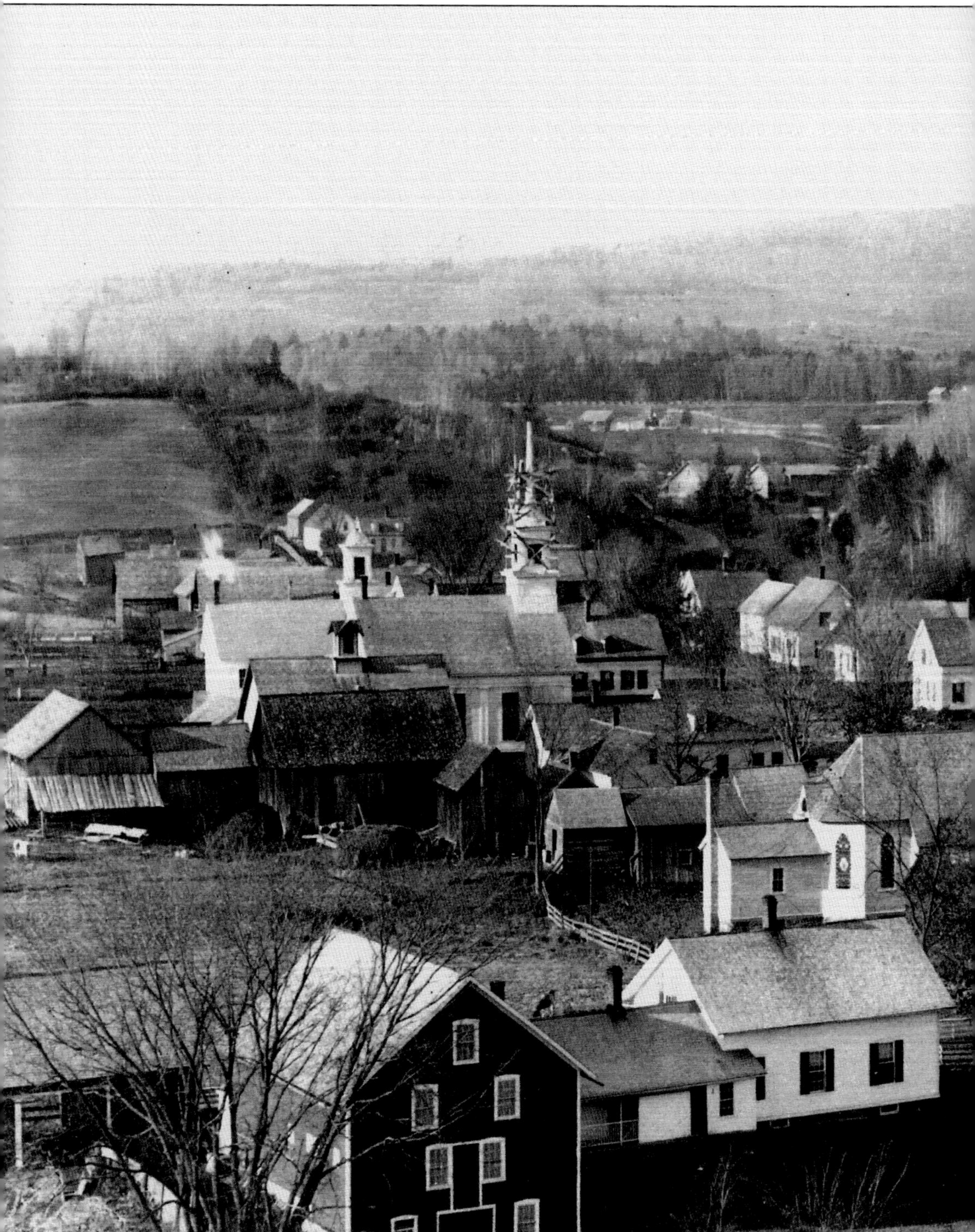

The two church spires belong to the Methodist church, center left, and St. Patrick's Catholic Church in Moretown. Changes that have occurred since this *c.* 1900 photograph was taken are the rebirth of woodlands on the hillsides, the paving of Main Street, and the disappearance of

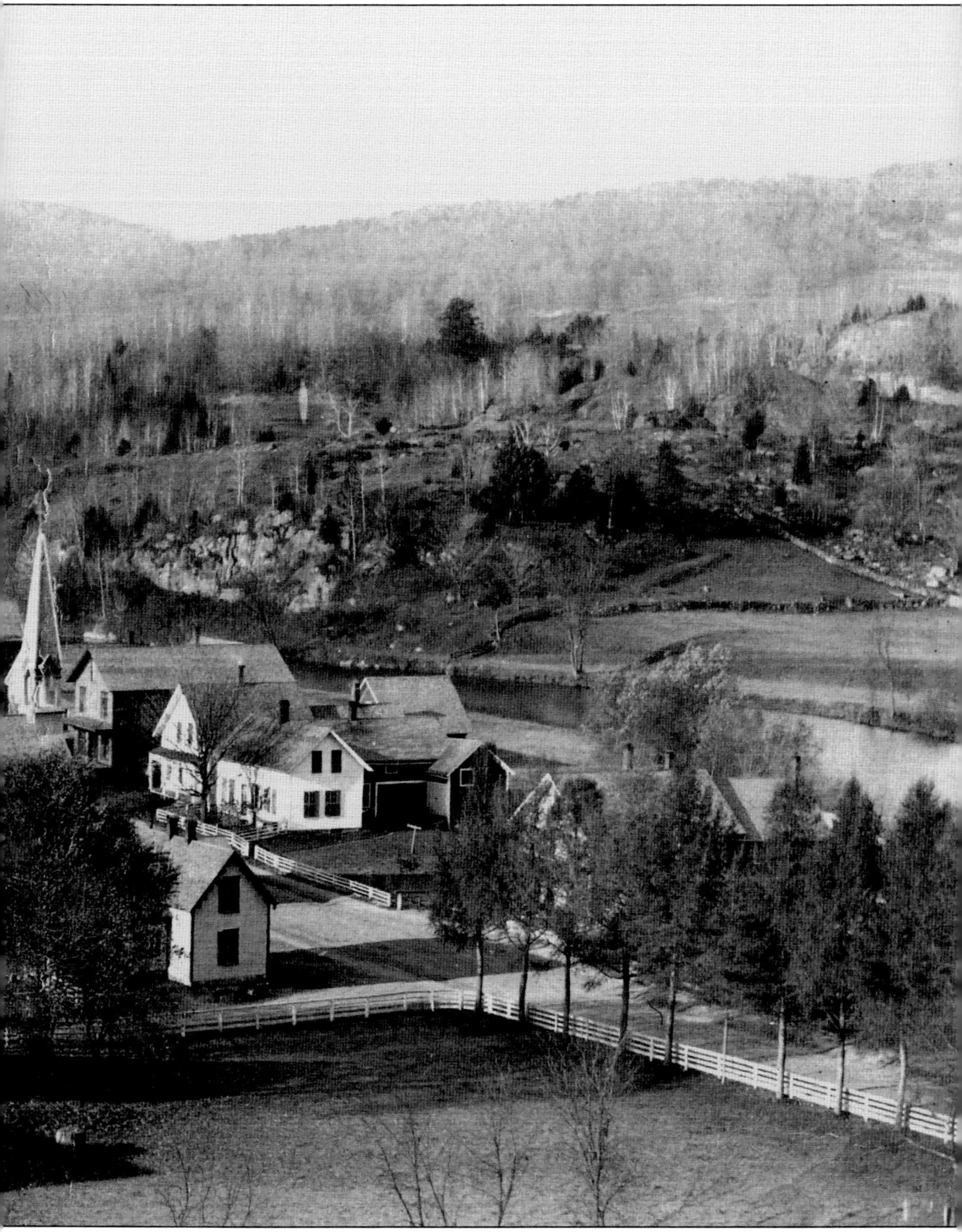

most of the barns in the backyards of homes. The house and barn in the foreground made up the early home of the Mad River Valley School, later named the Green Mountain Valley School, the ski academy now located on Bragg Hill in Fayston. (Courtesy of Moretown Historical Society.)

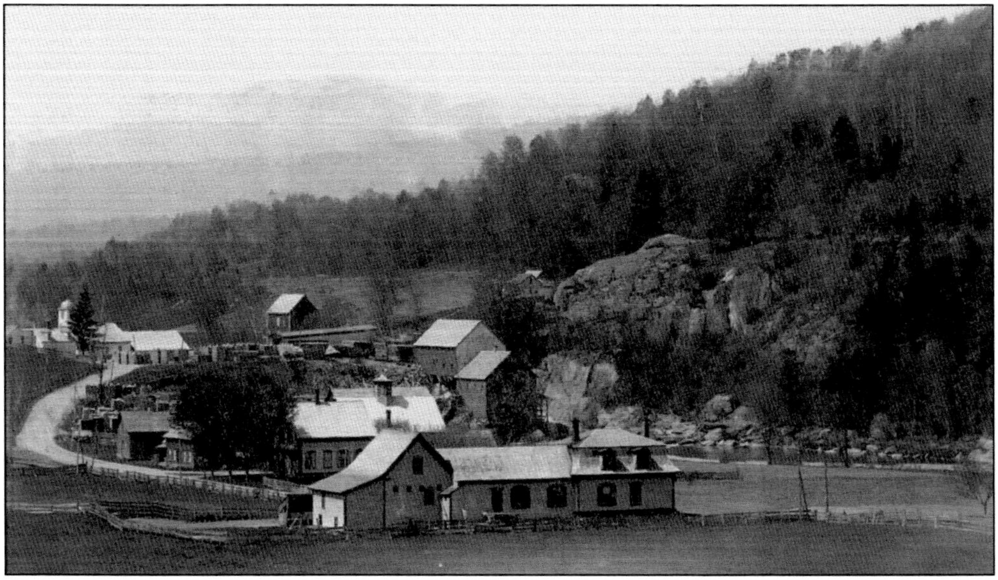

Moretown is seen here from the north end of the village, looking south along what is now Route 100B. The Buckley House, still standing and occupied, is in the foreground; the town hall, constructed in 1835, is at the far left. Moretown's largest population in the 19th century was recorded in 1840, when there were 1,400 residents—just 253 fewer than the 2000 census total. (Courtesy of Howard Ferris.)

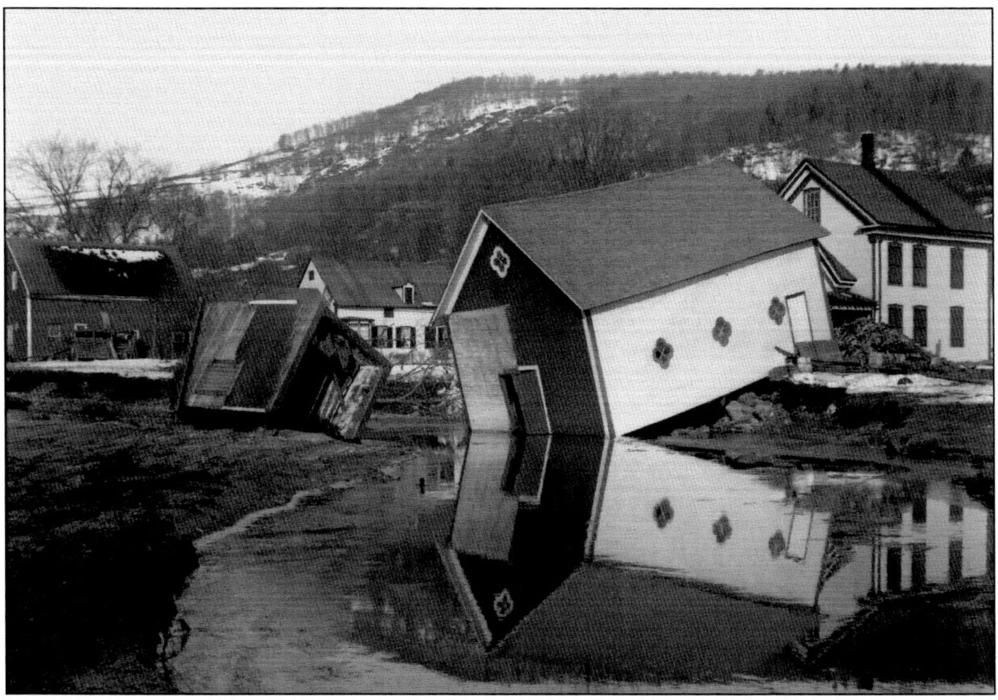

Call them floods, call them freshets—excessive rains and snowmelt still visit the valley, churning up what becomes the *really* Mad River, as evidenced by the tilt of the Fuller Barn in Waitsfield in this 1912 photograph. A major flood in 1830 caused many families to move uphill, away from the river. (Courtesy of Waitsfield Historical Society.)

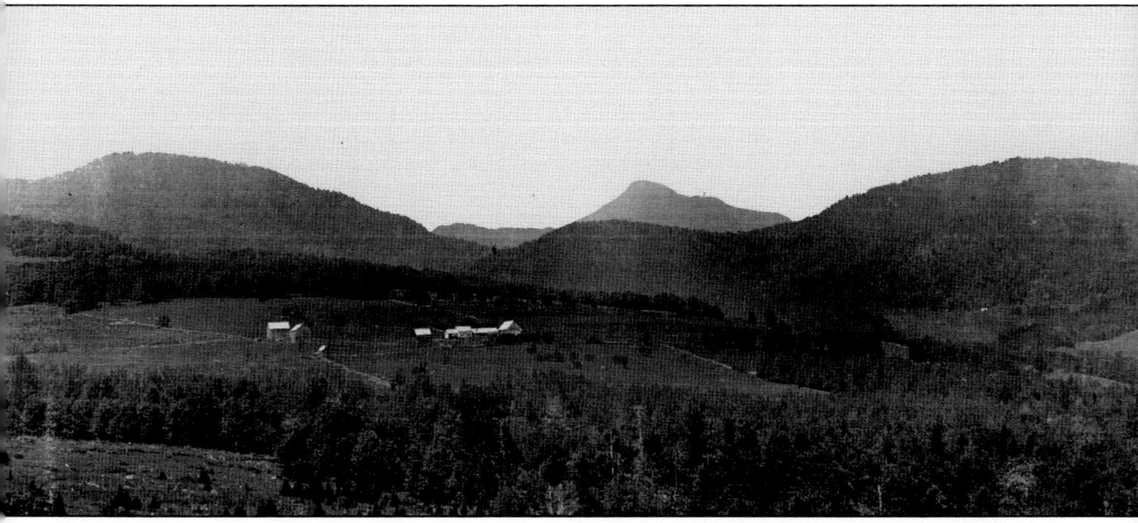

The thorny peak of Camel's Hump sits five miles north of Ward Hill in South Duxbury, where this photograph was taken. The distinctive 4,083-foot peak, straddling the borders of Chittenden and Washington counties and the towns of Huntington and Duxbury, has been a much-beloved landmark through civilized history. It has guided the way for Native Americans, the French explorer Samuel de Champlain (who is credited for naming it), and everyone since. For many farmers, "the Hump," also called "le Lion Couchant" (the Couching Lion), has been regarded as a somewhat reliable weather gauge: "If there's snow on top of Camel's Hump, you don't plant your seeds," said Alice DeLong, a former school teacher and keeper of local history, who is now in her 90s. Hikers reach the rocky and wondrous peak—which provides spectacular views of Lake Champlain, the Adirondack Mountains to the west, and the White Mountains to the east—via either the Long Trail or several other trails climbing from the eastern or western valley floors. (Courtesy of Alice DeLong.)

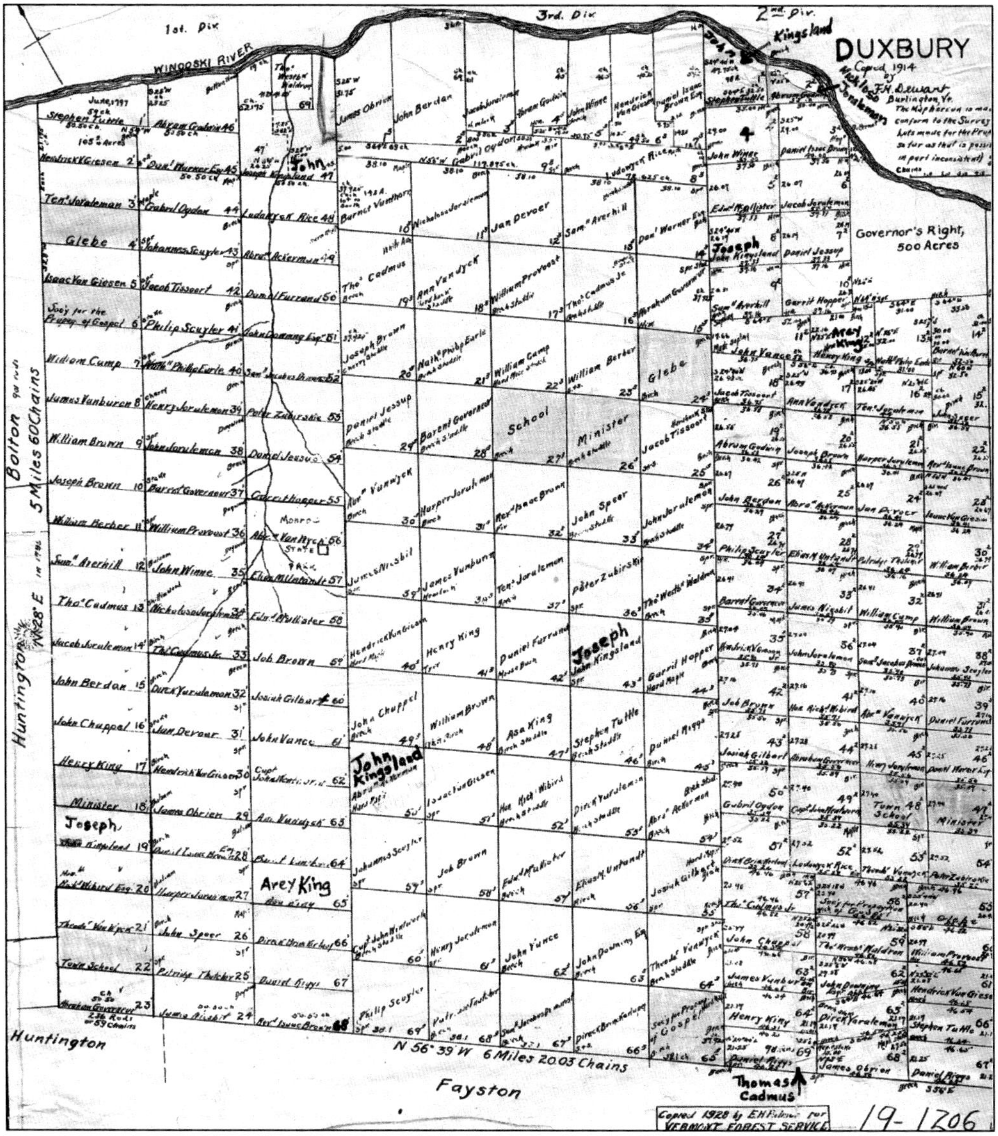

This map of early land grants in Duxbury made no distinction of topography, but earmarked several lots to be set aside for public use, such as for schools or churches. Grants were mapped similarly for the other towns in the valley. Duxbury in 1763 was divided into 71 shares: one share for each of the 65 proprietors; 500 acres for Benning Wentworth, the royal governor of New Hampshire; one for a school; one for a minister; and one for a house of worship. However, several property disputes arose, because magnetic north had not been considered in the early calculations. Subsequent surveys were needed. The first settlers were Walter Avery and Stephen Tilden. The first child, Lucy Bryant, was born in 1791. As you drive along Route 100 today through Duxbury, you will see small cemeteries along the road. They mark the locations of early hamlets. (Courtesy of Alice DeLong.)

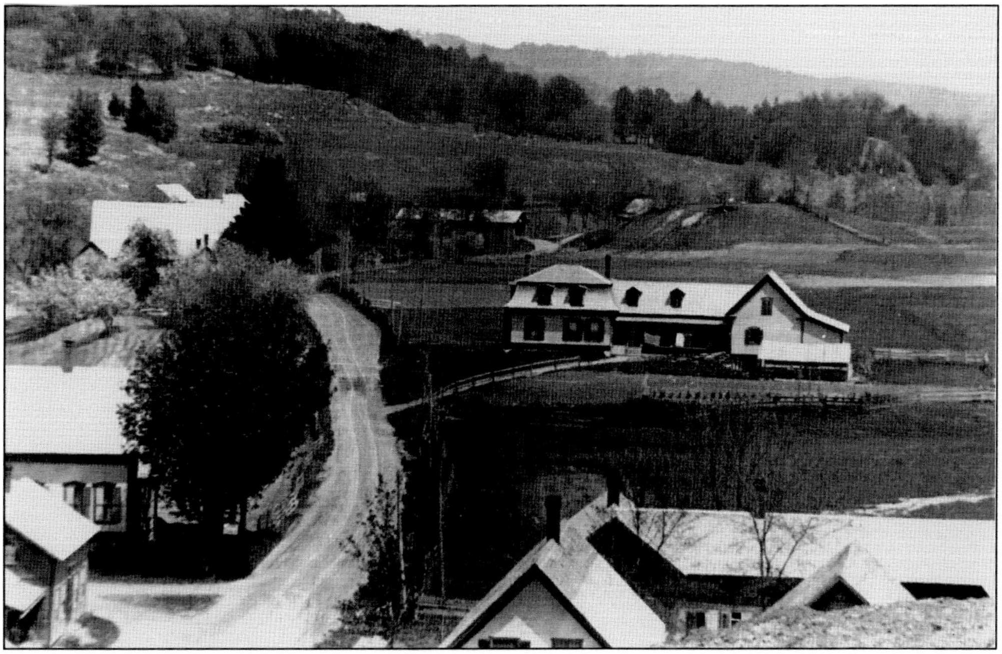

In the center of this view is the Buckley House, as it appeared in the late 1800s. This Moretown house is still occupied today. Just beyond it is the covered bridge that spanned the Mad River; it has since been replaced by a modern bridge, last rebuilt in 1990. (Courtesy of Moretown Historical Society.)

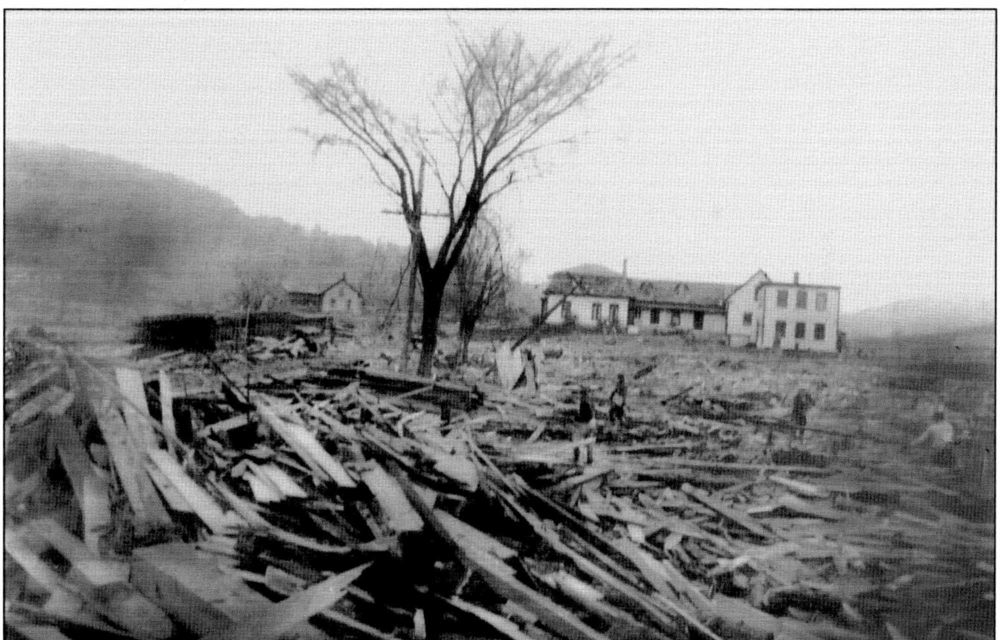

A scene of the same location shows piles of debris from the 1927 flood cluttering the road (Route 100B) and fields, as viewed going north out of Moretown Village toward Middlesex. The Mad River is to the left in the photograph, just a few hundred yards from the road. The Buckley House is in the background. (Courtesy of Moretown Historical Society.)

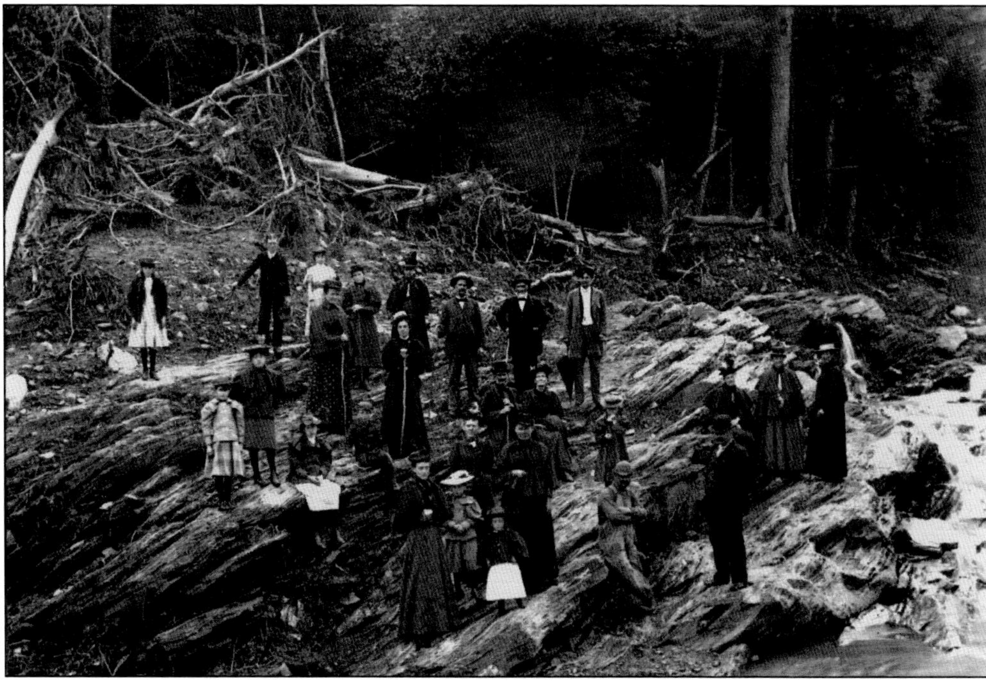

Hundreds of people came to Fayston to see the devastation caused by a mammoth slide of mud, rocks, and trees on July 14, 1897. The stream that flows down through the area between Sugarbush's Lincoln Peak and Mount Ellen is appropriately named Slide Brook. (Courtesy of Waitsfield Historical Society.)

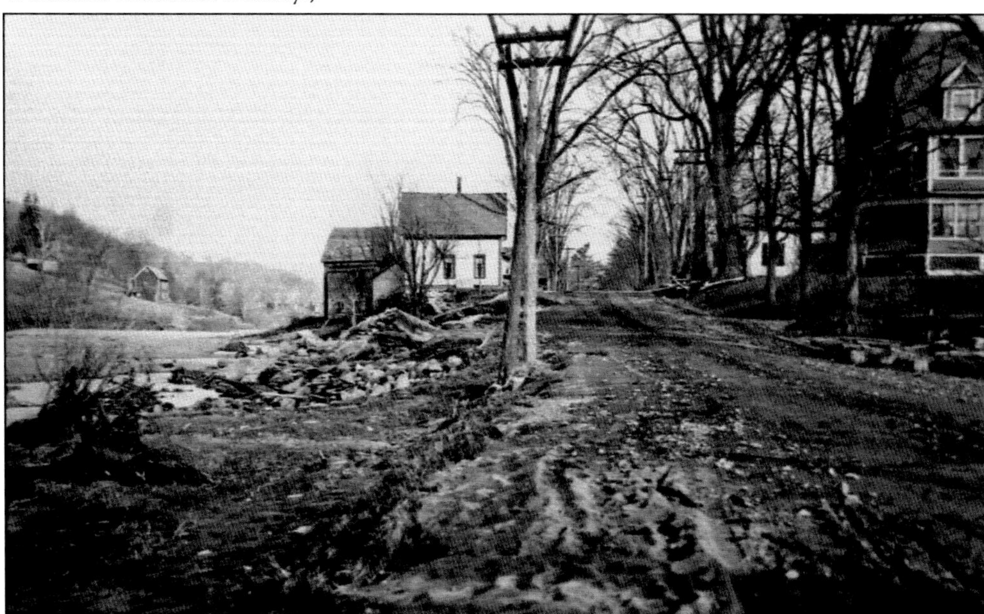

While most activity in the Mad River Valley, especially economic, has been dictated by the features of the land and the course of the river, the many floods have forced their will upon livelihoods also. This debris on what is now Route 100B in Moretown washed up from the flood of 1927, which destroyed most of the bridges and mills. (Courtesy of Moretown Historical Society.)

Two

LEARNING

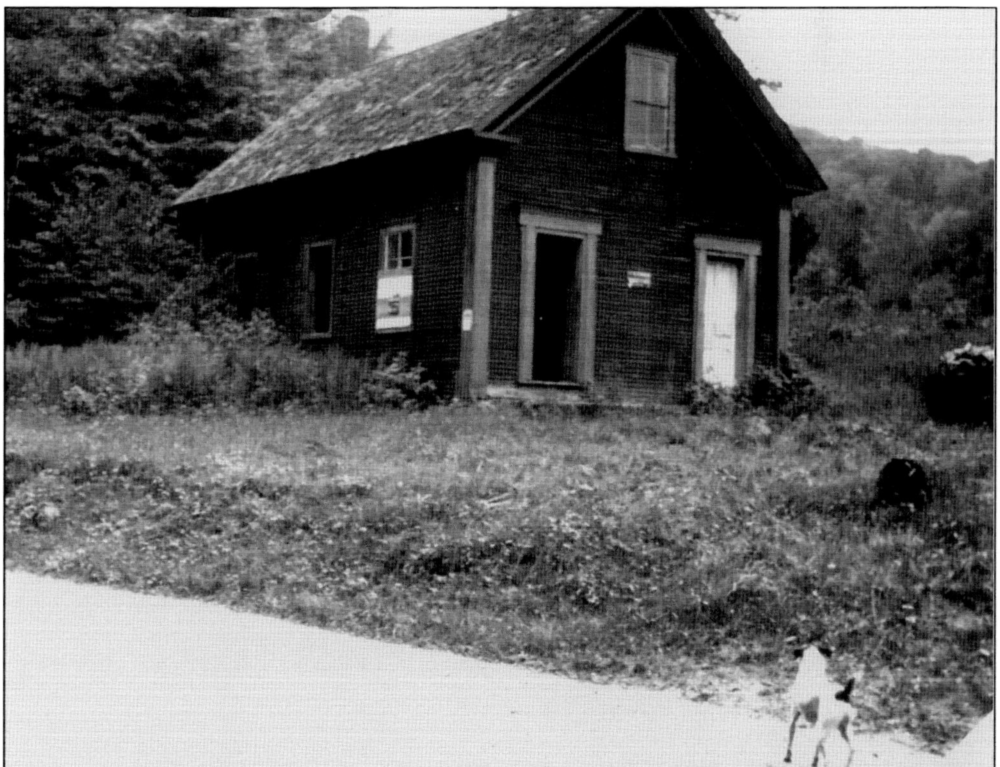

The Austin School was in District No. 9 in Warren, located at the beginning of the Stetson Hollow Road, just off Route 100. The deed to the lot owned by Daniel Austin stated that it was void when school was no longer held. Before 1805, all education in Warren was in the home. (Courtesy of Katherine Hartshorn.)

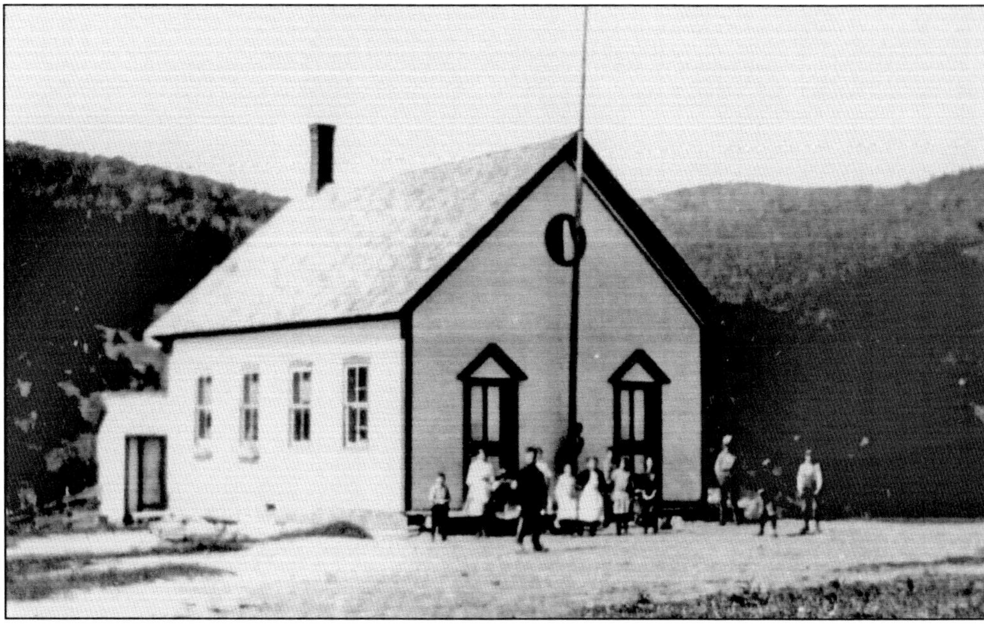

South Hollow School No. 6 is now a private home on the Lincoln Gap Road, below the West Hill Road in Warren. The school was closed in 1921 and was later sold to Orren and Nona Parsons Lovett. They lived there after selling their farm in East Warren. One of the school's last pupils, the late Clarence Hartshorn, husband of Warren historian Katherine Hartshorn, rode his horse to school every day, dismounted, and let the horse return home by itself. (Courtesy of Katherine Hartshorn.)

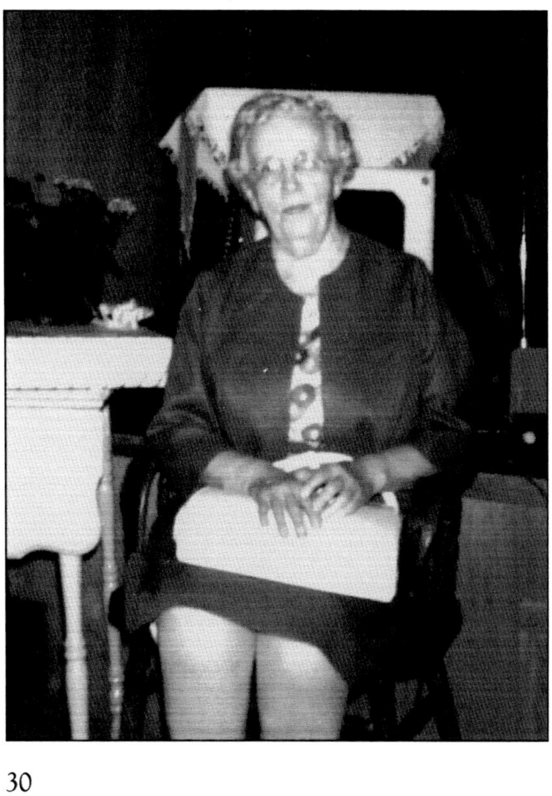

The teaching career of Ruth Phillips spanned both the eras of the one-room school and the consolidated district. She was one of the last teachers in the valley who was "boarded around," spending equal amounts of time living in the homes of students in Duxbury. Phillips retired in 1963. (Courtesy of Alice DeLong.)

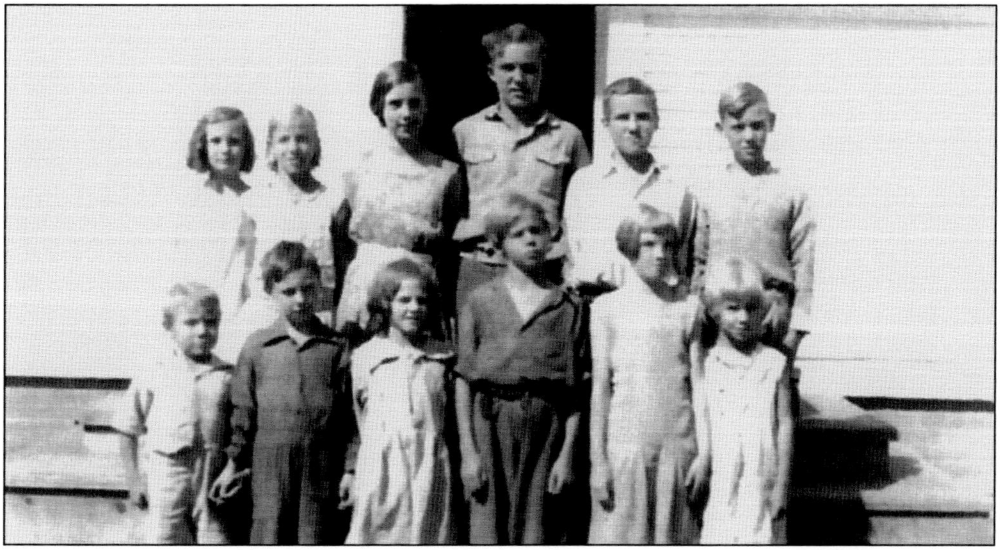

The Down River School was on the property of what is now the Golden Lion Motel on Route 100 in Warren. The old Route 100, prior to the 1927 flood, was located to the right of the school when traveling toward the covered bridge. The school building was moved by Clifton Corliss to become a real estate office at the entrance to Sugarbush Access Road. From left to right are the following: (first row) David DeFreest, Milfred De Call, Flora Walden, Fred Walden, Marjorie Thompson, and Eleanor DeFreest; (second row) Madelyn Eurich, Lois DeFreest, Evelyn McLain, Clesson Eurich, Donald DeFreest, and Roger Eurich. (Photograph by Kevin Eurich, courtesy of Katherine Hartshorn.)

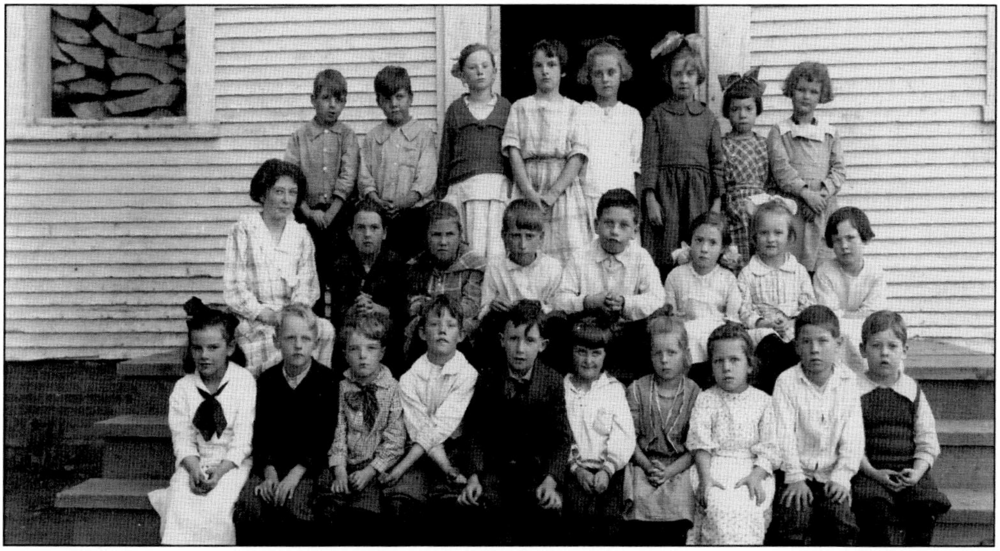

The first and second grades at the Warren Village School in 1920 were taught by Hazel Pierce. Pictured from left to right are the following: (first row) Marion Johnson, Richard Ralph, Sam Drew, Kenneth Maloney, Roland Hubbard, Helen Pray, Ruth Varner, Mary Murray, Eldon Delong, and Elwin Neill; (second row) teacher Hazel Pierce, Avis Stone, Merle Richardson, Warner Carliss, Lester Delong, Phyllis Carpenter, Mabel Mobus, and Beatrice Butler; (third row) Earl Stone, Clifton Murray, Hortense Luce, Gwendolyn Drew, Arlie Brooks, Lepha Long, Katherine Carleton, and Ruth Lovett. (Courtesy of Katherine Hartshorn.)

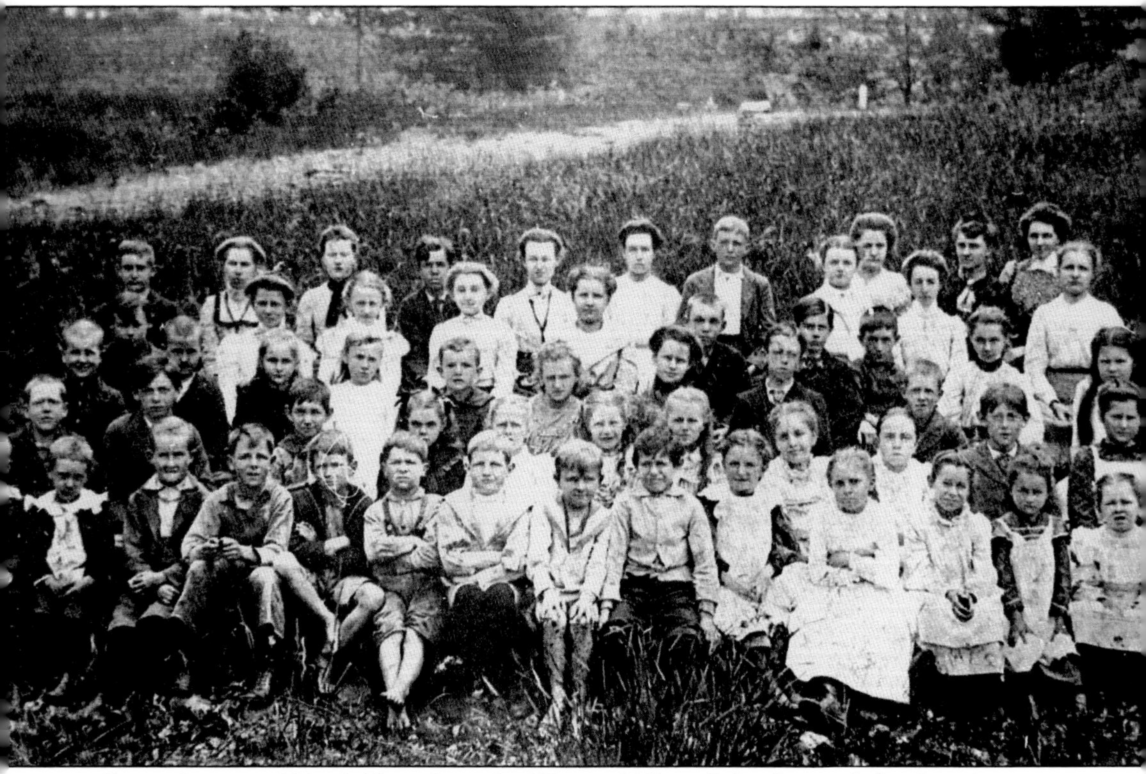

Shown here *c.* 1900, children from the Warren Village School attended either the primary department of grades 1 and 2, the lower department of grades 3, 4, and 5, or the upper department of grades 6, 7, and 8. Teachers identified in this photograph are Flora Sheppard and ? Anderson. Some of the pupils identified in this image are Earl Ralph, Carl Senor, Harold La Morder, Lee Miner, Dwight Long, Paul Miner, Henny Moore, Harold Parker, Paul Tienny, Jennie Benway, Florence Carpenter, Ora Parker, Kenneth Pierce, Earl Fuller, Jennie Miller, Clifford La Morder, Herbert La Morder, Rachel Murdock, Frank Kennedy, Grace Kennedy, Gladys Martin, Vaughn Brown, Elmer Pierce, Loren Fuller, Mary Tienny, Thaddeus Tienny, Ira Thayer, Clara Spaulding, Edith Gore, Lena La Morder, Loren Poland, Howard Wakefield, Roy Heath, Emma Blair, Mabel Poland, Vera Carpenter, Effie La Morder, Roy Russell, Lou Colby, Nona Parsons, Lloyd Long, Lydia Thayer, Blanche Miller, Clayton Miller, Amber Carpenter, and Flora Shepard. (Courtesy of Katherine Hartshorn.)

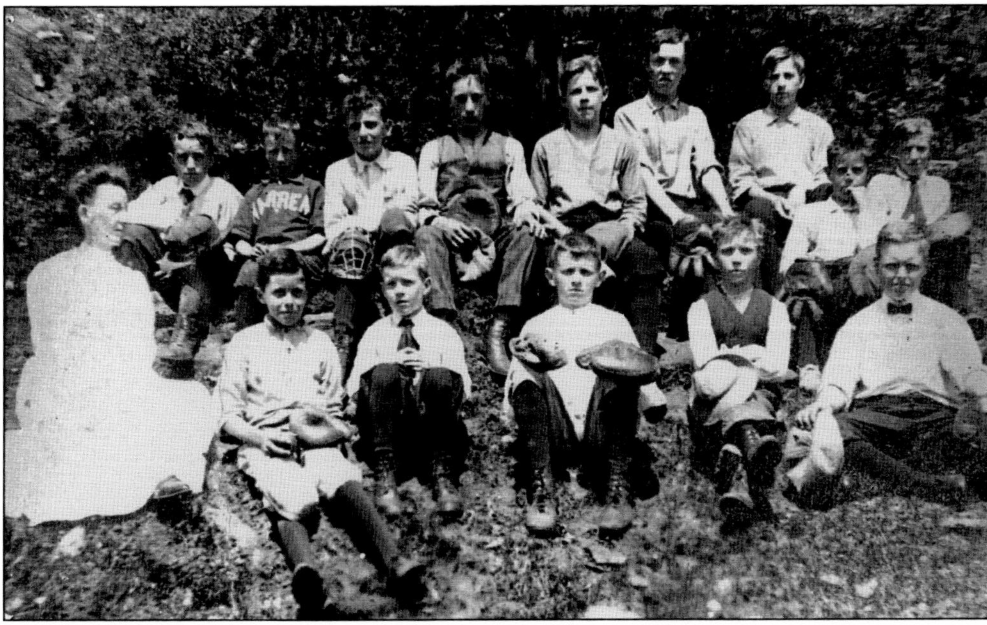

This Sunday school class in Warren was taught by Elma Spaulding, shown at the left in this c. 1909 photograph. From left to right are the following: (first row) Everett Colby, Theodore Greenwood, Lauren Long, Carroll Parsons, and Jasper Moore; (second row) Roger Gleason, Merrit Jones, Howard Spaulding, Leslie Parsons, Kenneth Tillotson, Wayne Pierce, Marshall Miner, Milo Miner, and Ralph Spaulding. (Courtesy of Katherine Hartshorn.)

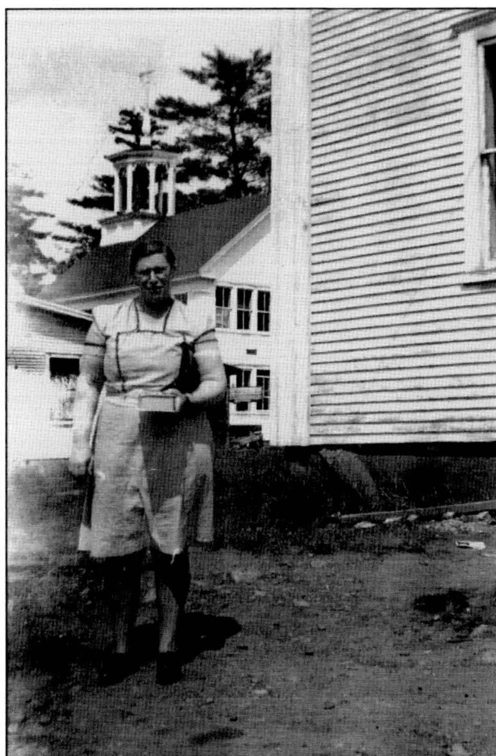

Alice Backus DeLong taught at the Warren Village School in the late 1940s, and by her account, taught all over the Mad River Valley during her career. By 1960, all of Warren's schoolchildren attended the village school, but 10 years later a new school was built at Brooks Field. (Courtesy of Katherine Hartshorn.)

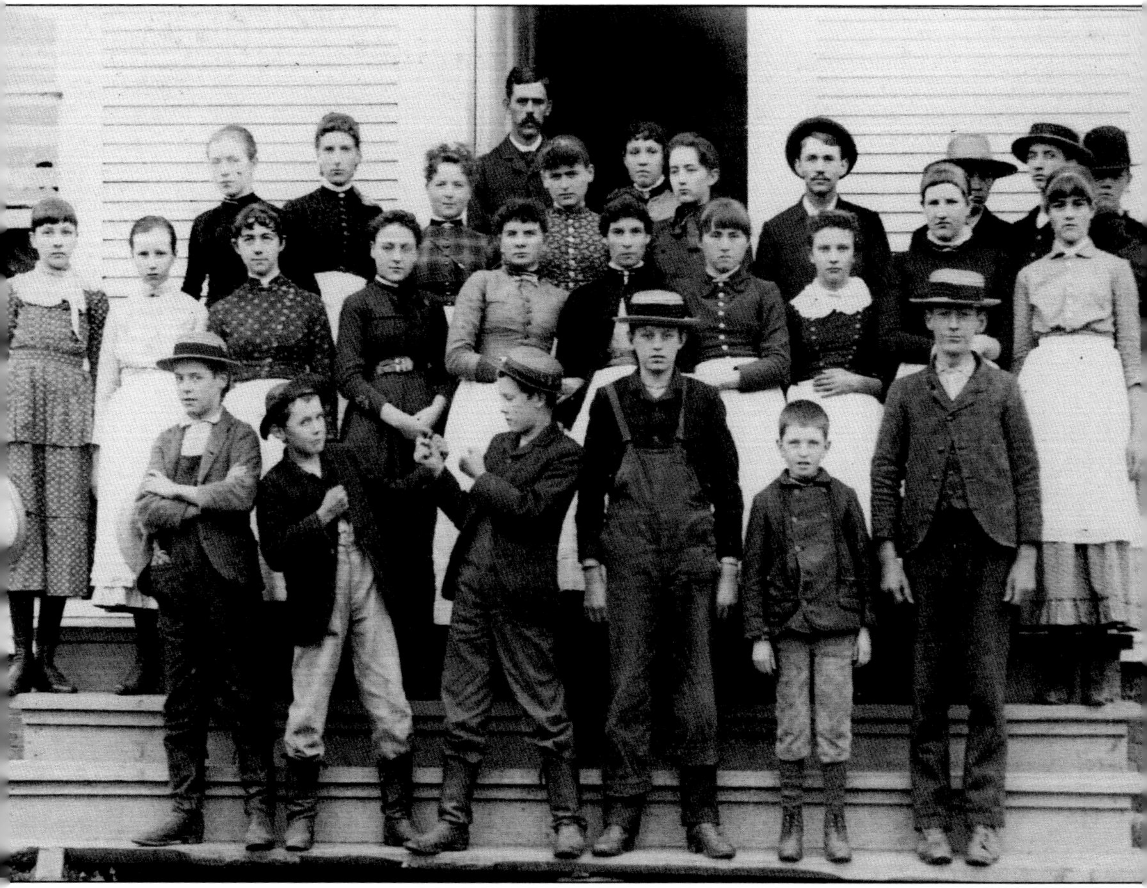

In the 1880s, while the Warren students in the second and third rows portray a trim and proper pose, their classmates in the first row provide a classic study of both the joys and pains of youth. In the front row, Jess McAlister and Will Martin, in their boxers' pose, cannot help showing off as look-alikes of John L. Sullivan and Gentleman Jim Corbett; and the two taller boys beside them, identified as Merton Hewett and Vern Perkins, are literally growing out of their sturdy school clothes. Although not everyone is identified, the individuals pictured here include the following: (first row) Leon Drew, Jess McAllister, Will Martin, Merton Hewett, George Williamson, and Vern Perkins; (second row) Minnie Slaton, Jennie Parker, Nell Spaulding, Ada Cuthbert, Lucinda Freeman, ? Johnson, Alice Martin, Belle Atkins, Jennie Grady, and Clara Shepard; (third row) Lettie Williamson, Nora Billings, Lydia Fuller, ? Stevens, Will Parsons, Nell Bucklin, Will Sargent, and Will Bean. (Courtesy of Katherine Hartshorn.)

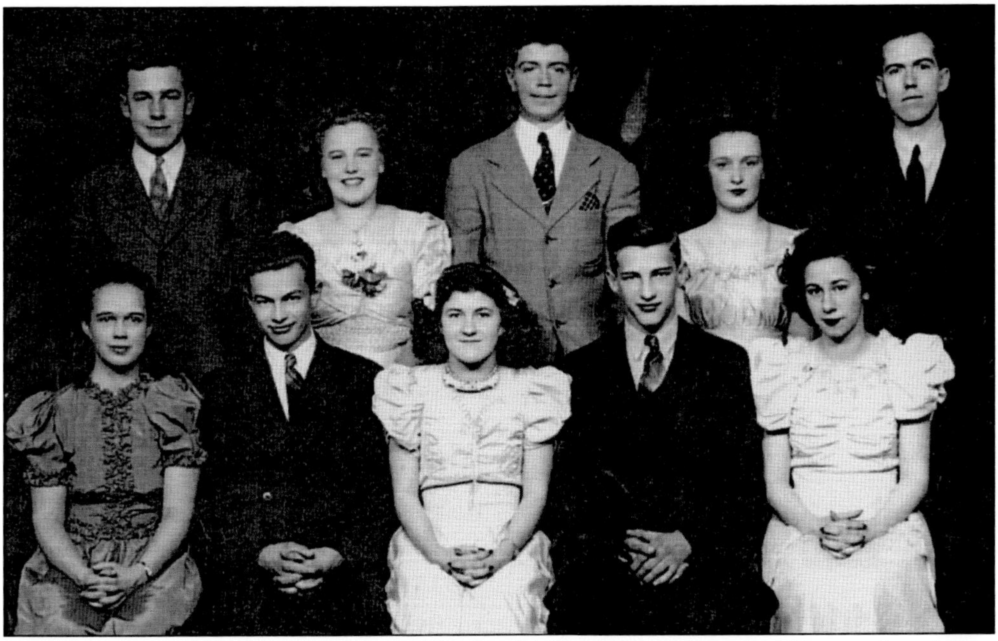

Graduates of Waitsfield High School in the World War II–era Class of 1943 were, from left to right, as follows: (first row) Priscilla Joslin, Robert Jones, Dorothy Harvey, Kenneth Phillips, and Florence Crary; (second row) Raymond Bissell, Georgena Conrad, Robert Griffith, and Constance LaVanway. At the end of the second row is school principal Russell Erwin. "Many of the boys went in the service. I would think about half of them joined up," said Dorothy Harvey Merchant, of Duxbury. (Photograph by Kevin Eurich, courtesy of Katherine Hartshorn.)

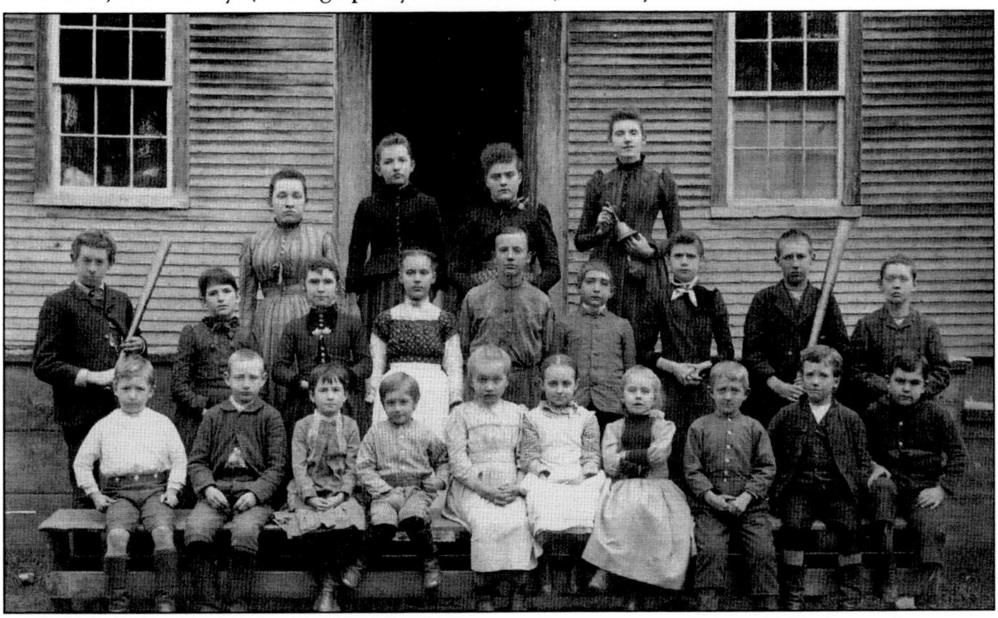

Students are pictured here in 1891 outside Fayston Lower School No. 4, which stood opposite the town cemetery on North Fayston Road. By 1844, Fayston was educating 262 pupils in several district schools, far more than the 167 students enrolled in both elementary school and Harwood Union High School in 1978. (Courtesy of Fayston Historical Society.)

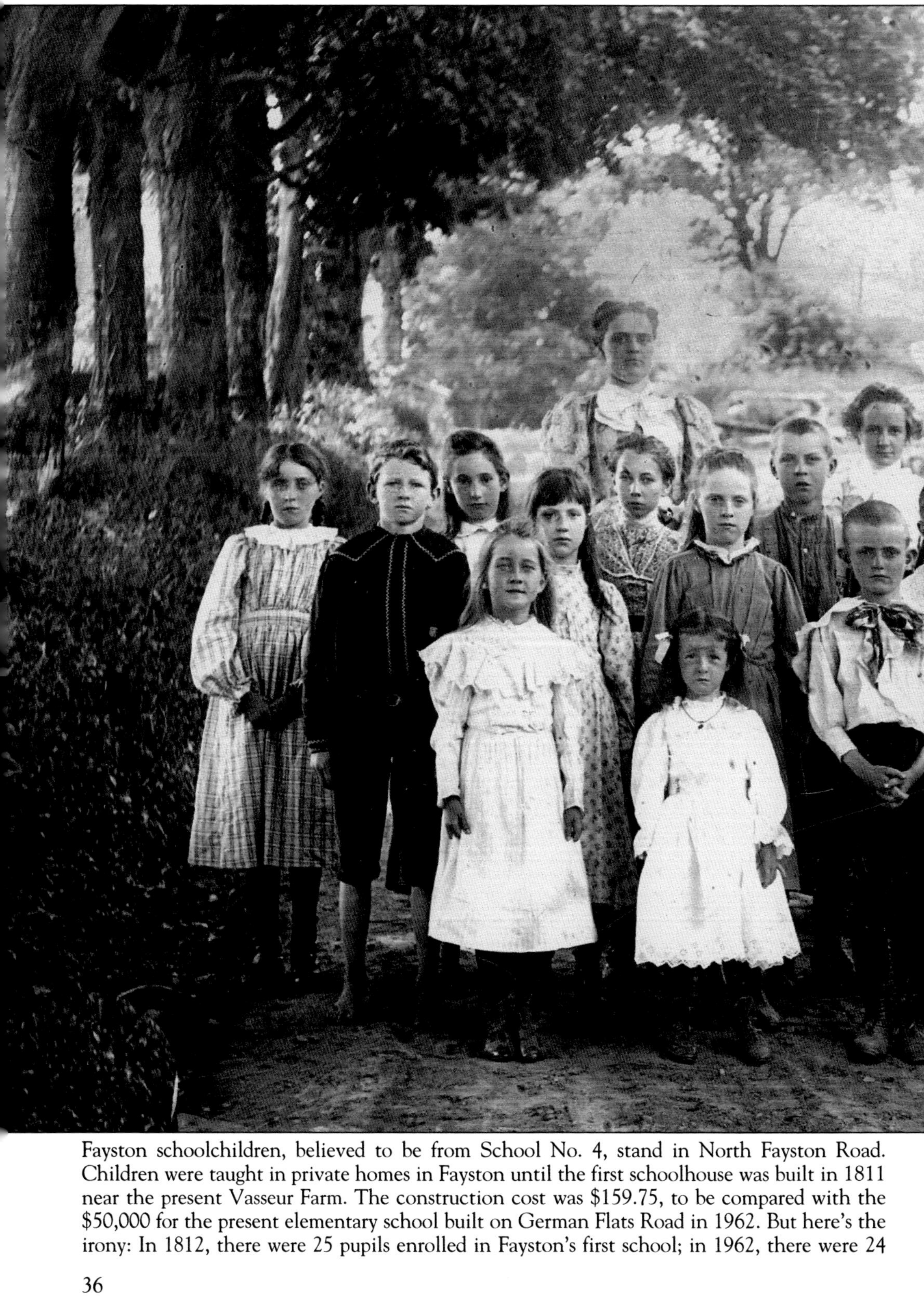

Fayston schoolchildren, believed to be from School No. 4, stand in North Fayston Road. Children were taught in private homes in Fayston until the first schoolhouse was built in 1811 near the present Vasseur Farm. The construction cost was $159.75, to be compared with the $50,000 for the present elementary school built on German Flats Road in 1962. But here's the irony: In 1812, there were 25 pupils enrolled in Fayston's first school; in 1962, there were 24

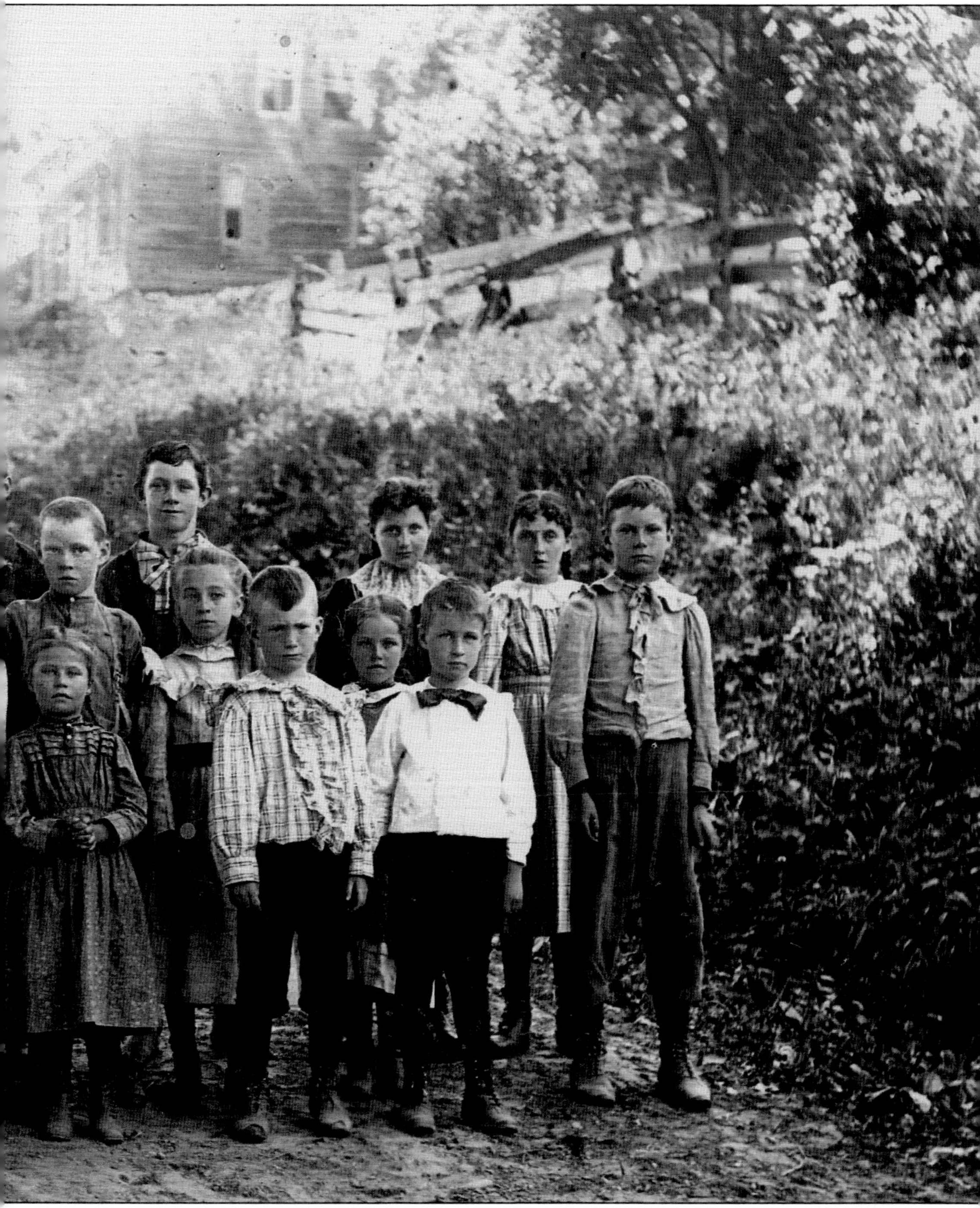

pupils occupying the new school. In 1844, there were 262 students in the town; and in 1978, there were 167 youngsters. After the Civil War, the area's population declined. Operating costs of the first schools were paid in grain or flax. Another form of early tuition payment was that families provided two-thirds of a cord of wood per scholar (as schoolchildren were called back then). (Courtesy of Fayston Historical Society.)

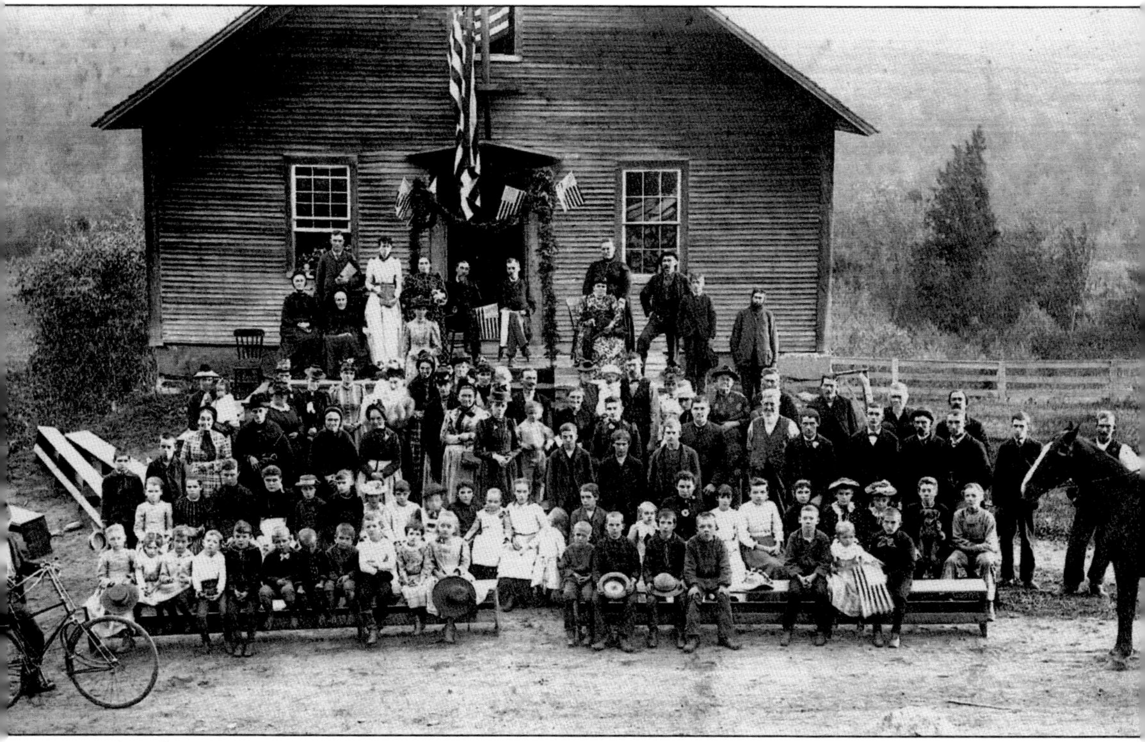

This flag-raising ceremony at Lower School No. 4 on October 2, 1891, was a community celebration attended by young and old. Flora Glass was the teacher. Early on in the town's history, Fayston children attended schools in Waitsfield. By 1860 there were 10 Fayston districts: No. 2 School was on North Fayston Road, north of Shepard Brook; No. 3 School was near Fayston Center; No. 1 School was on Bragg Hill; and No. 6 School was on German Flats Road. Shown in 1891, the Lower School No. 4 was opposite the town cemetery on North Fayston Road; the building is now a private home. (Photograph by J. J. Towle, courtesy of Fayston Historical Society.)

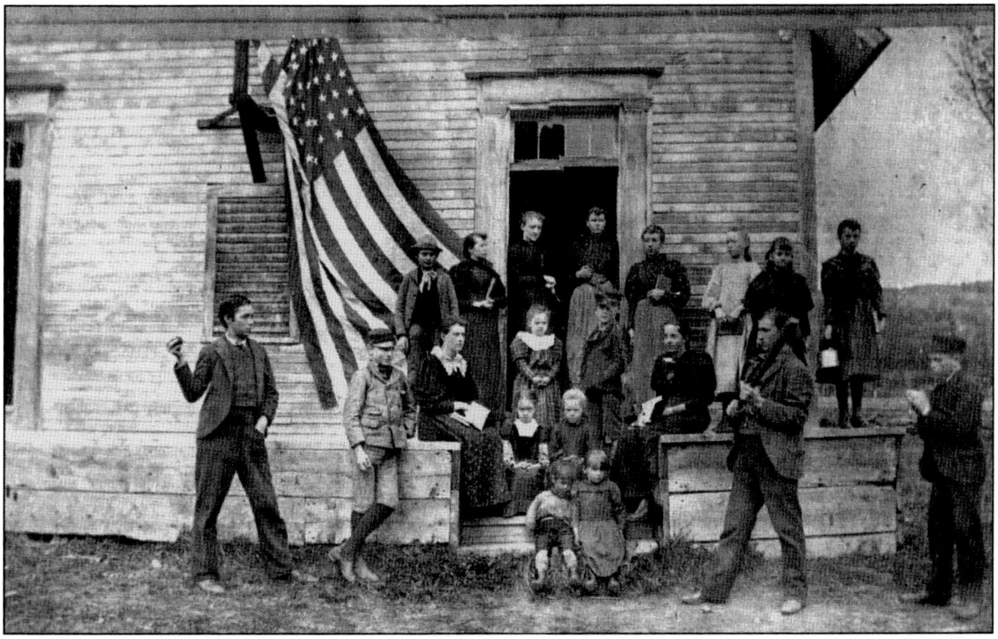

Fayston kids from the fall term of 1905 take a short respite from classwork at the No. 2 School, north of Shepard Brook on North Fayston Road. There were 10 school districts in town by the beginning of the Civil War. (Courtesy of Fayston Historical Society.)

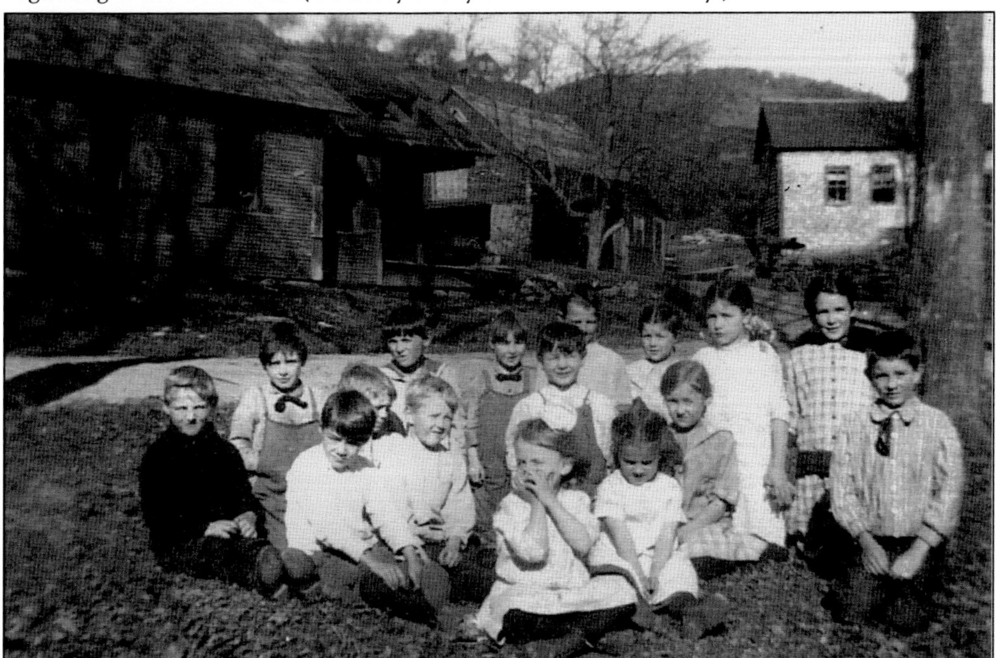

The original No. 9 School in Fayston is the abandoned building seen at the left. It is located across the road from the school building's present site on the north side of what is now Route 17. The building is now occupied by Burley Partnership, an architectural firm. Schoolchildren sometimes arrived at the No. 9 School in the area's earliest-known school bus: a horse-drawn wagon with canvas sides, driven by Melvin Long. (Courtesy of Fayston Historical Society.)

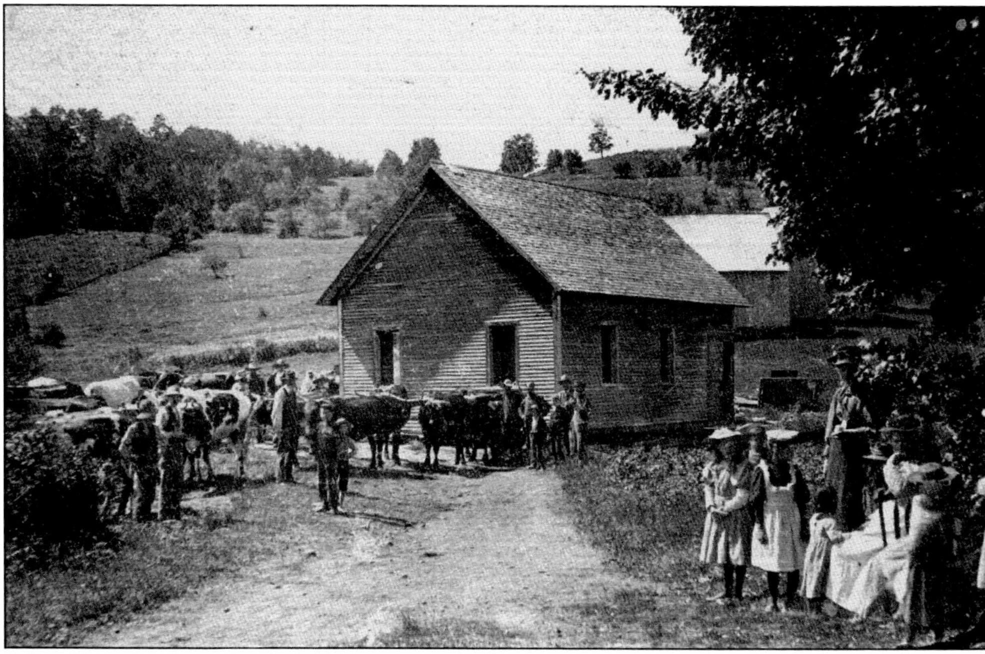

School No. 3 is being hauled by oxen to its new location on the east side of the road in Fayston Center in 1897. These small, one- or two-room buildings were frequently moved around the valley to suit changing population centers. (Courtesy of Fayston Historical Society.)

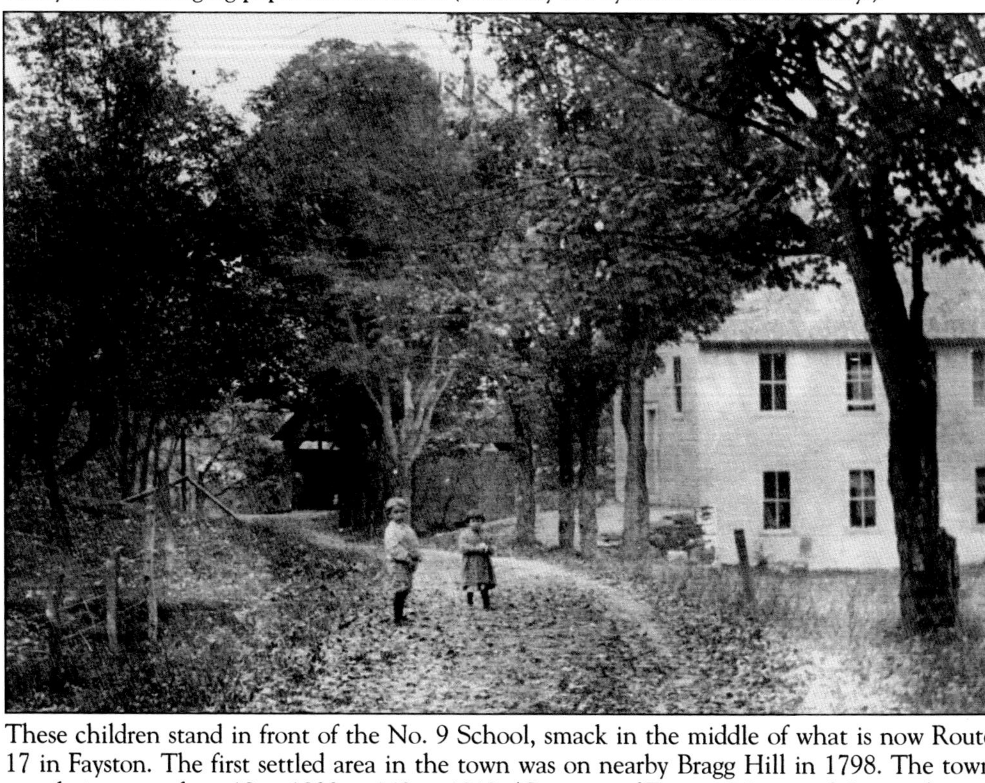

These children stand in front of the No. 9 School, smack in the middle of what is now Route 17 in Fayston. The first settled area in the town was on nearby Bragg Hill in 1798. The town population grew from 18 in 1800 to 149 in 1819. (Courtesy of Fayston Historical Society.)

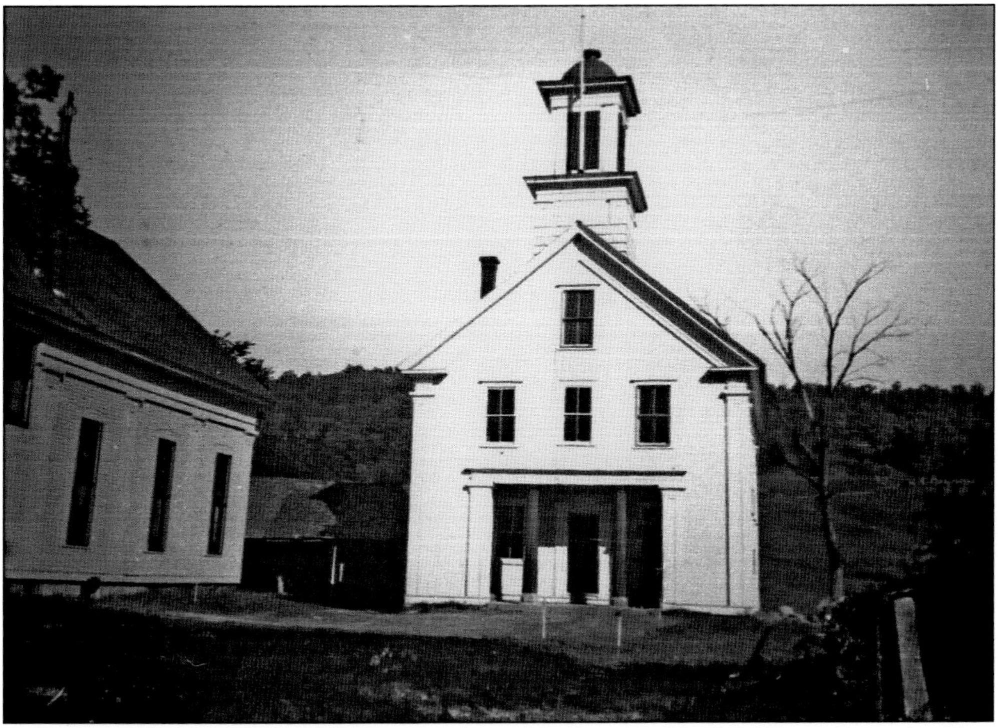

The handsome old village school in Moretown lasted until 1932, and it stood on the same site as the present elementary school. At one time in the late 1800s, Moretown had 15 school districts. It was not until 1960 that the elementary schools were merged into one in Moretown Village, where six teachers taught eight grades. (Courtesy of Moretown Historical Society.)

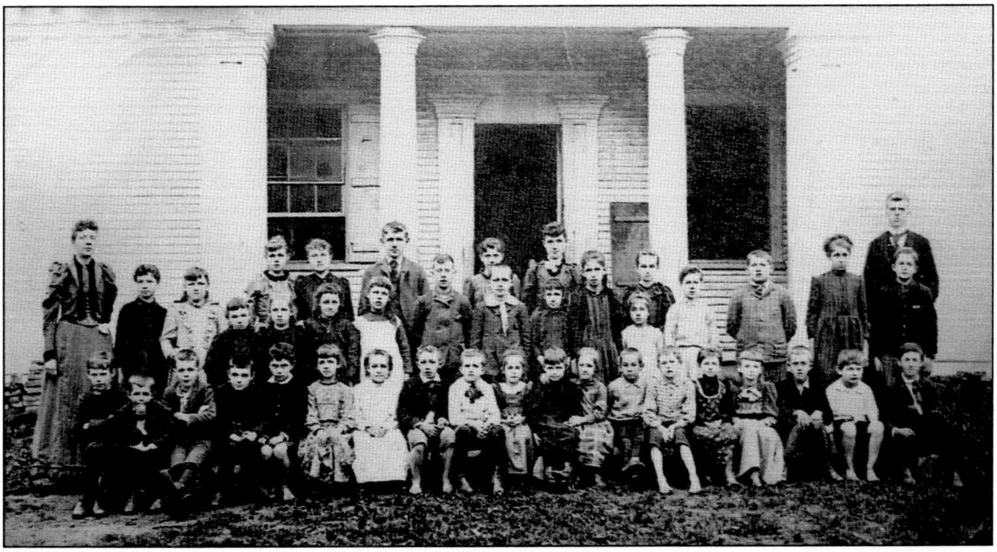

Eight grades were taught in the old village school in Moretown, as indicated by the number of students that appear in this photograph from the 1880s. There were two rooms and two teachers for the entire school. A report said that in the late 1800s, male teachers were paid $6.67 a week, while females were paid $4.31. Total enrollment for the whole town in 1888 was 226 pupils. (Courtesy of Moretown Historical Society.)

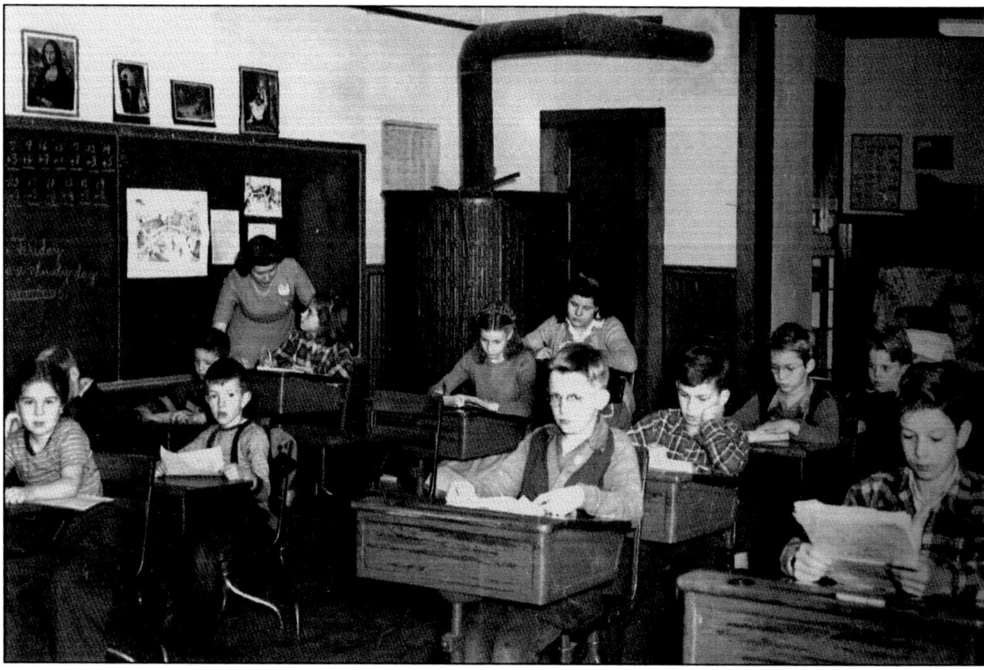

The monstrous stove in the corner of the Rockbridge School on Route 2 in Moretown kept the chill off the shoulders of the Class of 1947. Standing is substitute teacher Laurel Eddy Young. The children shown in this image are listed from front to back, beginning with the row closest to the blackboard. They are as follows: (first row) Teddy Grout (partially hidden), Roger E. Lemery, and Marlene Poland; (second row) Rosalie Noyes, Billy Clifton, Lillian Corriveau, and Barbara Lemery; (third row) Francis Grout, Billy Russell, Freddy Grout, Tommy Barry, and Buddy Eastman; (fourth row) Henry Corriveau. (Courtesy of Helen Eastman Utton.)

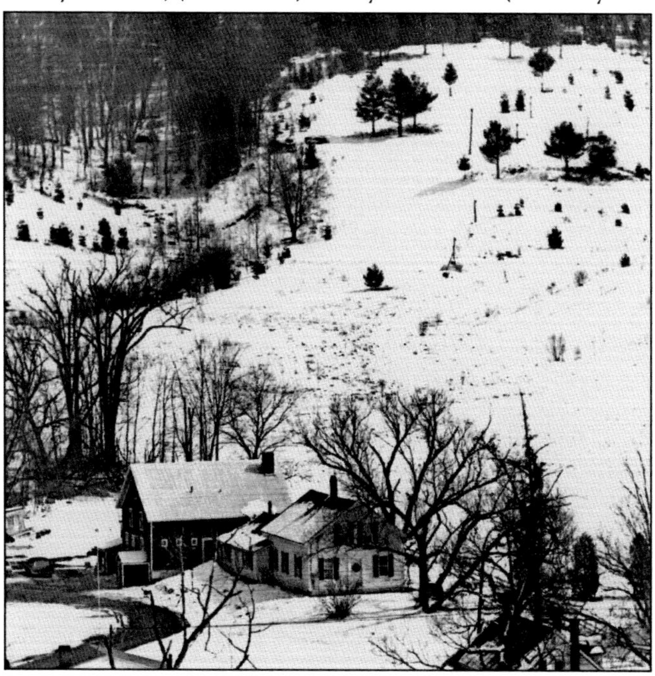

The original site of the Green Mountain Valley School was in Moretown at the home of John Schultz, who along with Bill Moore helped Al Hobart set up the academy. The school has sent many graduates to the U.S. national ski team, including Sarah Billmeier, A. J. Kitt, Doug Lewis, Katie Monahan, Jeremy Nobis, and most recently, Daron Rahlves, who was ranked No. 5 overall on the World Cup race circuit in 2003 and 2004. (Courtesy of Green Mountain Valley School.)

Three

MAKING A LIVING

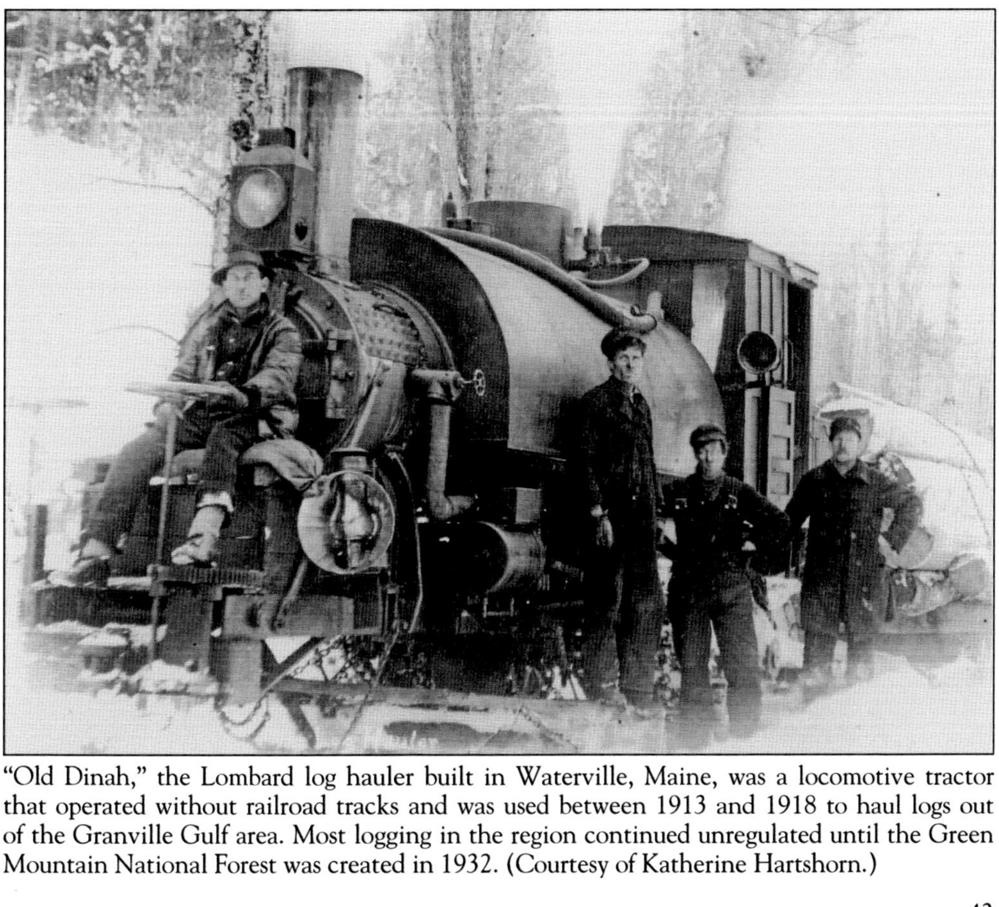

"Old Dinah," the Lombard log hauler built in Waterville, Maine, was a locomotive tractor that operated without railroad tracks and was used between 1913 and 1918 to haul logs out of the Granville Gulf area. Most logging in the region continued unregulated until the Green Mountain National Forest was created in 1932. (Courtesy of Katherine Hartshorn.)

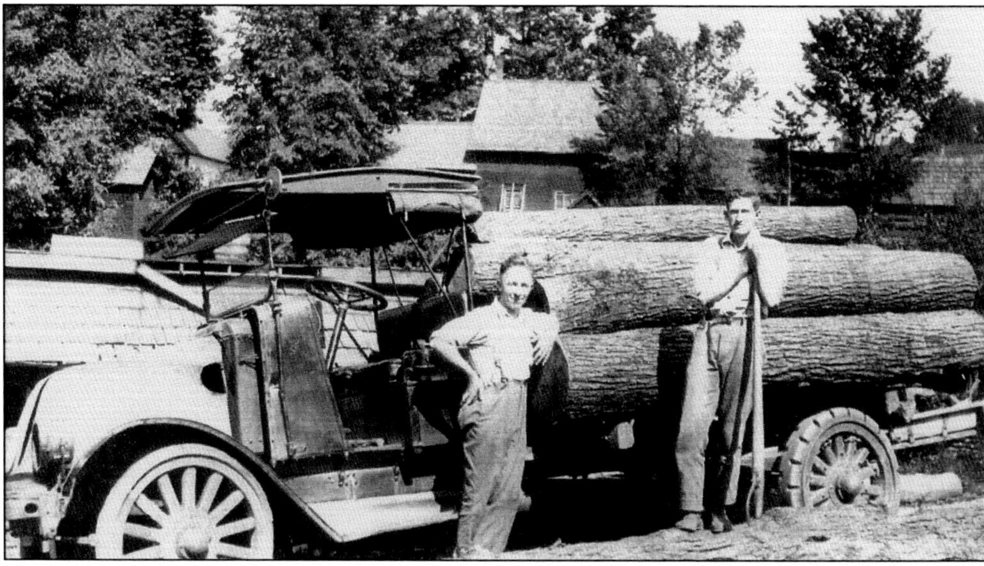

Henry Brooks (left) and Gardner Hayes are shown with the "Cast-Iron Wonder," a logging truck they used in the mid-1920s. Seen in the background is a steam-and-water-powered mill in Warren that burned in 1936. Since the national forest was created, it has grown to almost 400,000 acres, across nearly two-thirds the length of Vermont. (Courtesy of Katherine Hartshorn.)

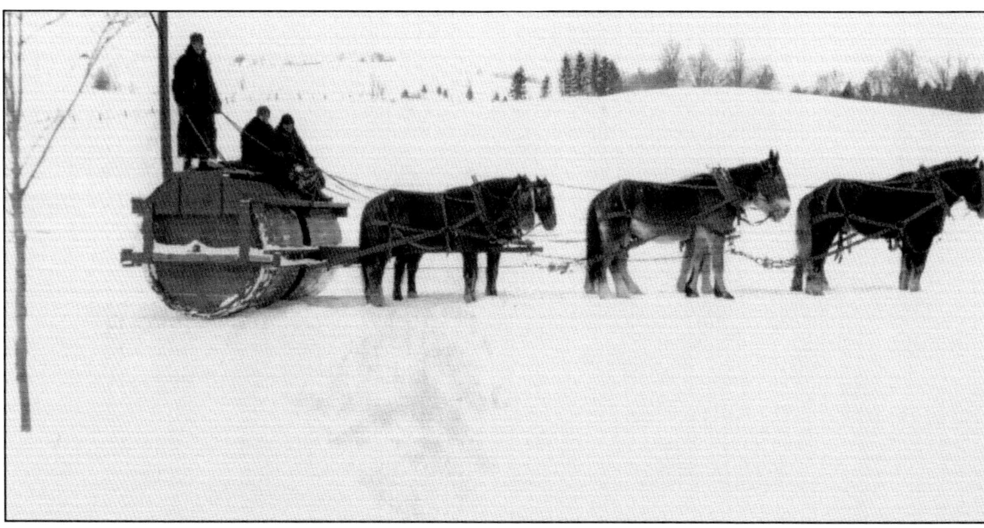

A snow roller and six mules handled by the Duxbury road crew kept the snow packed nicely on the major roads where sleighs and wagons traveled. A different problem altogether concerned the many covered bridges crossing the streams. There, crews busily shoveled snow onto the bridges to make the surfaces slick enough for sleighs to slide on.

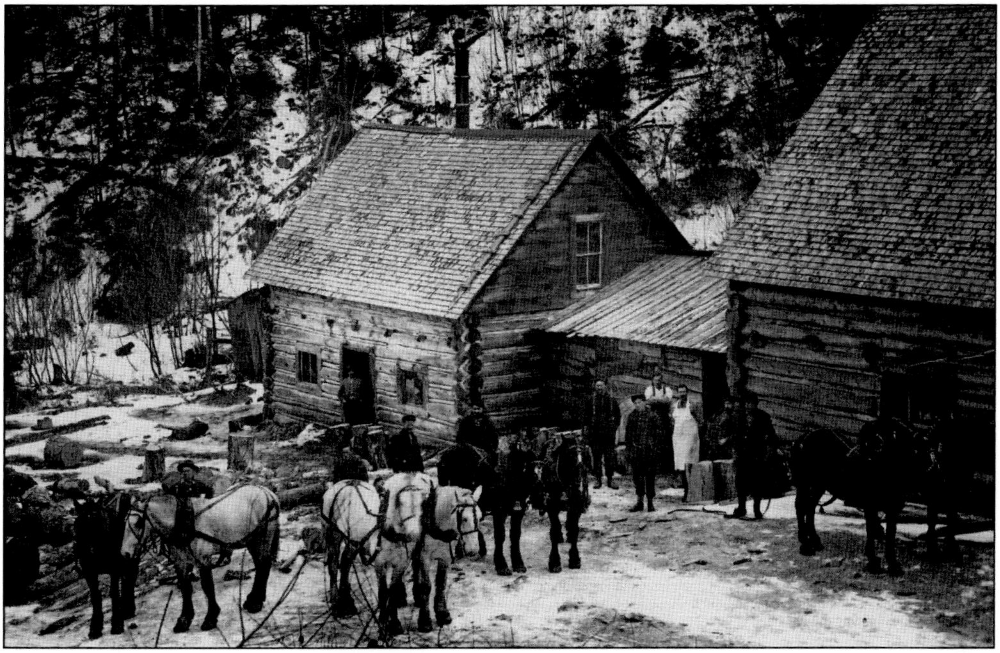

An old logging camp known as Camp 15 was located in Austin Hollow. Earl and Jessie Hanks were cooks there and many men from Warren worked the woods. Logs were hauled through the Granville Forest south to Granville, and from there they were floated down the White River to White River Junction. (Courtesy of Katherine Hartshorn.)

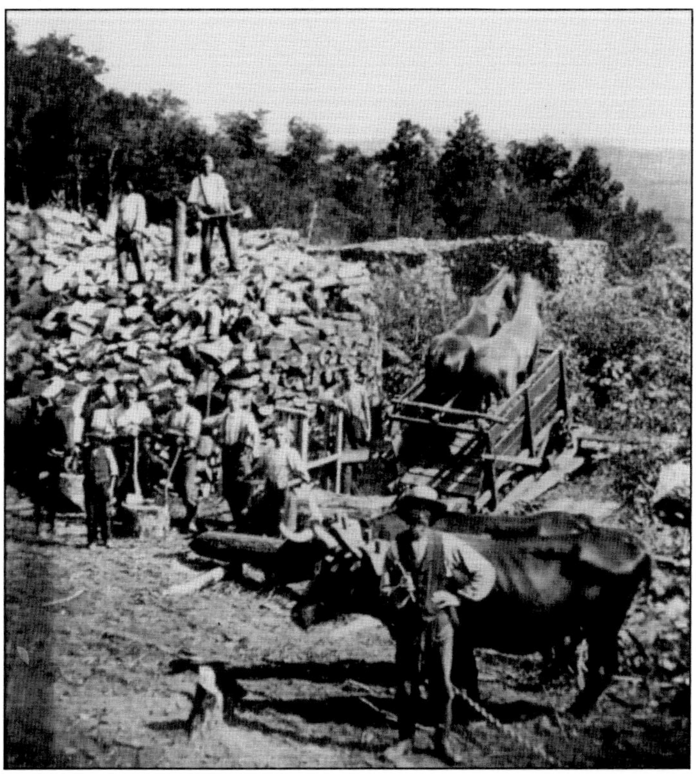

Horse-powered ramps were a portable means of putting power where it was needed in the late 1800s and early 1900s. The horses seen here are generating power for a machine that splits wood. Logging in the upland forests was a steady means of income for many farmers during the non-growing months. (Courtesy of Waitsfield Historical Society.)

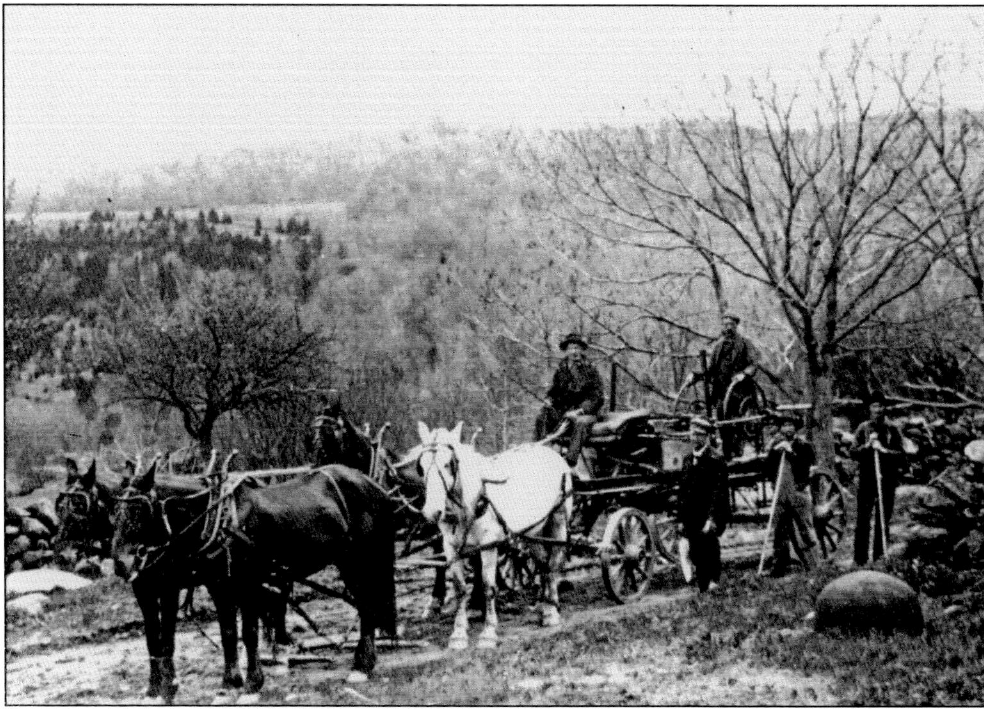

A Fayston work crew near the present site of Mount Ellen was photographed by Ernest Chase in 1903. In the wagon are, from left to right, driver Robert Livingston, and Win Dana, the road machine operator. Standing from left to right are Pline Dana, Arthur Livingston, and a man identified only as "Ramblin' Sam." (Courtesy of the Fayston Historical Society.)

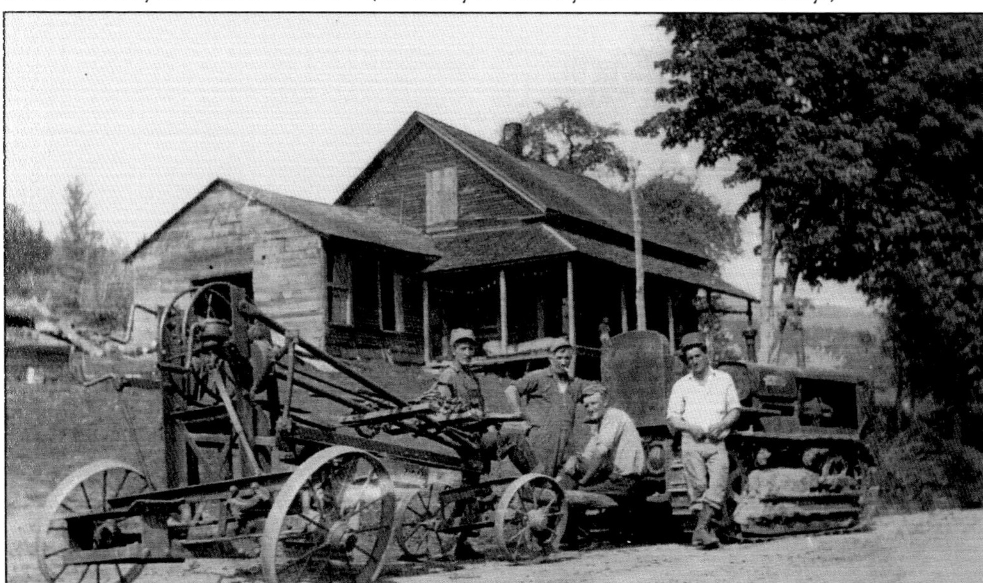

This was a retirement party for the old Fayston road grader, which probably occurred between 1943 and 1946. Shown in this image are, from left to right, Ernest Nelson, Jim Griffin, Dennis Griffin, and Greg Viens, whose house at the foot of Dunbar Hill in North Fayston is in the background. (Courtesy of the Fayston Historical Society.)

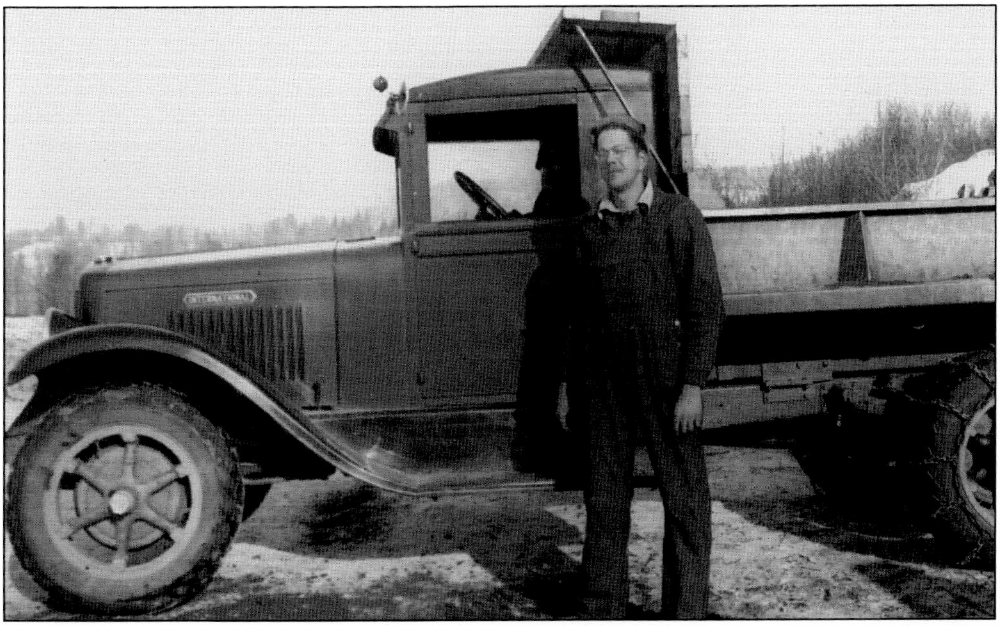

In addition to running the family feed mill in Waitsfield, Riford Joslin worked in the 1930s with the Civilian Conservation Corps (CCC) on construction of the large dams at Waterbury, Wrightsville, and East Barre. The CCC was also instrumental in cutting some of the first ski trails in Vermont. (Courtesy of Stephen Joslin.)

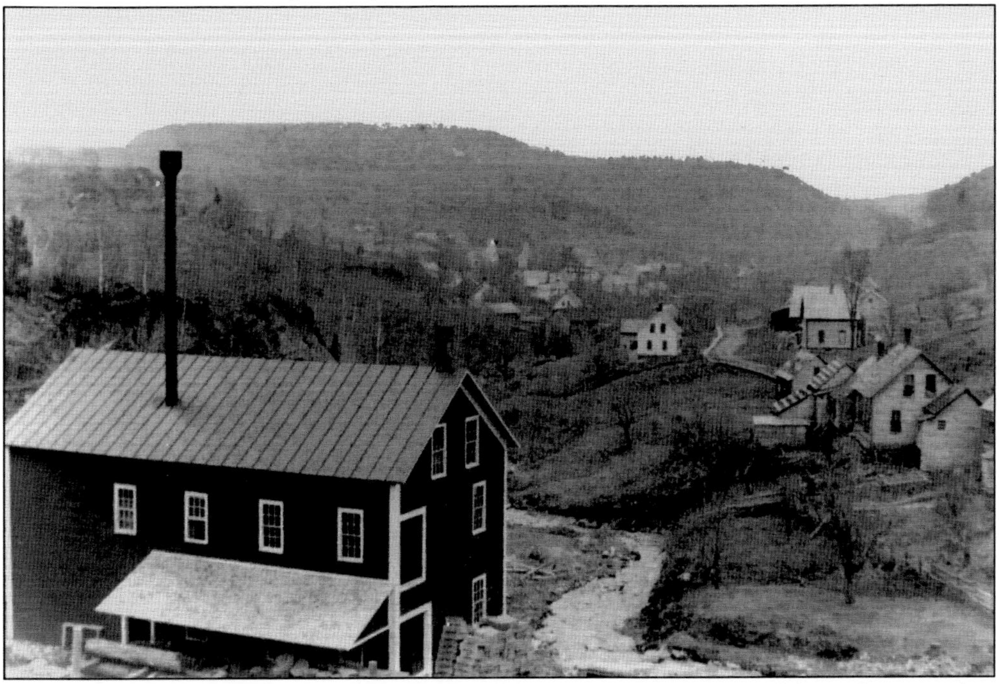

Over the years, this factory owned by H. W. Lyfords in Warren was used for making window sashes and doors, clothespins, pail handles, and tubs. Three or four employees could produce up to 30,000 butter tubs a year. The steam-powered mill was located on Clay Brook near the foot of West Hill Road. (Courtesy of Katherine Hartshorn.)

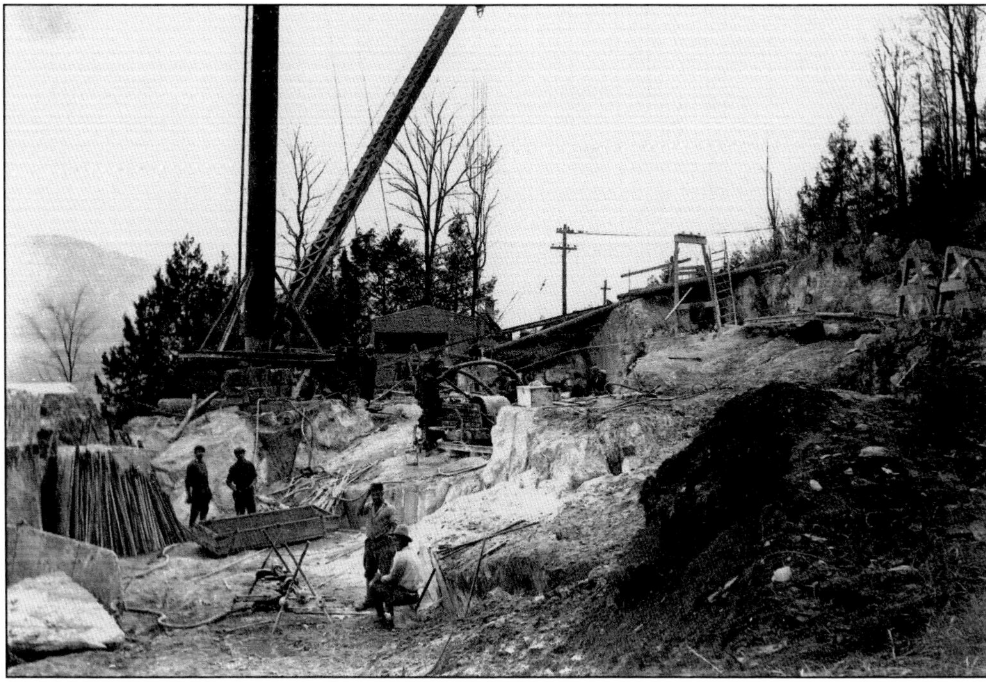

A verd antique (serpentine marble) quarry was located on Ward Hill in Duxbury. This type of marble was in great demand in the first half of the 20th century for use as countertops for soda fountains. (Courtesy of Alice DeLong.)

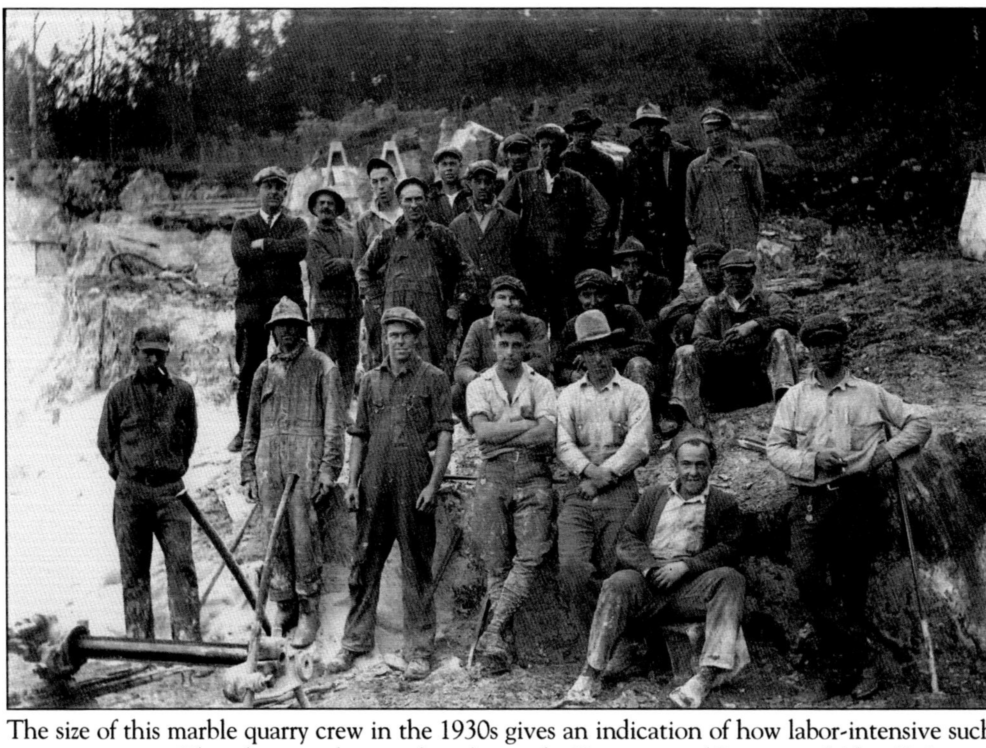

The size of this marble quarry crew in the 1930s gives an indication of how labor-intensive such enterprises were. This photograph was taken during the Depression. (Courtesy of Alice DeLong.)

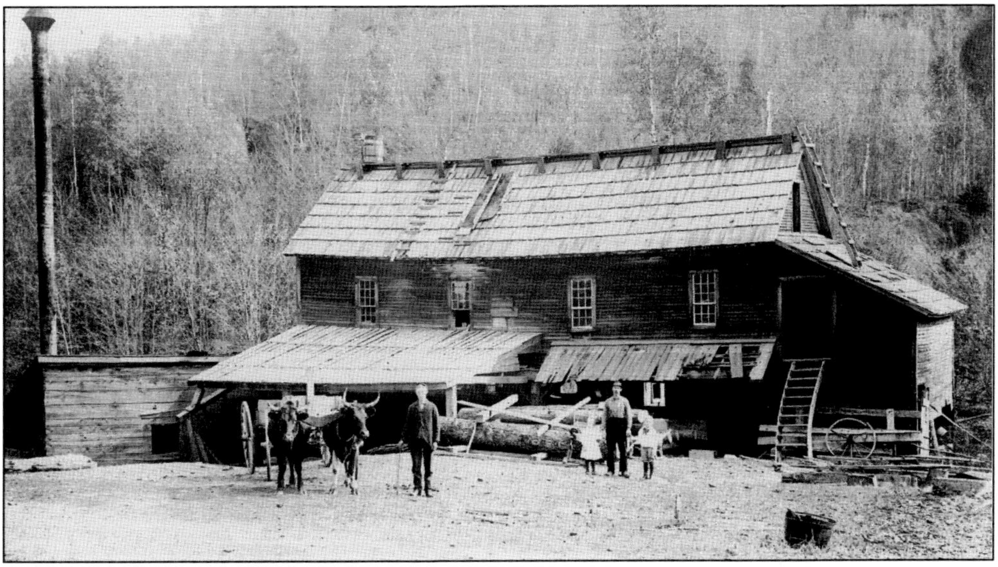

In 1908 Will Parsons's sawmill in Warren was at the south end of Warren Village, just below the Stetson Hollow Road. The trio on the right consists of Will's son Roy and his children Roma and Floran. Next to the oxen is Parsons's nephew Roy. The ruinous flood of 1927 hastened the end of water-powered industry in the valley. In that flood, Warren Village lost the dams at all four mills: the Stetson Mill, the Bradley Mill, the Grist Mill, and the Plyne Parker Mill. (Courtesy of Katherine Hartshorn.)

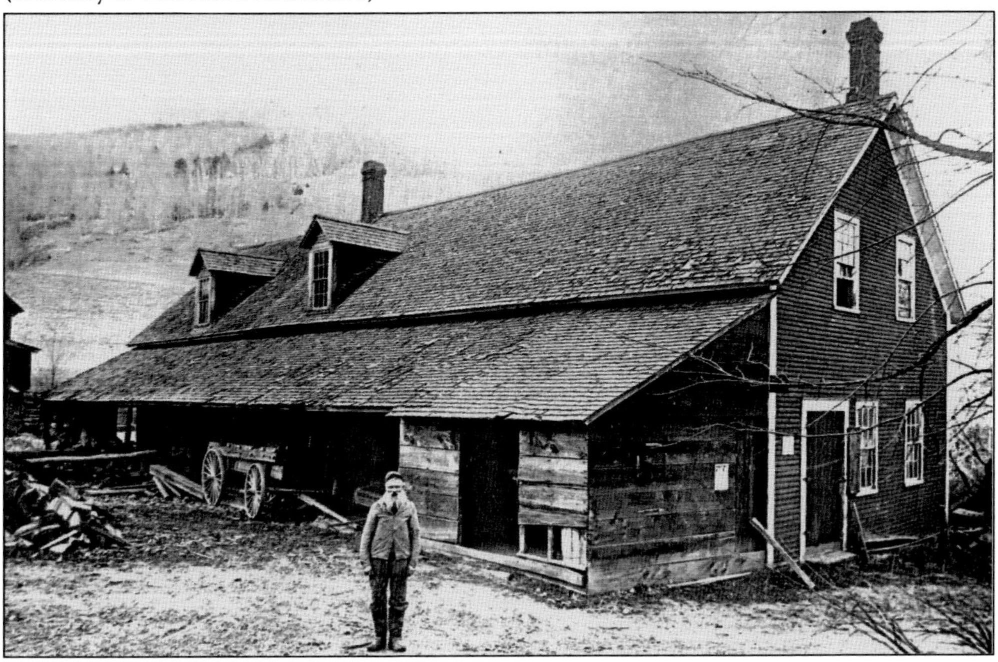

Built by Carlos Sargent *c.* 1845 as a scythe and edge-tool factory, this mill was rebuilt by John Bradley (in the photograph) after it burned in the spring of 1880. Bradley's sons Mason and Nelson took over the operation in 1884 and added clapboards, shingles, and bobbins to the product line. The Bradley Mill was located in the south end of the village of Warren, just north of the junction of Route 100 and Main Street. (Courtesy of Katherine Hartshorn.)

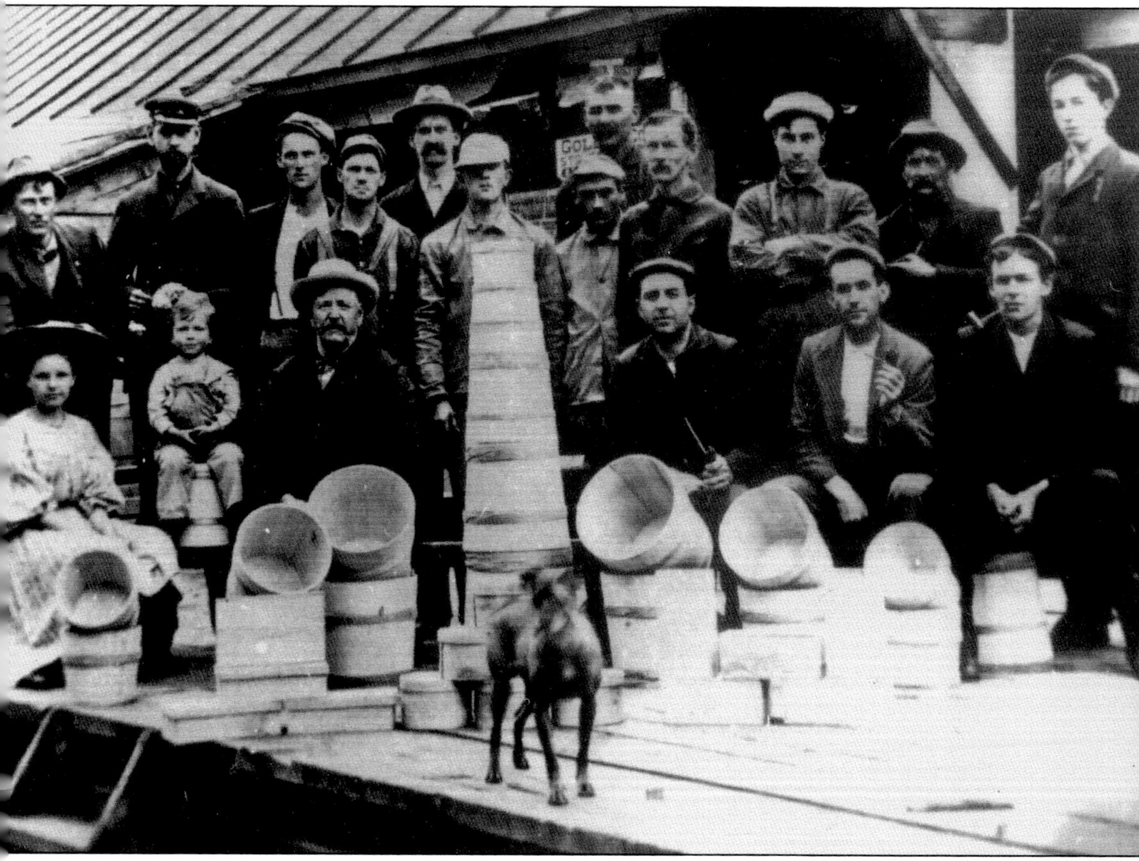

The Plyne Parker sawmill and shingle mill, which was first built in 1777 in Warren, was rebuilt in 1877 for sawing coarse lumber, shingles, and dressing boards. Parker, over the years, owned three mills in town. The clapboard mill was on the Mad River just below Freeman Brook. A lumbermill and gristmill stood across from one another on the Mad River, just south of West Hill Brook. At the apex of the mill period in Warren, the mills produced pail handles, butter tubs, wooden bowls, hoe handles, downspouts, clapboards, and shingles. The individuals pictured here include Marjorie Jones, Merrit Jones, Plyne Parker, Floyd Blake, Perle Carpenter, Don Stone, Charles Stone, Frank Shaw, Ed Van Deusen, Herman Catchapaw, George Robinson, Maurice Sterling, Allison Bradley, Dr. Edwin W. Slaton, Will Tompkins, and Vern Stone. (Courtesy of Katherine Hartshorn.)

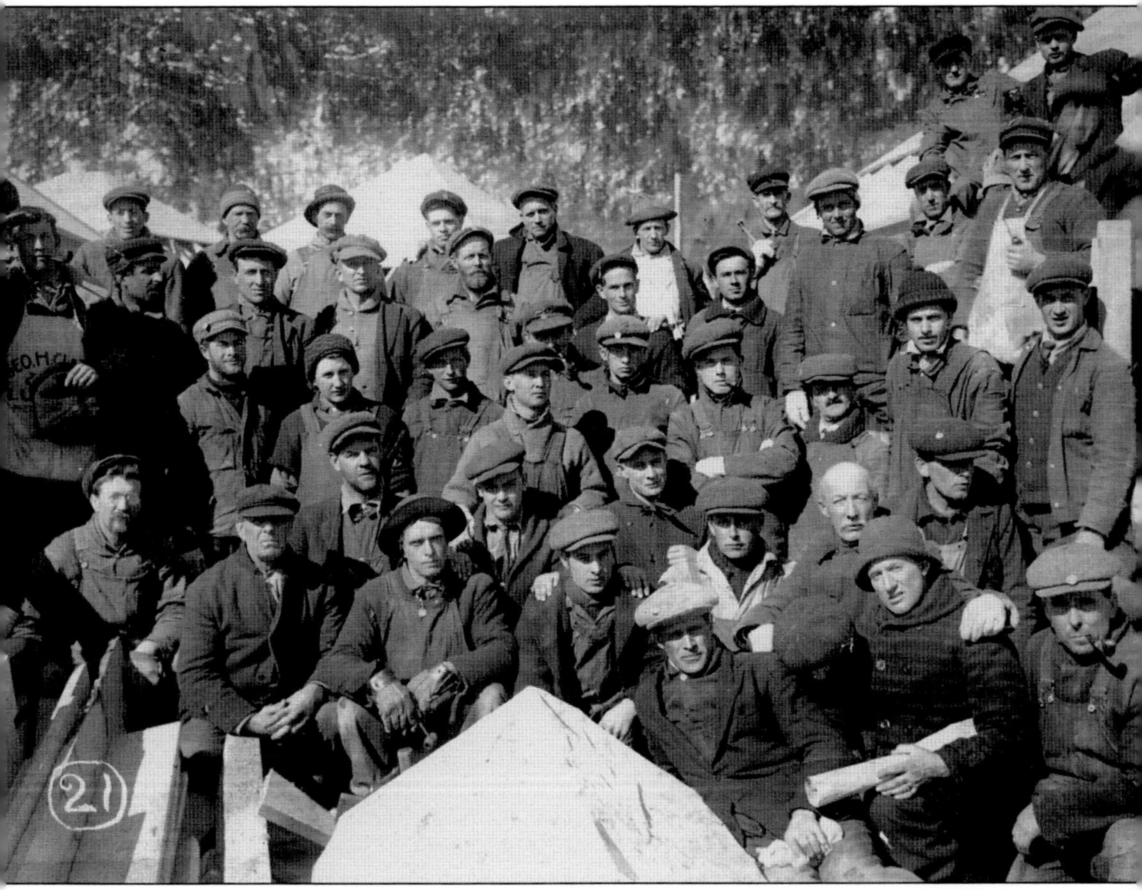

This photograph shows the work crew at the Parker and Ford Mill, which was located on the west side of the present Route 100, south of the village of Warren. Parker's mills were the largest in town. The Daniel Austin Mill was north of the village, where the Trout Hollow development is now located. In 1927, it belonged to Mary Adna Bradley. It was only used for storage of lumber by Parker and Ford at the time. In 1910, it was home to the Plyne Parker board mill, and before then it was the Parker and Slayton Lumber Company. In 1873, the mill was listed as the Daniel Austin Mill. People who worked there in 1910 were Joe Pierce, Orvil Jones, Charles Parker, Bub Miner, Audrey Hubbard, Pete Luce, George Walden, and Plyne Parker. It was flooded out in 1910. (Courtesy of Warren Library.)

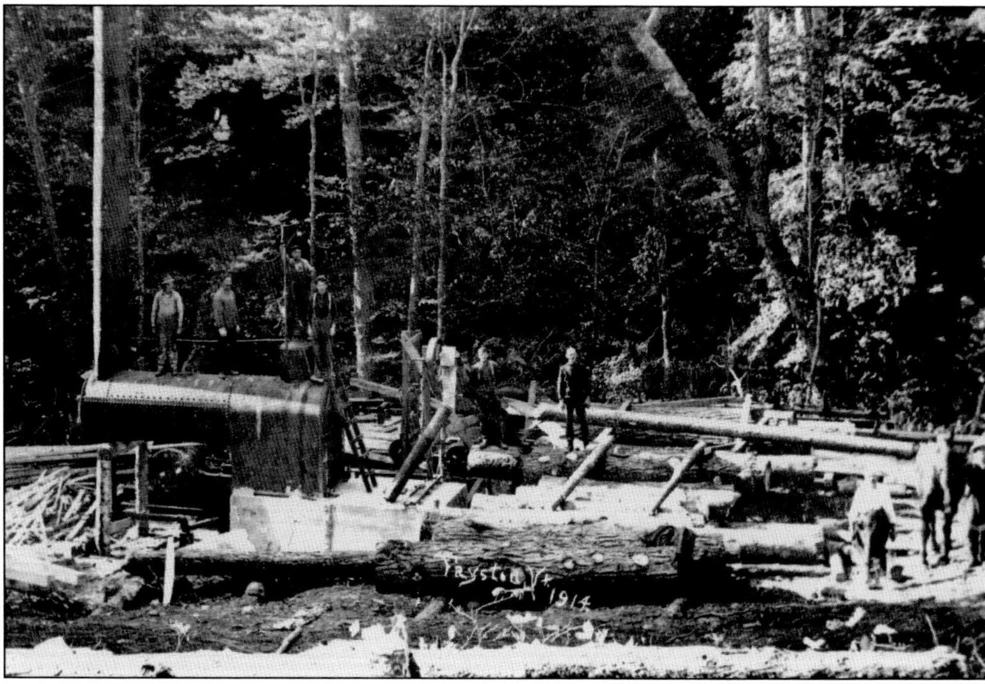

This steam-powered sawmill owned by C. D. Billings was being built in 1914 at the site of the present Hyde Away Inn on Route 17. An 1891 map showed seven lumbermills and a cooper shop in Fayston. All were powered by water and were mostly located along the Shepard and Mill Brooks. Workers often stayed overnight at the mills in camps set up there. (Courtesy of the late Reba Hall.)

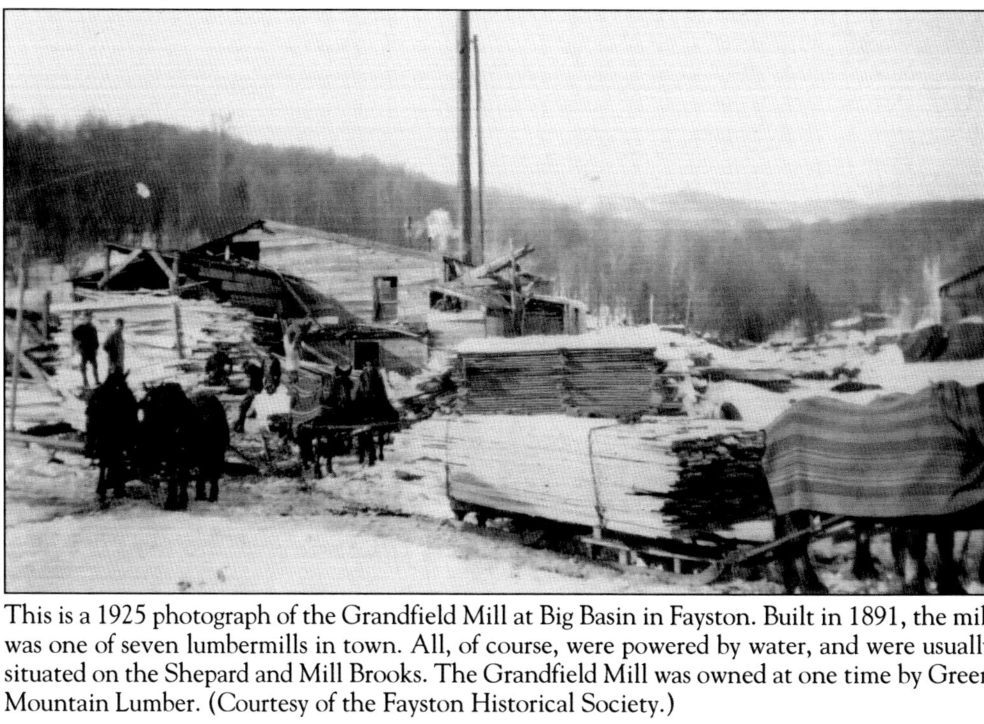

This is a 1925 photograph of the Grandfield Mill at Big Basin in Fayston. Built in 1891, the mill was one of seven lumbermills in town. All, of course, were powered by water, and were usually situated on the Shepard and Mill Brooks. The Grandfield Mill was owned at one time by Green Mountain Lumber. (Courtesy of the Fayston Historical Society.)

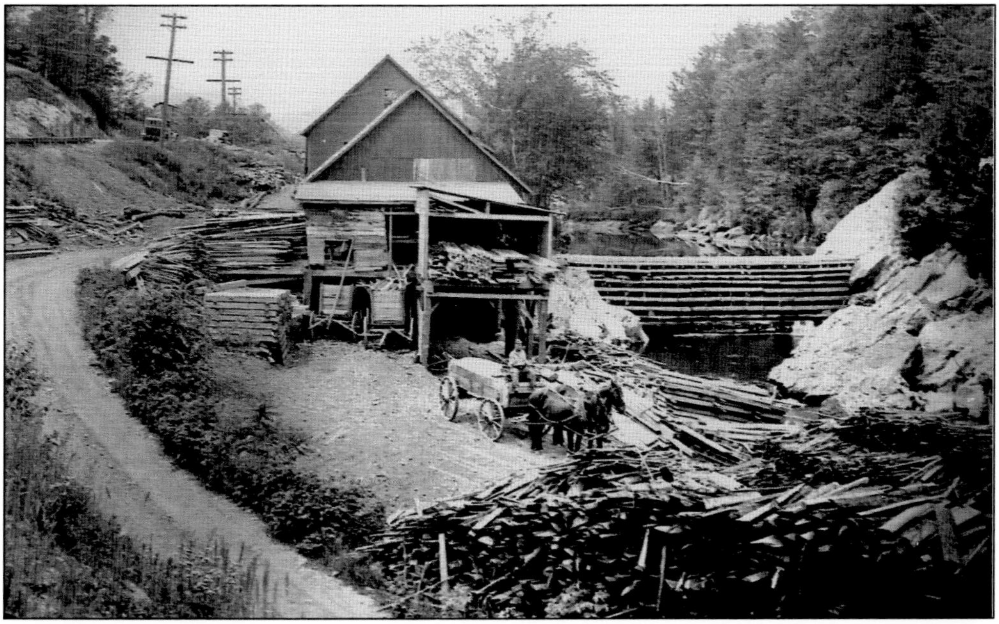

The Ward Upper Mill in Moretown burned down February 3, 1961. Its history includes the manufacture of boxes and chair parts, which were shipped to Gardner, Massachusetts, for assembly. The forerunner of the Ward Lumber Company mills was the Hiram O. Ward box factory and gristmill in the village. (Courtesy of Moretown Historical Society.)

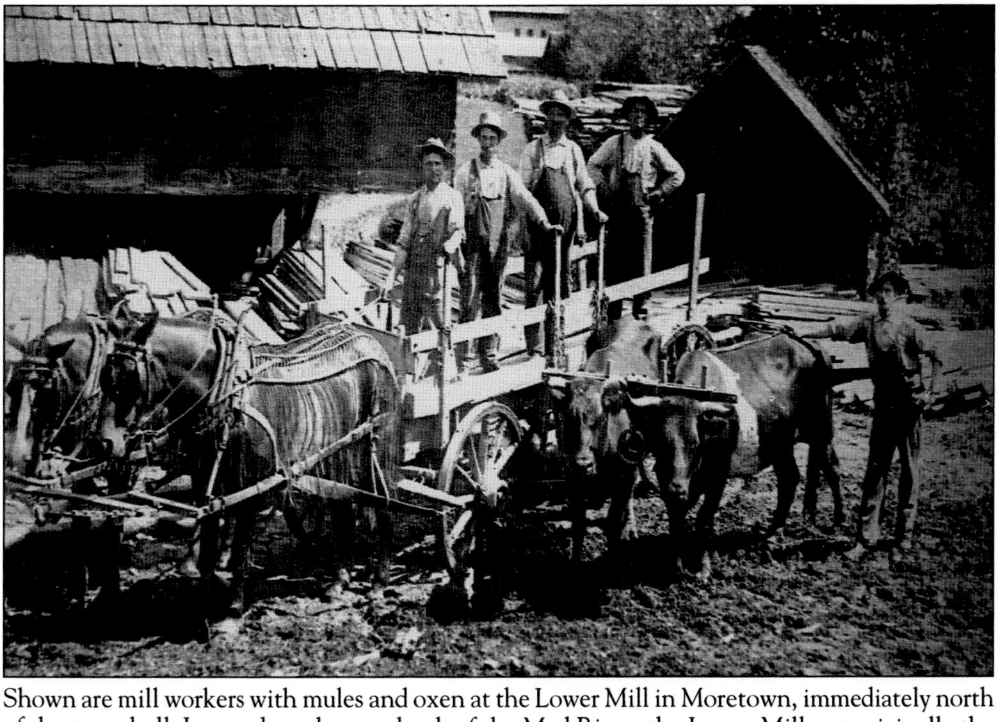

Shown are mill workers with mules and oxen at the Lower Mill in Moretown, immediately north of the town hall. Located on the east bank of the Mad River, the Lower Mill was originally the Tripp and Tenant Mill, which was destroyed by fire, then rebuilt. The fire also destroyed the nearby home of John Taylor. (Courtesy of Moretown Historical Society.)

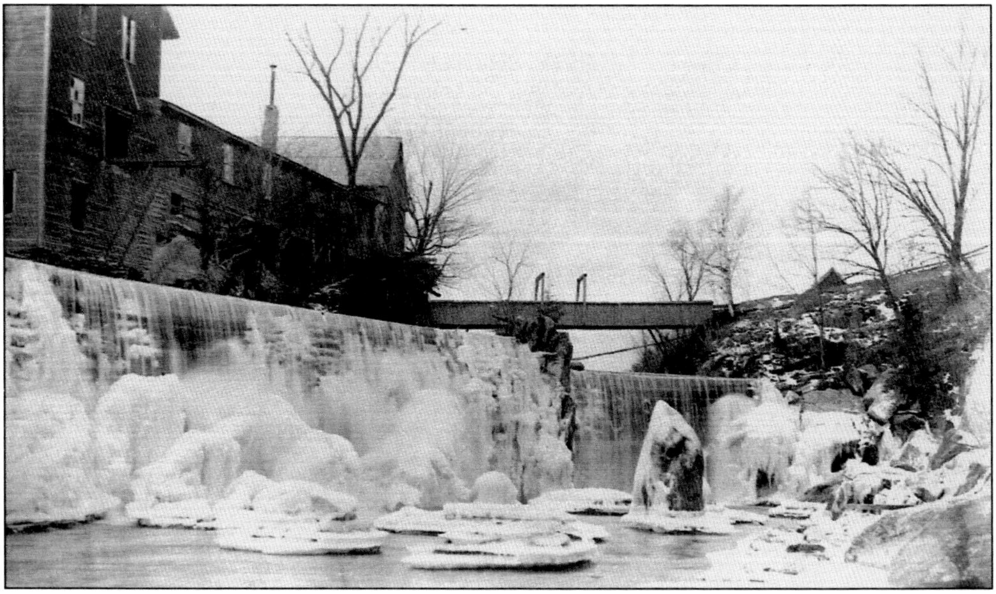

Shown is the Tripp and Tenant Mill, which was the Lower Mill taken over by Ward's in the 1880s. Ward Lumber Company bought the sites of the Fassett Mill, the Tripp and Tenant Mill, and the Parker Mill after their destruction by fire. The Wards had previously operated a mill in Dowsville. (Courtesy of Moretown Historical Society.)

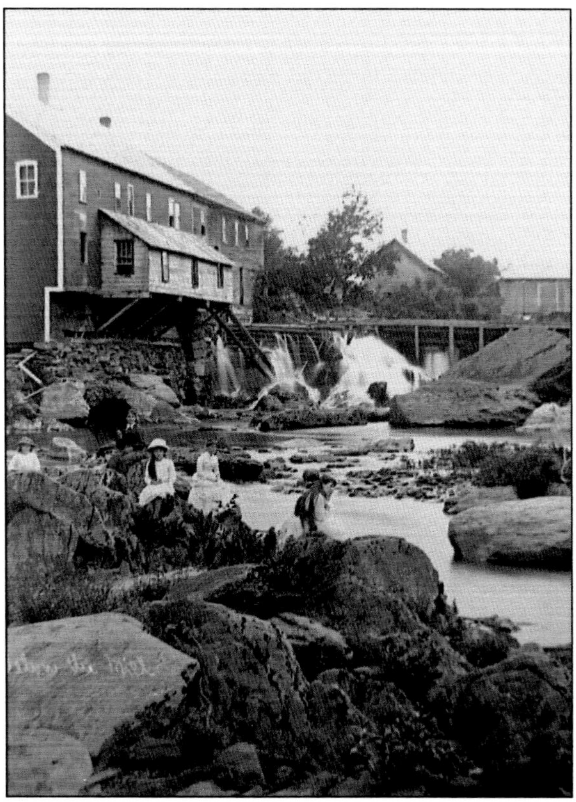

A Sunday afternoon at the old Upper Mill in Moretown is shown here, with the water from the crib dam thundering upon the rocks. At the right is the covered bridge that spanned the Mad River on what is now Route 100B, just north of the Moretown cemetery. (Photograph by G. H. Dale of Waterbury, courtesy of Moretown Historical Society.)

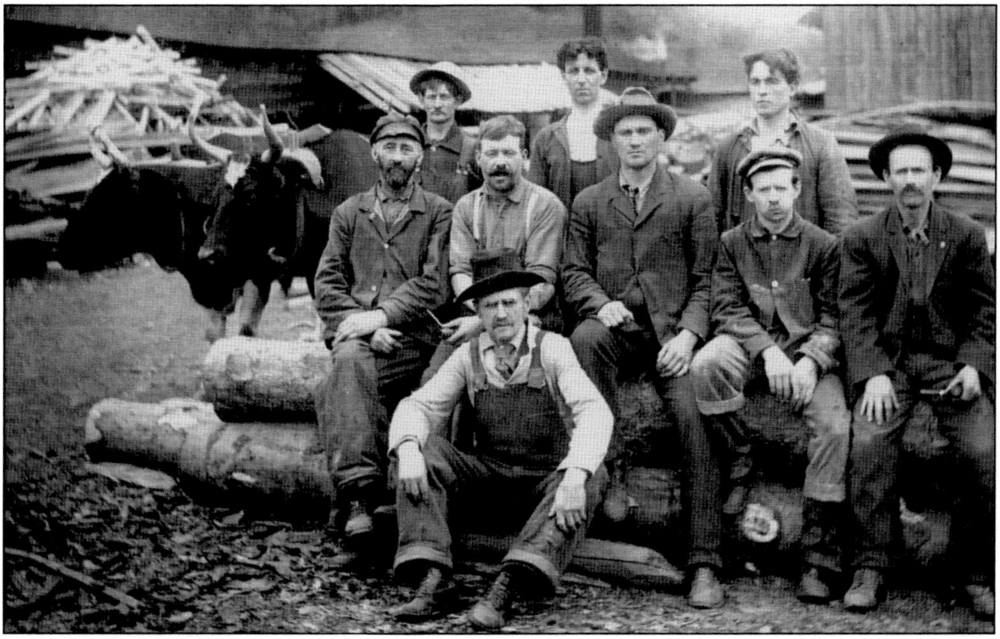

Burton Ward's lumber gang is pictured at one of the Moretown mills. The Wards had massive holdings in the Mad River Valley, most of it forested land. An article in the *Burlington Free Press* in November 1937 reported that the company had planted 800,000 spruce and pine in the forests it owned, of which 14,000 acres were in the Mad River Valley. (Courtesy of Moretown Historical Society.)

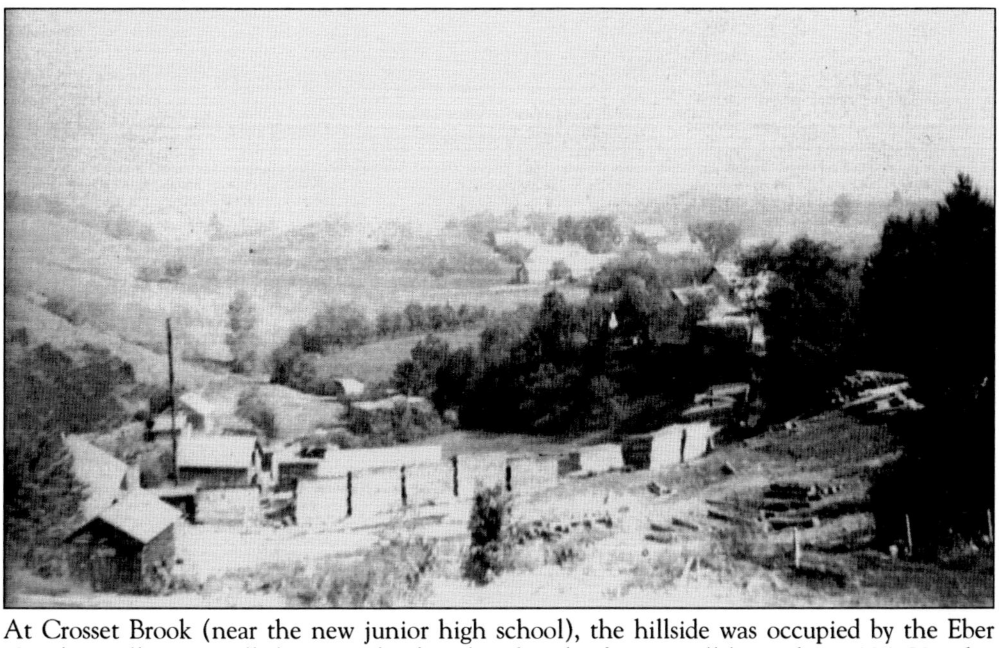

At Crosset Brook (near the new junior high school), the hillside was occupied by the Eber Huntley Mill, a sawmill that Huntley bought after the former mill burned in 1886. Huntley made dressed lumber, chair stock, and hardwood flooring, and employed seven or eight men in the mill plus a crew in the woods. The mill handled 500,000 feet of lumber a year. Huntley was a former town clerk of Duxbury. (Courtesy of Alice DeLong.)

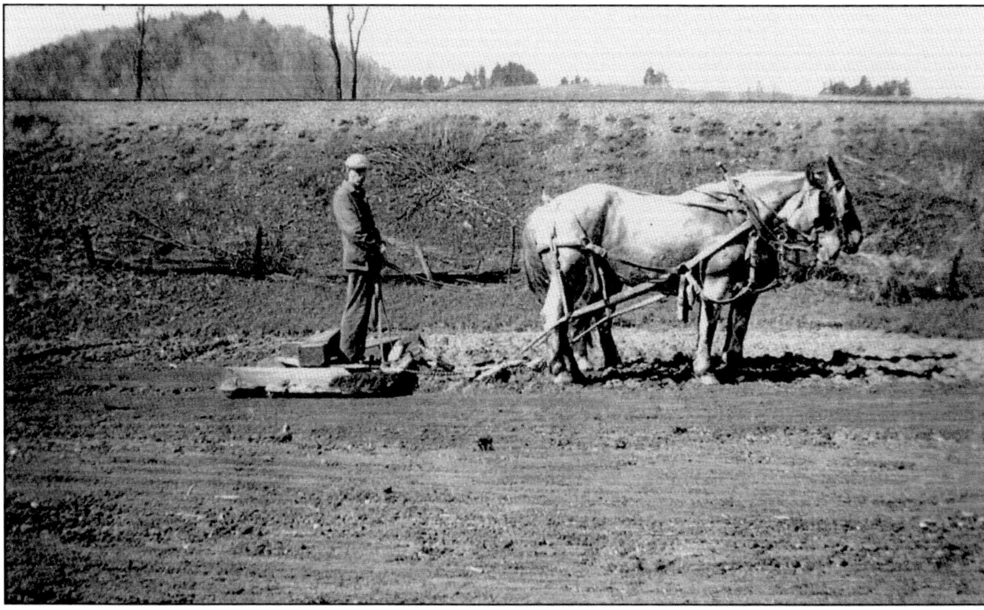

A stone boat that had railroad spikes on its bottom was used to pack seeds into the ground. Some of Vermont's first settlers were farmers who had come in search of more-fertile soil than what remained on the farmed-out acres they had left in southern New England. The newcomers were met in most places by flinty fields that were hard to plow. (Courtesy of Alice DeLong.)

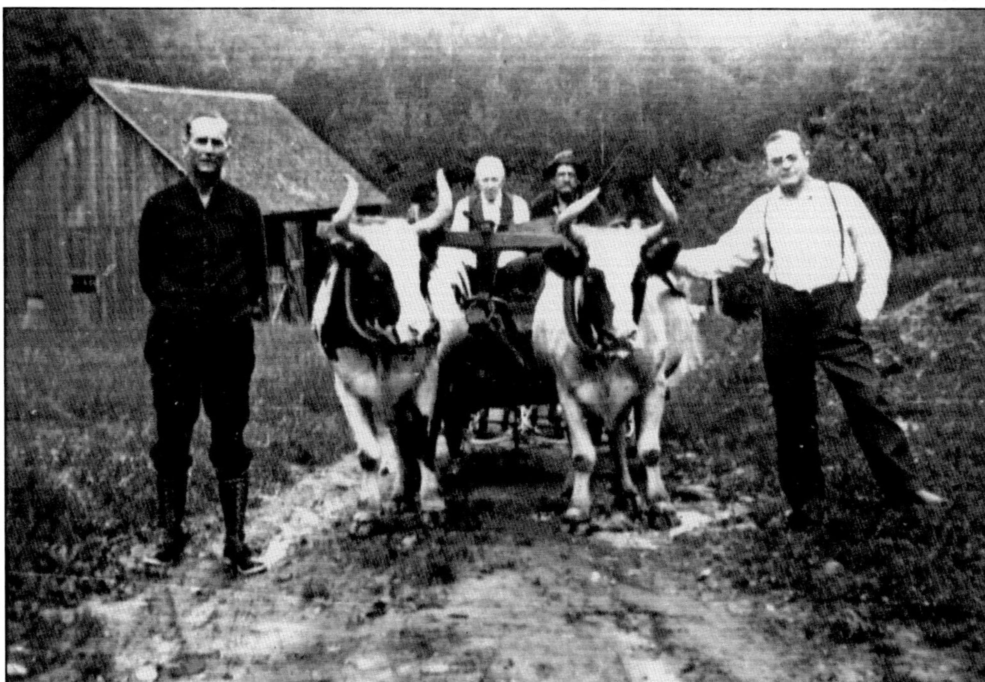

Oxen, which are fully grown steer, were often the bovine engine of choice in the 18th and 19th centuries. Andon Smith is the white-haired gentleman riding in this cart, which was photographed in front of Smith's barn in the Stetson Hollow area of Warren. (The other men are not identified.) (Courtesy of Katherine Hartshorn.)

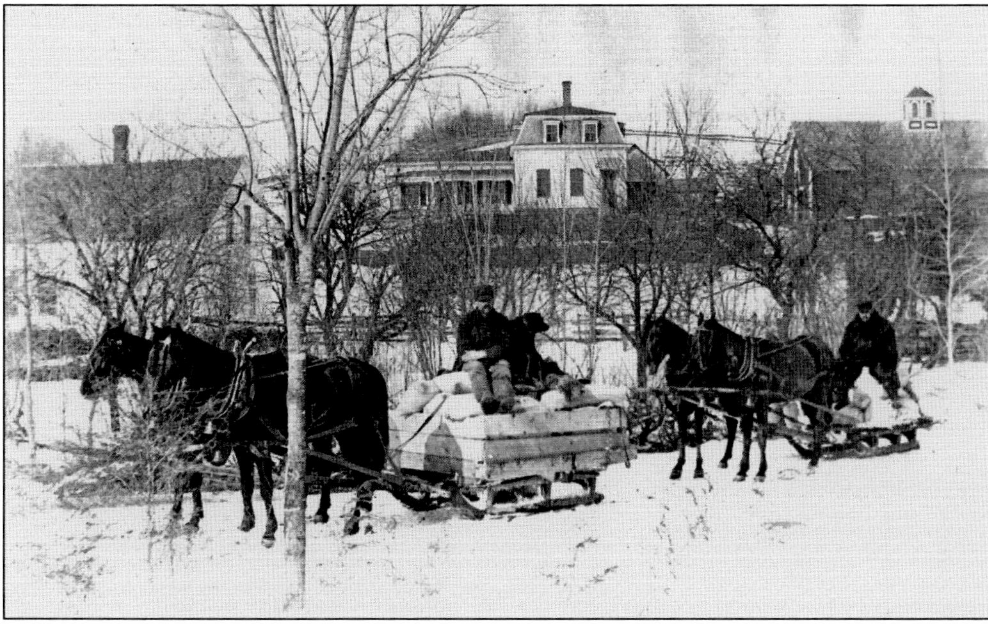

Here, Audrey Hubbard (left) and Gabe Senor are bound for the gristmill c. 1910; the Jones-Mobus House is one of the houses in the background. Plyne Parker's gristmill was located on the Mad River north of Freeman Brook, in the north end of Warren Village. Parker also owned a lumbermill on the west side of the river. (Courtesy of Katherine Hartshorn.)

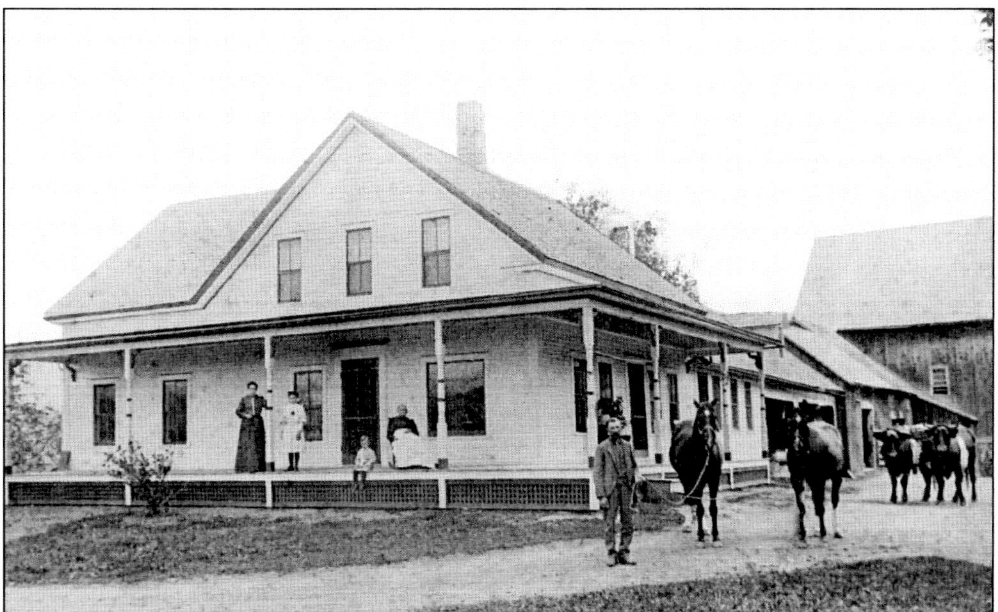

On the front porch of the Meadow Crest Farm in Waitsfield in 1910 are, from left to right, Jennie Palmer, Gladys Palmer, Harry Palmer, and Melissa Wheeler Barnard. Fred Palmer stands at the front with the horses. The Palmer ancestors helped settle the Mad River Valley in the 18th century. The farm, at Meadow and North Roads in Waitsfield, is part of the Mad River Valley Rural Historic District. (Courtesy of Fred Messer.)

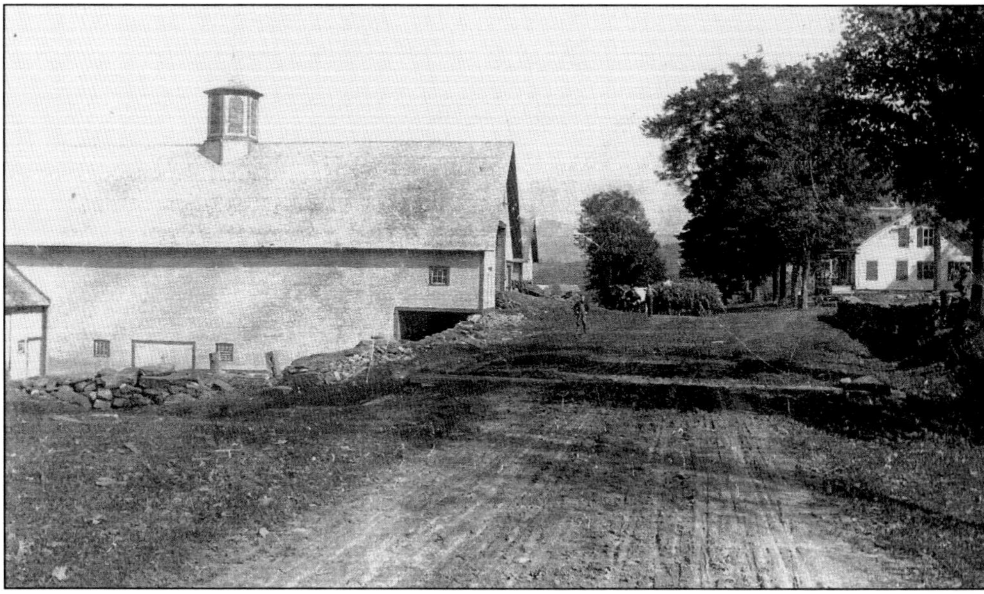

Shown here is the Geiger Farm on the Waitsfield Common Road. The barn was built in 1882. Toward the latter half of the 19th century, the emphasis of farming in the Mad River Valley changed from sheep to cows. In 1803, in Waitsfield there were nearly 700 sheep and about 165 cows. Less than 25 years later (1826), there were 3,200 sheep and little more than 550 cows. By 1908, there were only 113 sheep, compared to 1,843 cows. (Courtesy of Fletcher Joslin.)

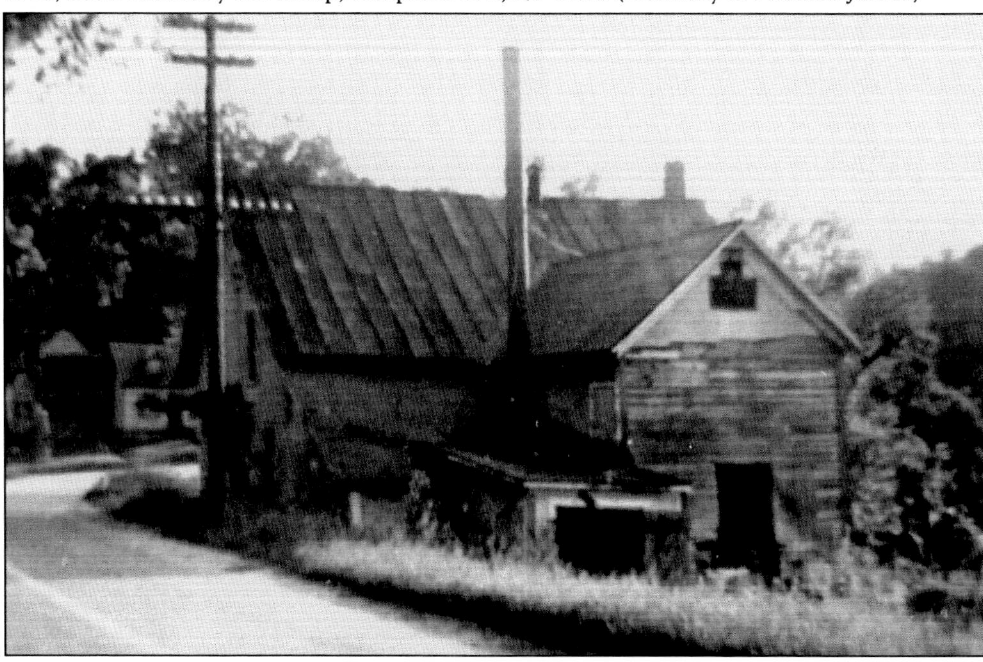

The old creamery in Moretown was located at the site of the Moretown Village swimming hole on Route 100B. The creamery was in operation until the mid-1930s and was managed by Birney Griffith. Many farmers sold their milk and cream there. Butter was made and sold at the creamery, along with fresh cream. A spring on the property furnished the creamery with ice-cold water. (Courtesy of Moretown Historical Society.)

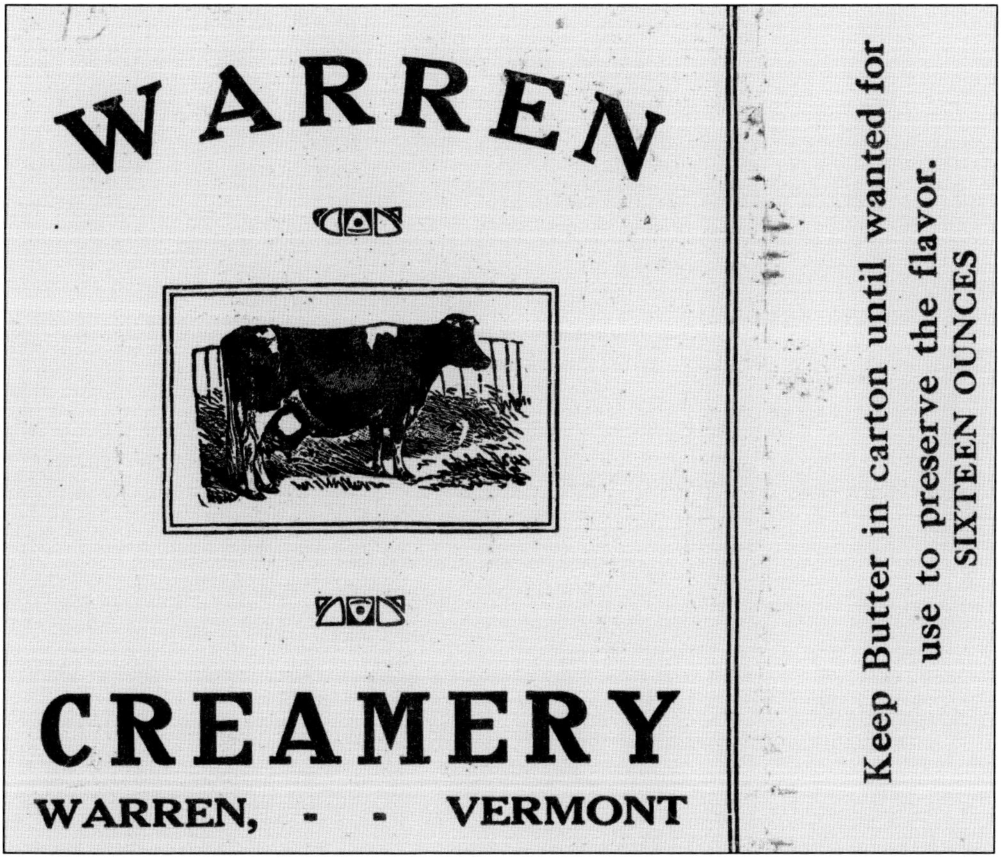

The Warren Creamery attached these labels to its butter boxes. The creamery was established in East Warren in 1892, but was moved to the village in 1900. In the 1890s, the valley had four different creameries. In Waitsfield there was a co-op creamery and Harry Belden's Mad River Creamery. The foundation remains of Moretown's creamery can be found at the swimming hole on Main Street in the village. Changing times marked the real demise of creameries due to the fact that whole milk could be trucked out of the valley for processing, usually to Waterbury or at other points for shipment. Then, the introduction of DeLaval separators enabled farmers to separate milk from cream at their farms rather than at the creameries. The Hood Milk Company began picking up fluid milk at various distribution points for shipment to Boston, but in later years, milk was picked up directly from the new steel bulk tanks at the farms by refrigerated trucks. (Courtesy of Katherine Hartshorn.)

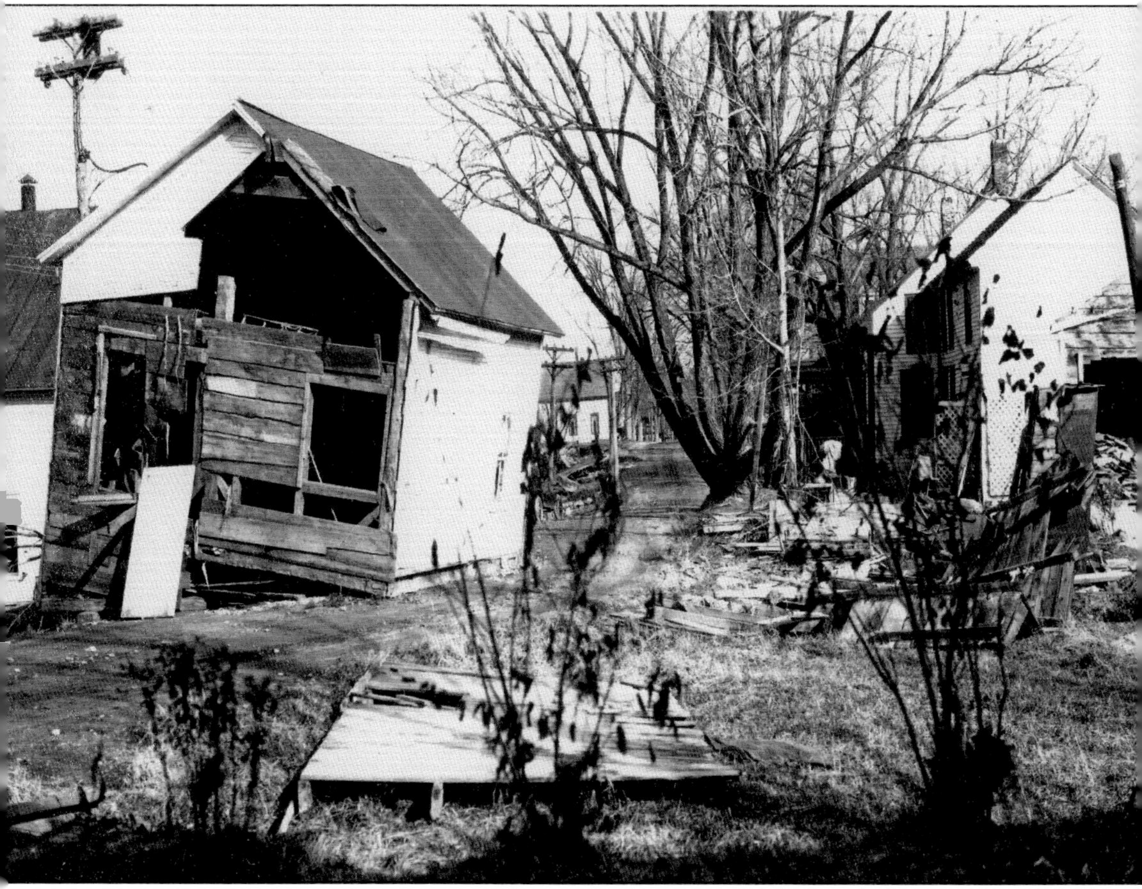

A portion of the Moretown creamery (shown on page 58) was deposited in the middle of what is now Route 100B during the disastrous flood of 1927, which swept away almost an entire mill industry on the Mad River and put many people out of work. The monetary damages in all of Vermont totaled $25,026,355. Even worse, 55 persons lost their lives, including 12 in Waterbury, 8 in Duxbury Corners, and 5 in Moretown. A poignant account of the 1927 flood, printed in the "Brief History of Moretown 1963," related that a home with three people in it was dislodged from the banks of the Winooski River, into which the Mad River empties at the border of Moretown and Middlesex: "All three were carried away when their house, with lights burning, sailed down the river, seen by many as it tossed its way along the miles." A couple and their grandson perished. (Courtesy of Moretown Historical Society.)

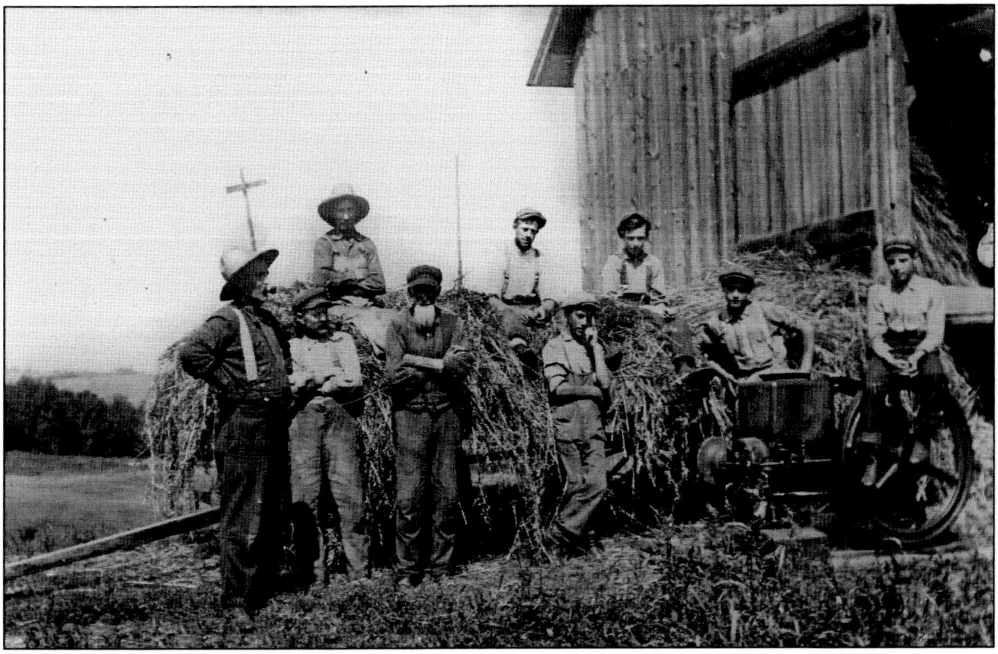

Almond Gove's for-hire threshing machine, shown here at Blair's Barn in Warren in 1914, moved from farm to farm at every harvest. Pictured are Edgar Towne, Carl Buzzell, Erwin Willsol, Almond Gove, Herb Blair, Jim Blair, Walter Parker, Dennis Gove, and Elmer Gove. (Courtesy of Warren Library.)

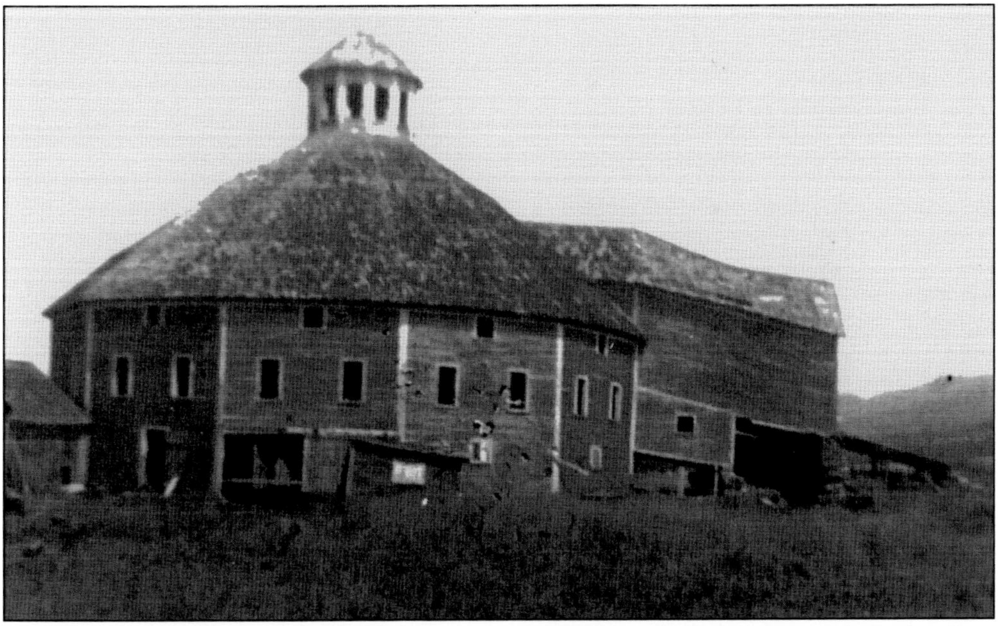

Art Mobus's round barn was constructed by one of the McLaughlin brothers and stood at Four Corners in East Warren. Round barns were considered more economical because they held more storage with less wall space, were easier to clean, and, mythically, eliminated corners where the Devil might hide. This barn was later pulled down by a tractor and replaced by a free-stall barn, built by Rudolph Elliot. (Courtesy of Warren Library.)

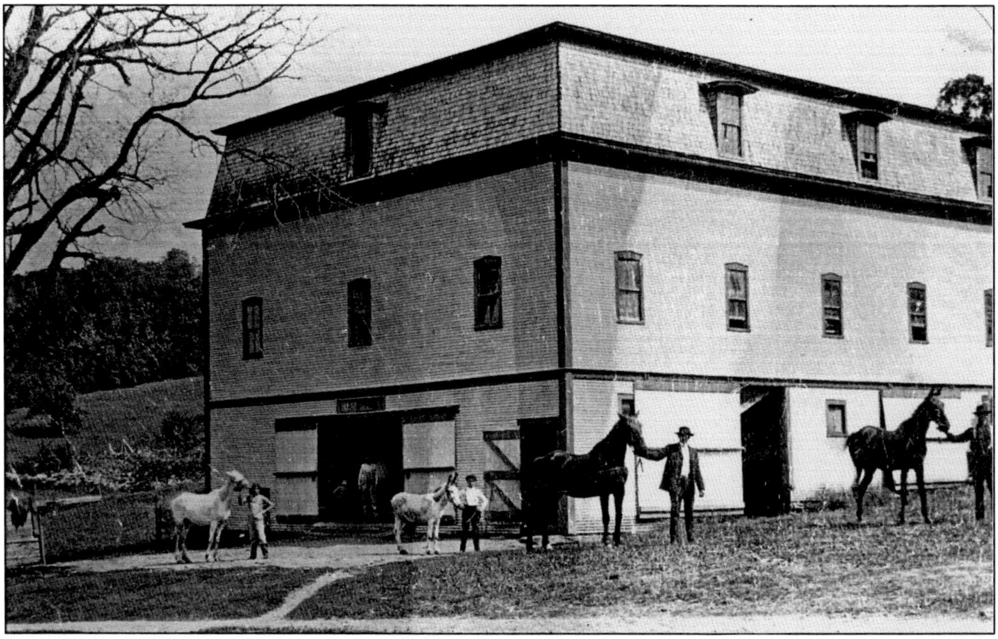

The large and handsome Mobus Barn in East Warren was destroyed by fire in 1904. Fred Mobus was the son of John and Kate Mobus, who came from Germany originally. The family's descendants have continued to play a major role in the development of the valley. (Courtesy of Warren Library.)

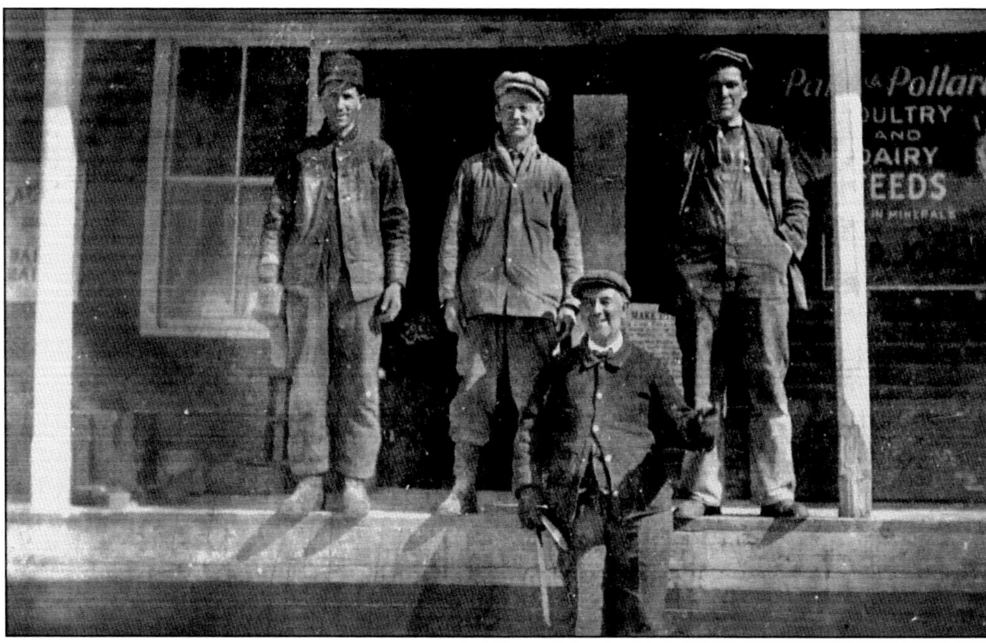

Stephen Perry Joslin (top right) operated a family feed mill and store on Bridge Street. The others in the photograph are, from left to right, Herb Smith, George Patterson, and Walter Moriarty. The latter owned a sawmill directly behind the Joslin store. The mills were powered by a canal that ran under Bridge Street before flowing back into the Mad River. The canal has since dried up. (Courtesy of Fletcher Joslin.)

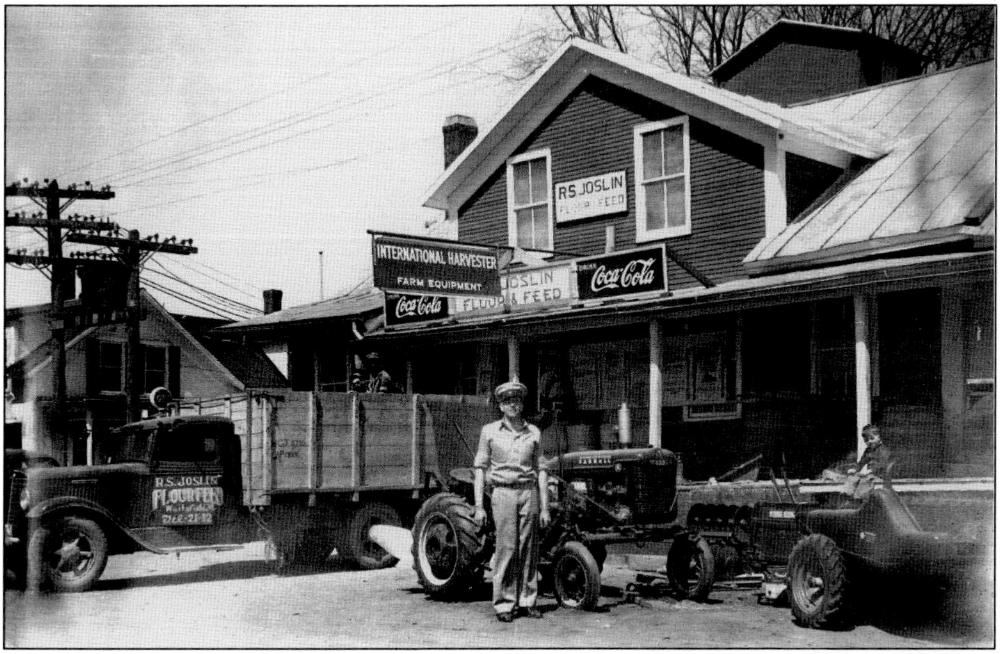

Riford Joslin stands in this 1940s view of the Joslin feed mill and store, which burned down in 1944. It had been located on Bridge Street where the Miramar Ski Club is today. The Joslin family has been a presence in Waitsfield since the 1790s. (Courtesy of Stephen Joslin.)

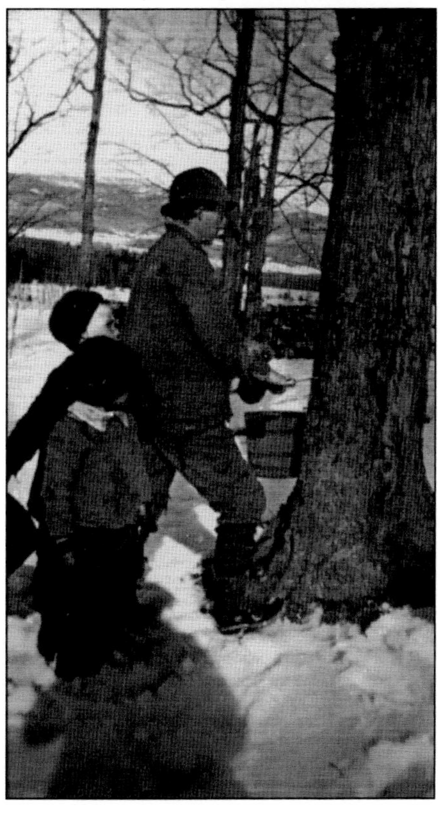

Albert Whitworth taps a maple tree on the DeFreest Farm in Warren. Sugaring is a rite of spring, and maple sugar has been a principal valley product from the time of the first settlers to the present day. At one time, sugar makers who lacked local markets sold to the Cary Maple Sugar Company and other firms like it. (Courtesy of Warren Library.)

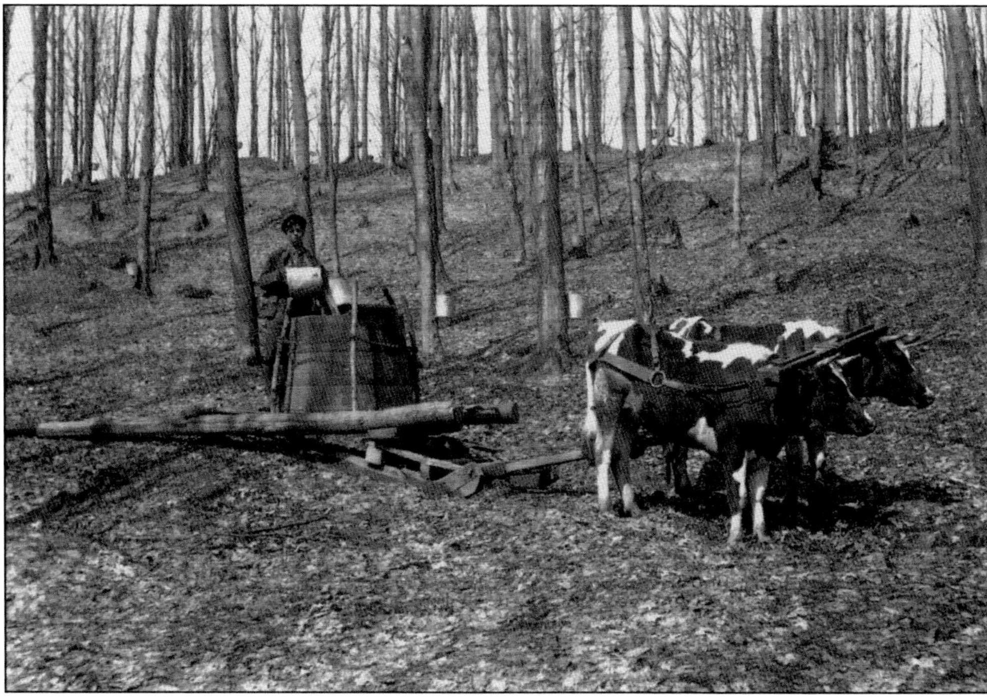

Gathering maple syrup in Duxbury. Here is an 1845 entry from the maple sugar diary of Duxbury mill owner James Crossett: "March 1, Got sap spouts. March 4, sharpened sap spouts. March 16, made 25 pounds sugar. March 25, made 103 pounds sugar. March 29, made 187 2/3 pounds sugar. April 25, finished sugar. Made 1,532 pounds sugar." (Courtesy of Alice DeLong.)

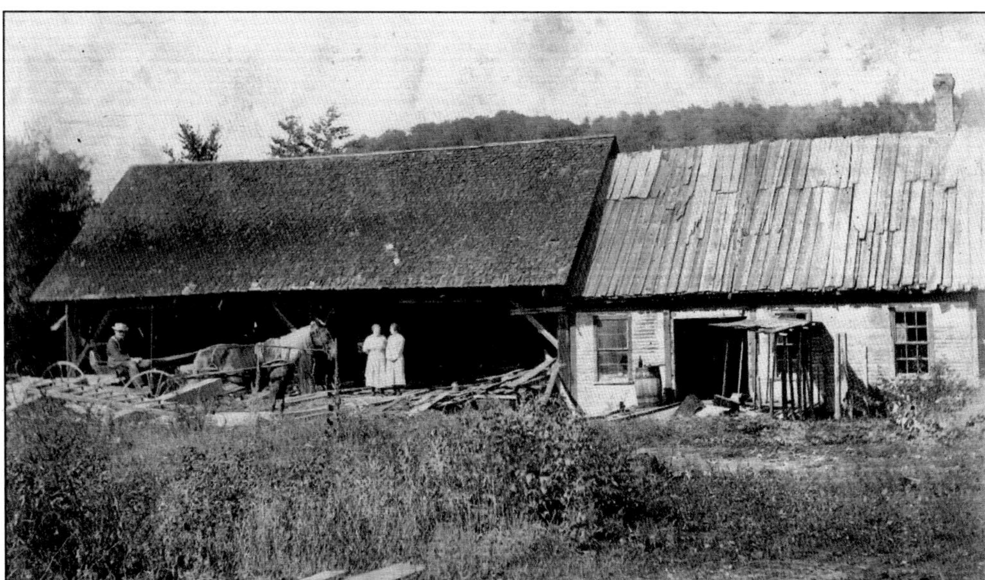

Murray's Cider Mill in South Duxbury was located on Dowsville Brook, which passes under present-day Route 100, south of Harwood Union High School. Pictured from left to right are Warren Murray, Maggie Battles, and Edna Lodge. (Courtesy of Alice DeLong.)

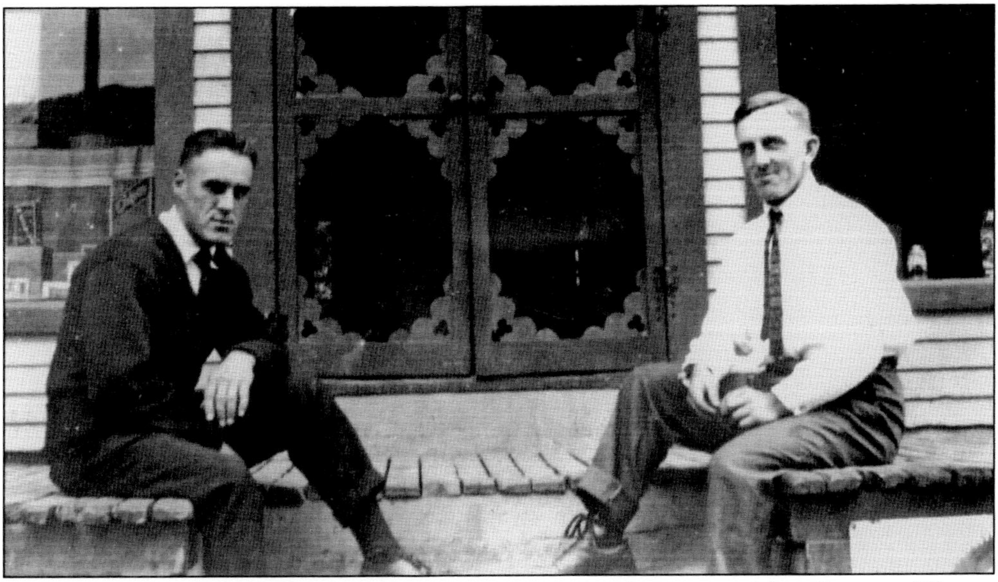

Lawrence Ford (left) and Harold Parker were proprietors of a store on Main Street in Warren that formerly was the Spaulding store. The site later became the parking lot for guests of the Pitcher Inn, which is one of 75 buildings within the town's historic district. The fact that the railroads bypassed the Mad River Valley is a major reason why its villages have maintained their character. The railroads brought with them rapid and often haphazard development. (Courtesy of Katherine Hartshorn.)

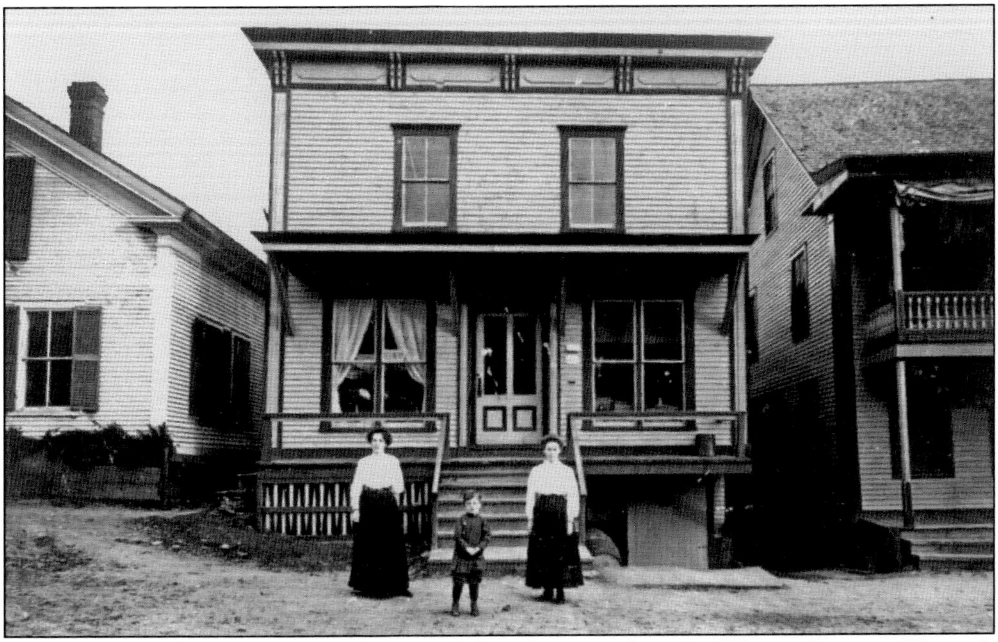

The Bragg Millinery Store (center), located directly across from the Warren Store on Warren's Main Street, sold women's hats, bonnets, laces, ribbons, and sewing supplies. The Spaulding store and Warner Moore's hardware store were in the same neighborhood, as were several sites that are still standing: the United church, the village cemetery, the town hall, and the municipal building and library (formerly a schoolhouse). (Courtesy of Katherine Hartshorn.)

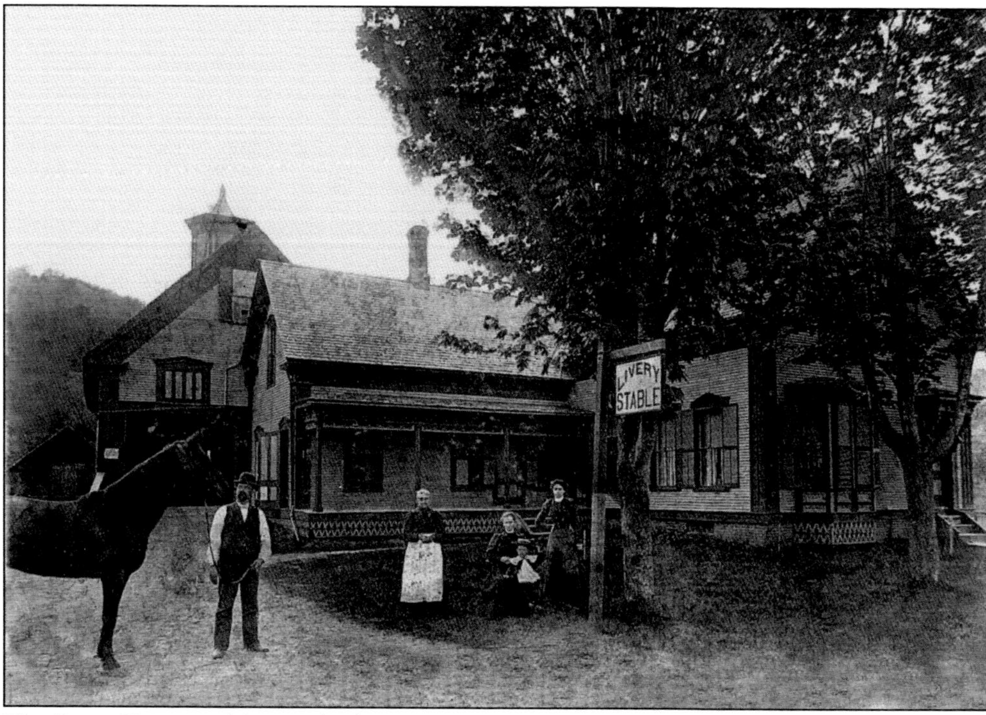

The Ferris House and barn, which were part of a livery stable and undertaking business, still stand on Main Street in Moretown, just across the street from the town garage. Tom Ferris stands in the driveway in this handsome 19th-century photograph. (Courtesy of Howard Ferris.)

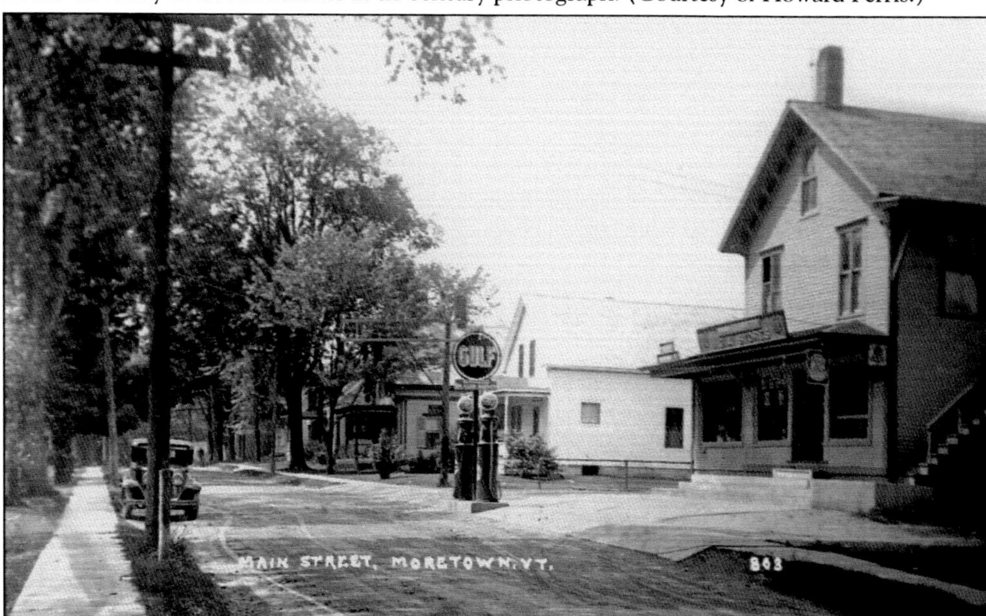

The Moretown Upper Store was located across Route 100B from the Methodist church. This photograph was taken in the 1930s, before Route 100B was paved. Where once there were several commercial businesses on that side of Main Street in the village, today there are none. (Courtesy of Moretown Historical Society.)

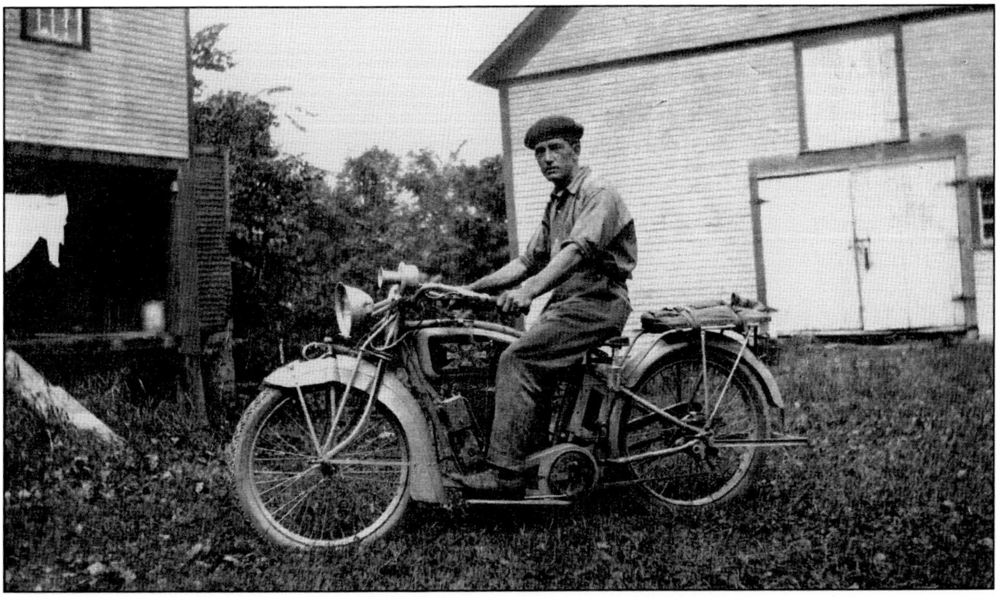

Alton Farr is pictured with an Excelsior 1916 model motorcycle. He took over the management of the fledgling Waitsfield & Fayston Telephone Company in 1906, despite a dire prediction from his former employer at New England Telephone & Telegraph that Farr would "never make a go of an independent company." That company celebrated its 100th year in business in 2004. (Courtesy of Waitsfield and Champlain Valley Telecom.)

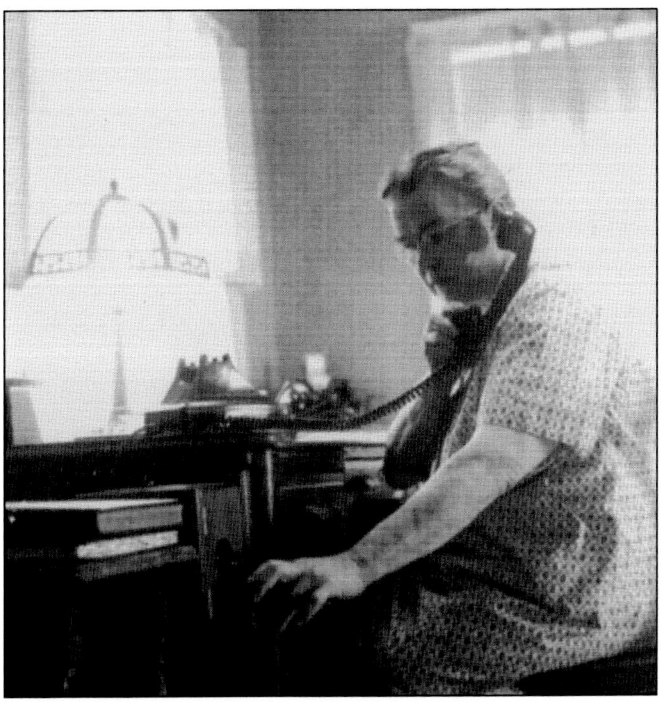

Eunice Farr is pictured at her desk in the office of her home, where the Waitsfield telephone company operated prior to 1966. She was a widow and single parent when she took on the job of leading the company that her husband had operated for many years. Eunice kept the books, ran the switchboard, and made repairs. (Courtesy of Waitsfield and Champlain Valley Telecom.)

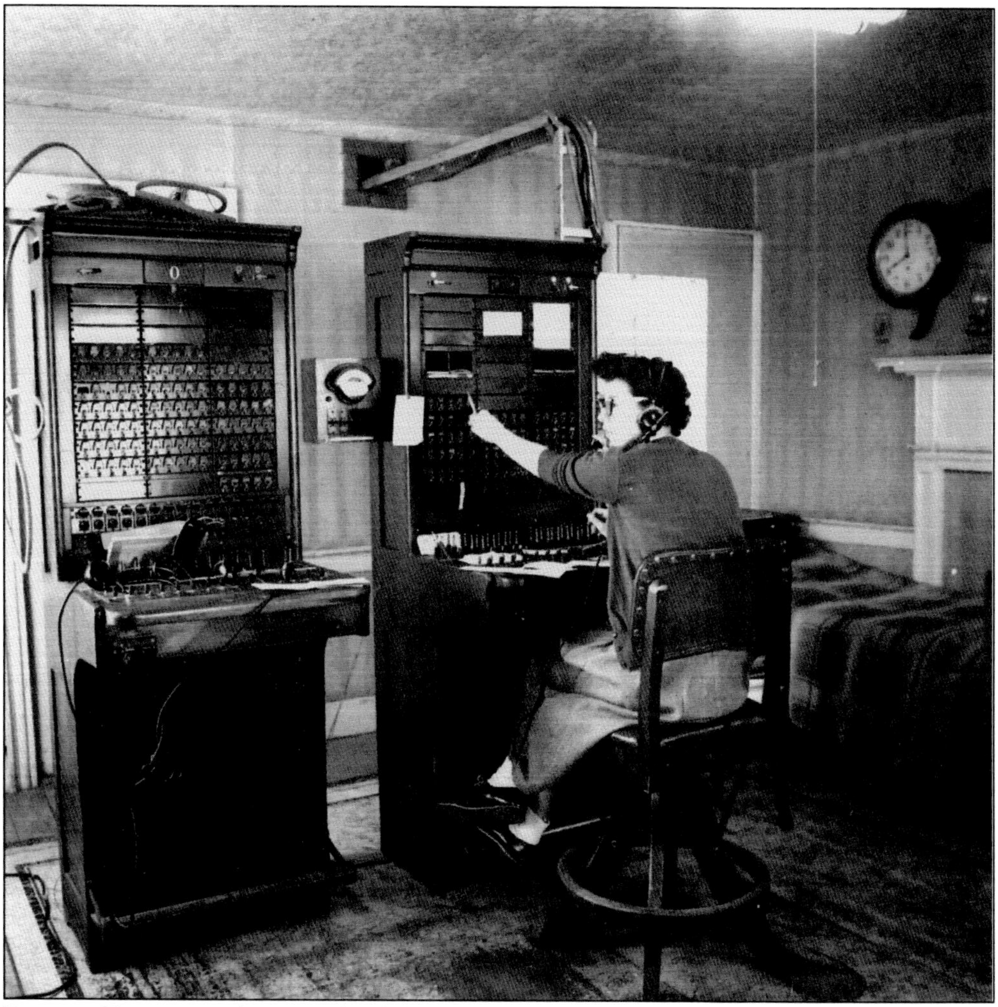

Ramona Shaw sits at the controls of the telephone company switchboard. She worked for the company from 1949 until 1961, when dial conversion took place. The story of the family that owned Waitsfield and Champlain Valley Telecom, which celebrated 100 years in the Mad River Valley in 2004, is not just unique in Vermont history, but nationwide as well. Starting and continuing as a family operation, it survived every attempt at takeover, while managing to advance a contemporary technology; the Waitsfield company was the envy of the industry. For many years the company operated out of the back porch of the home of Alton and Eunice Farr. Their daughter Eleanor and son-in-law Dana Haskin run the business today, maintaining a close relationship to customers that was first nurtured by Alton Farr. An example of Farr's workday tenacity is that in the wake of the flood of 1927, he made repairs up the line by canoe. (Courtesy of Waitsfield and Champlain Valley Telecom.)

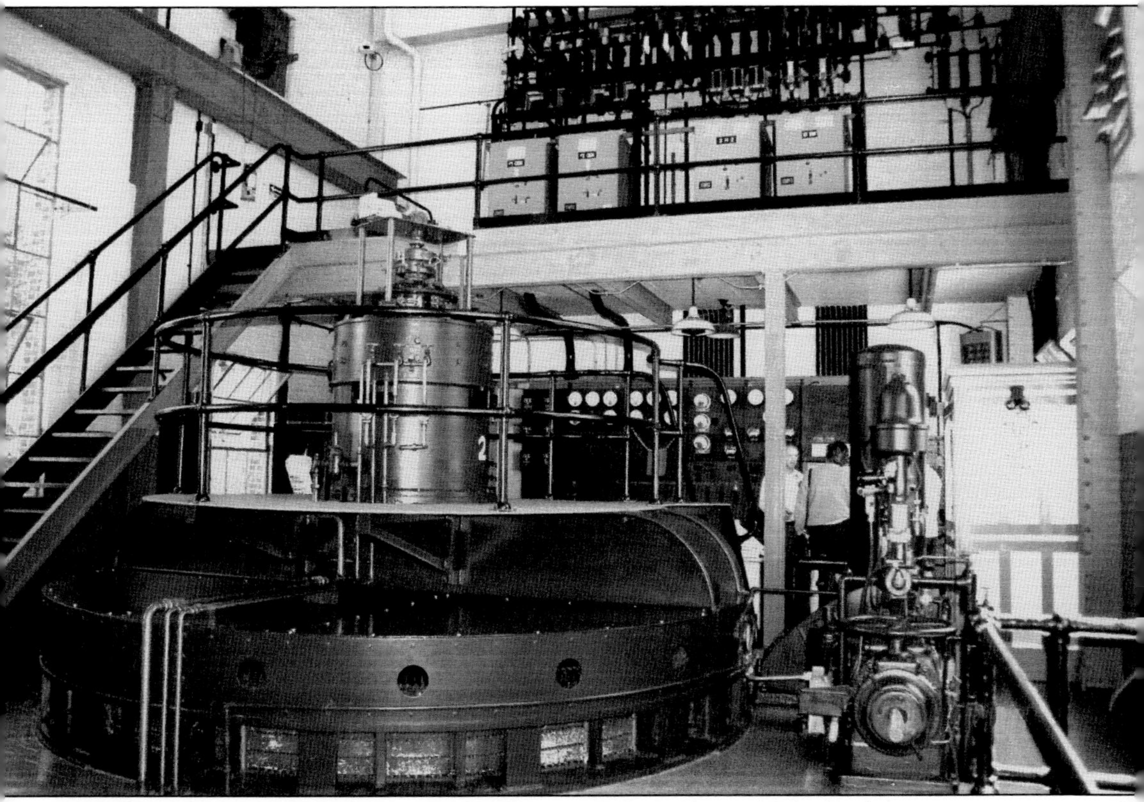

The sole water-powered industry in the Mad River Valley today is the hydroelectric generating facility near the junction of the Mad River and Winooski River. The plant has a 12-meter dam and a turbine generator rated at 1,250 kilowatts, and it is part of the grid from which Green Mountain Power operates. During a low-water time in 1999, new water-intake rakes were installed at the facility. Hydroelectric generation is considered one of the most efficient methods of energy conversion. Large plants can be made close to 100 percent efficient. Hydroelectric power generation is particularly useful for peak load generation, because hydro generators can be switched in and out more quickly than other generators. Other advantages of hydro generators are that they can work well on a small scale, as is the case in Moretown, and they do not contribute to the pollution of air or water. (Photograph by Ellie Hilferty.)

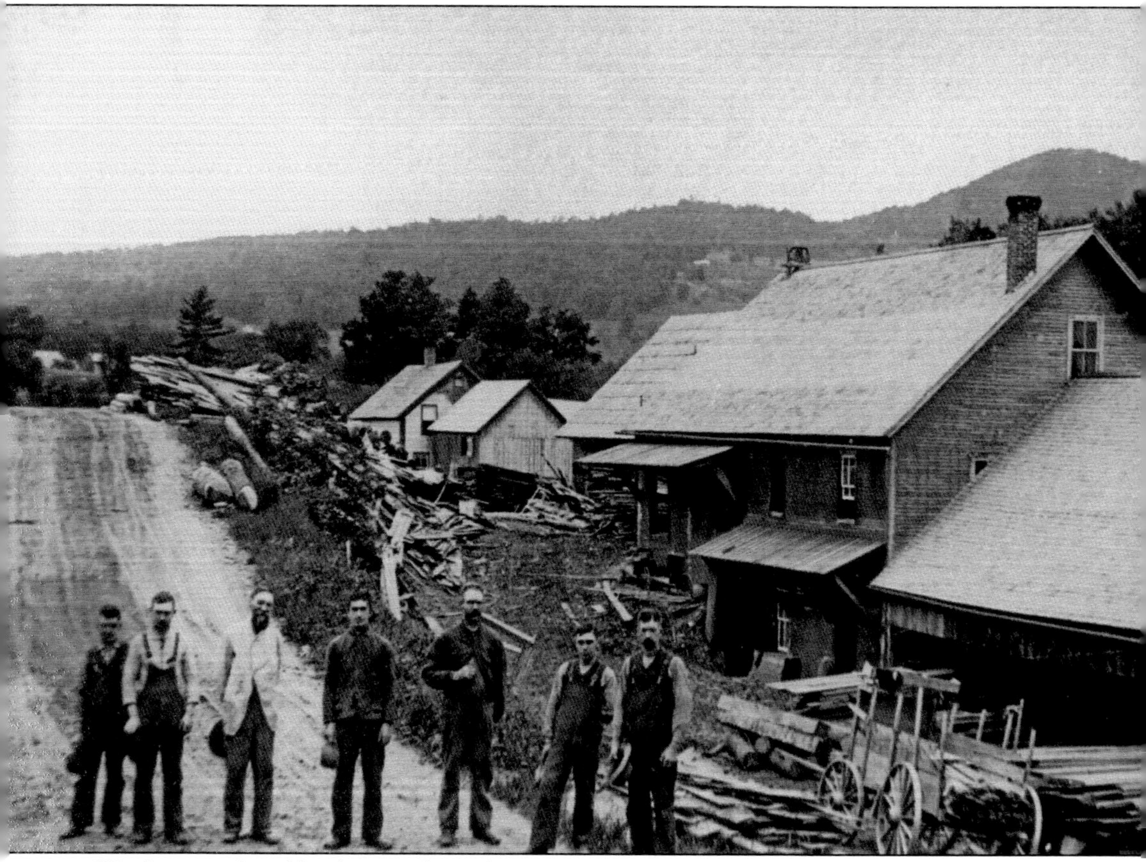

Workers employed by the Ward Lumber Company take time off to pose for this portrait, using the Upper Mill as a backdrop. Fires ravaged many mills along the Mad River, and this one was no exception. After one fire in 1955, a new mill was built across the road (which is now Route 100B). This building was later sold and renovated into a restaurant. It is now a private home. During its most prosperous era, early in the 19th century, Moretown Village had a harness shop, a tin shop, a carriage shop, a livery stable, a blacksmith shop, a general store, a hardware store, a dressmaker, a hotel, a cider mill, a gristmill, a lumbermill, a clapboard mill, a wheelwright, a creamery, and a distillery for making whiskey. (Courtesy of Moretown Historical Society.)

Four

PEOPLE AND PLACES

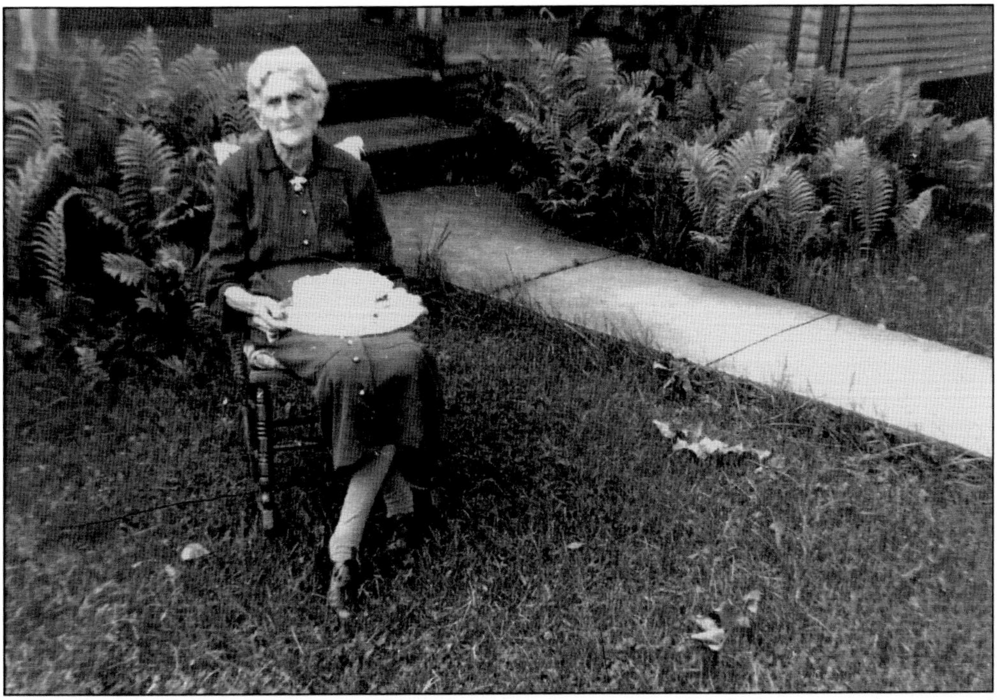

The sometimes-nagging contemporary question, "Who's minding the kids?" was easily answered in a town like Warren, where close-knit neighbors watched, protected, and guided. Frances Shaddock, who lived in the village center on Main Street, was known by everyone in town, kids and adults alike, as Aunt Frank. (Courtesy of Katherine Hartshorn.)

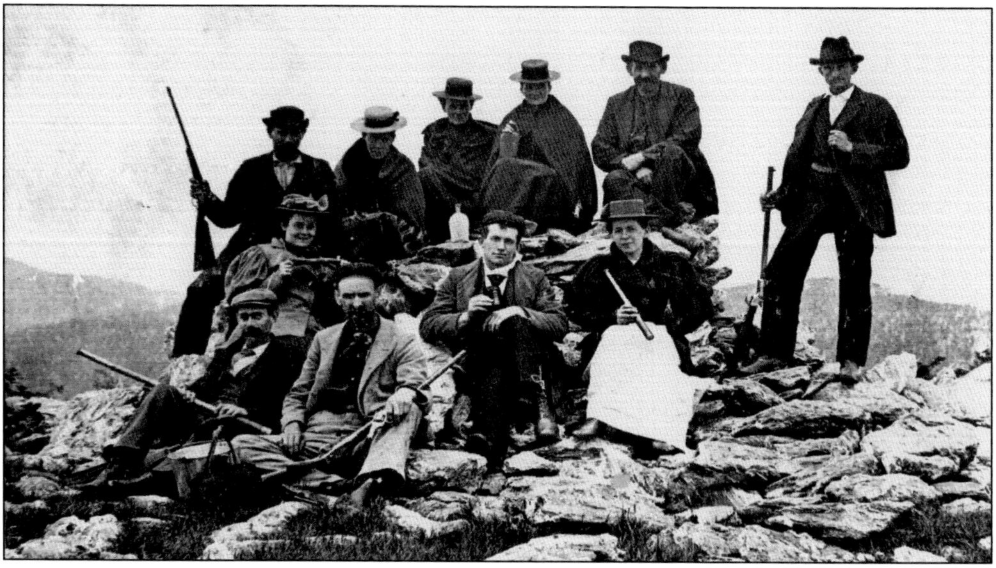

An 1895 outing on Mount Abraham, known as Potato Hill, is shown here. Pictured from left to right are the following: (first row, seated with guns) Oriel Hanks and Charlie Hanks; (second row) Erma Buttles Hanks, and Mr. and Mrs. John Buzzell; (third row) Walter Luce, Addie Bradley, Hattie Mathews, Anna Hartshorn, Frank Hartshorn, and Arthur Hartshorn. Hiking on the Long Trail was always popular, but the trail did not become officially designated until after the formation of the Green Mountain Club in 1910. (Courtesy of Warren Library.)

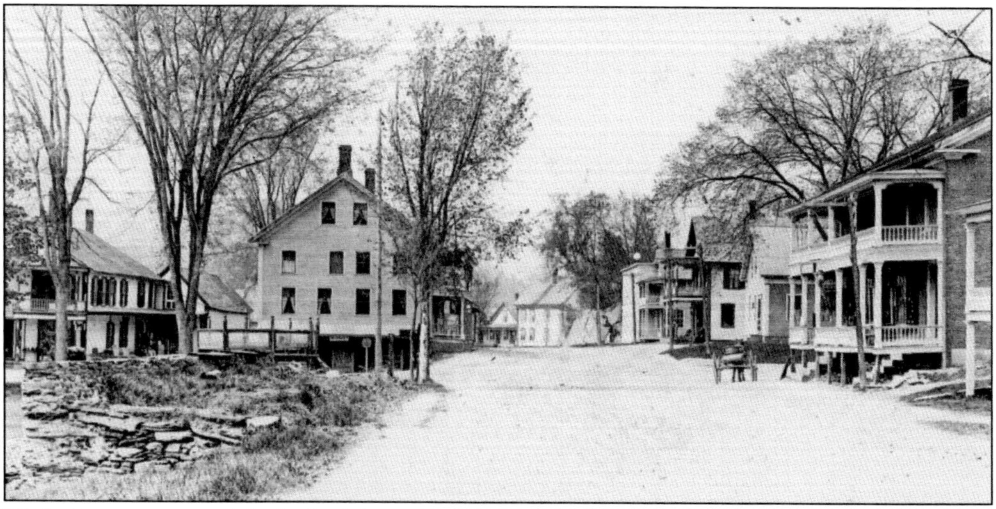

With the exception of the Joslin Memorial Library, which was not built until 1913 on the lot at the left, Main Street in Waitsfield looks pretty much the same today as it did in this photograph from 1907. The original main thoroughfare through town bears very little trace today. It lay a few hundred yards west of the present street, beyond the ledges visible from the road. It was on this road that the first settler of the town, Gen. Benjamin Wait, had his home, which was moved in the 1830s to its present location on Route 100 and is now home to the Sugarbush Chamber of Commerce. What are now the main routes in the village were not established until 1837. The intersection with Bridge Street (pictured above) remained the center of commerce for the entire valley for many years—at least until shopping malls were built in Irasville. (Courtesy of Waitsfield Historical Society.)

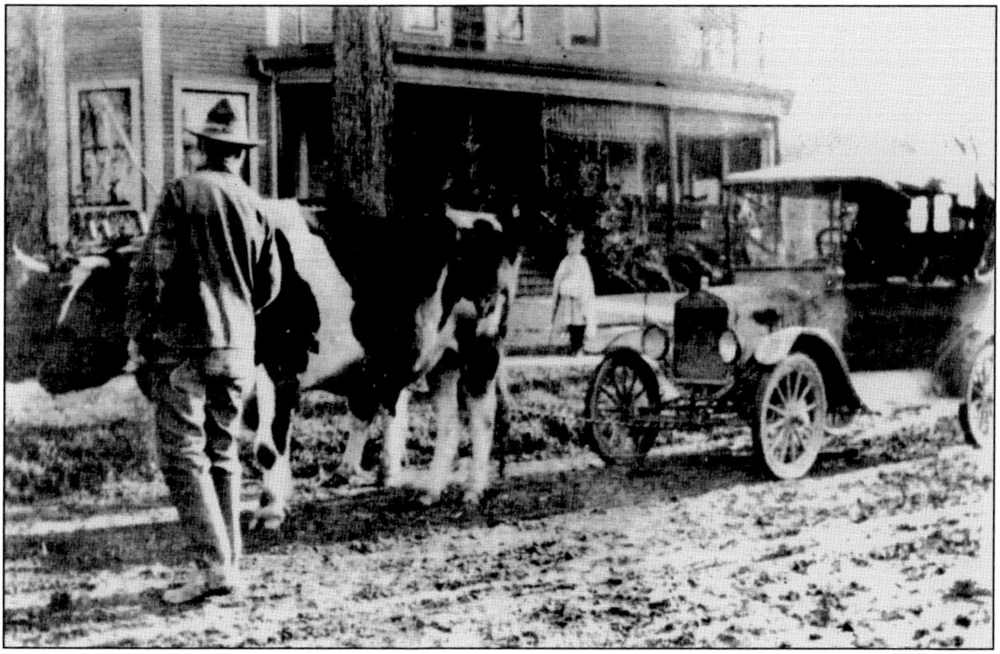

The depths of humiliation were reached in the early 1900s when automobile owners suffered the fate of having their precious new vehicles towed out of trouble by a couple of horses. Imagine the pain of the man who owned this vehicle, humbled by a couple of ladies. (Courtesy of Moretown Historical Society.)

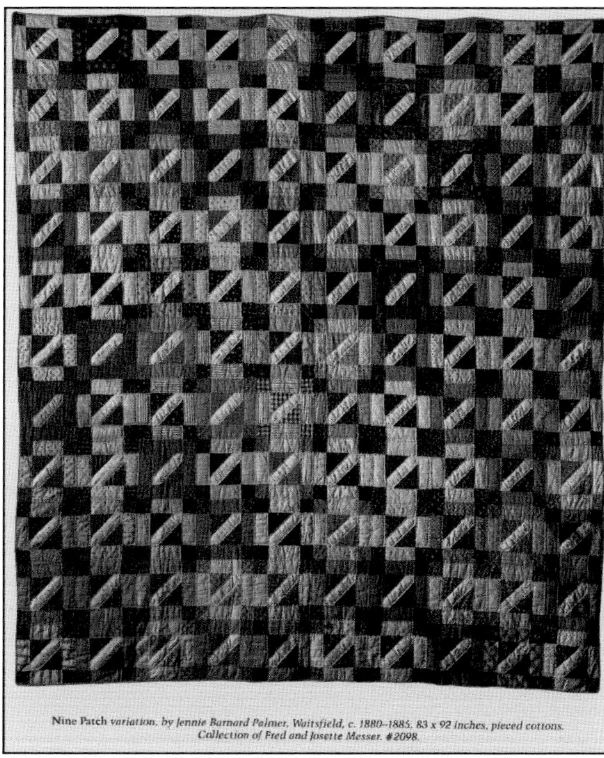

Many years ago, people who purchased maple syrup made in the Mad River Valley received a small patch of cloth along with their bottles of syrup. Some of those patches were later collected by Jennie Palmer Messer, who saw to it that a signature quilt was made. The description beneath this photograph reads: "*Nine Patch* variation, by Jennie Barnard Palmer, Waitsfield, c. 1880–1885, 83 x 92 inches, pieced cottons. Collection of Fred and Josette Messer." (Courtesy of Fred Messer.)

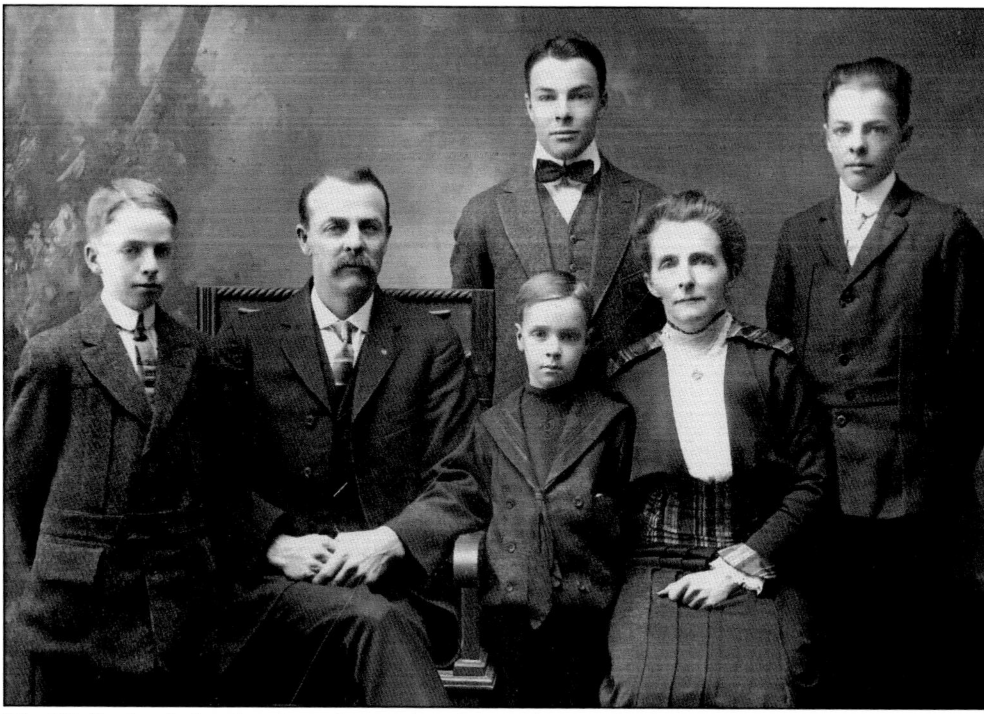

The Wallis family has lived in a large white house that was built in 1800, on what is now Route 100, since the end of the Civil War. Family members pictured here are, from left to right, Clifford Wallis, George Wilbur Wallis, Otis Wallis, Harold Wallis (behind Otis), Adele Bragg Wallis, and Everett Wallis. (Courtesy of Anne Wallis-Bull.)

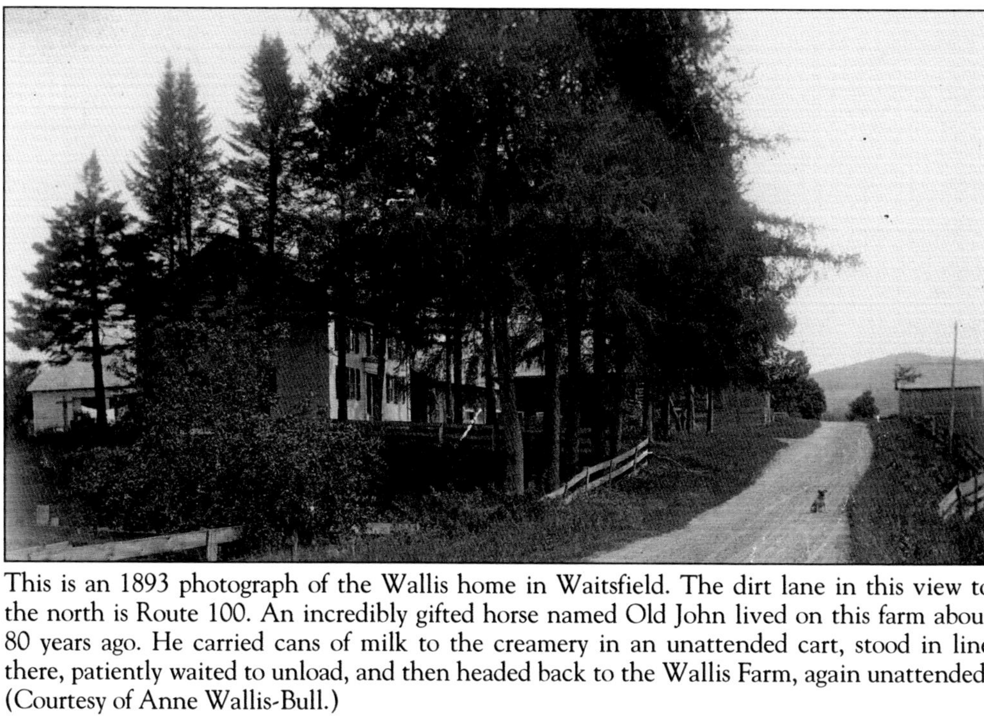

This is an 1893 photograph of the Wallis home in Waitsfield. The dirt lane in this view to the north is Route 100. An incredibly gifted horse named Old John lived on this farm about 80 years ago. He carried cans of milk to the creamery in an unattended cart, stood in line there, patiently waited to unload, and then headed back to the Wallis Farm, again unattended. (Courtesy of Anne Wallis-Bull.)

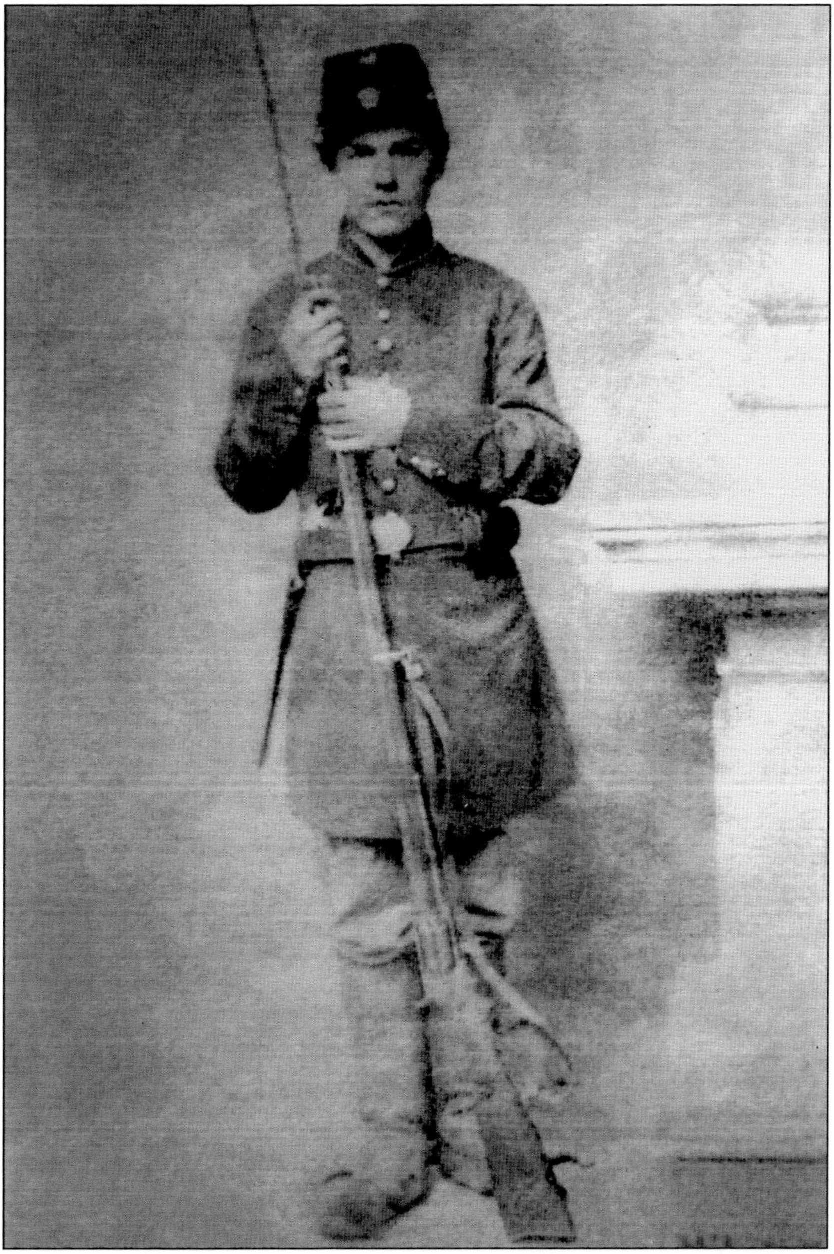

Civil War soldier Edwin Joslin, shown here in 1862, was one of 87 men from Waitsfield who joined the Union Army; proportionally, this number is equivalent to 10 percent of the village's male population at the time. Of the 87 men, 10 died in battle and 10 others died of diseases contracted during the war. From Moretown, 122 men enlisted in the Civil War. Like Waitsfield, that number may have represented about 10 percent of the population. At least seven Moretown natives died during the war. As a state, Vermont's contribution in the war effort far exceeded that of other states, based on percentage of population. From the state, 1,832 were killed or mortally wounded during the war. A total 4,700 were wounded. Vermonters took part in more than 35 separate battles, and 32 men from the state were awarded Medals of Honor. (Courtesy of Waitsfield Historical Society.)

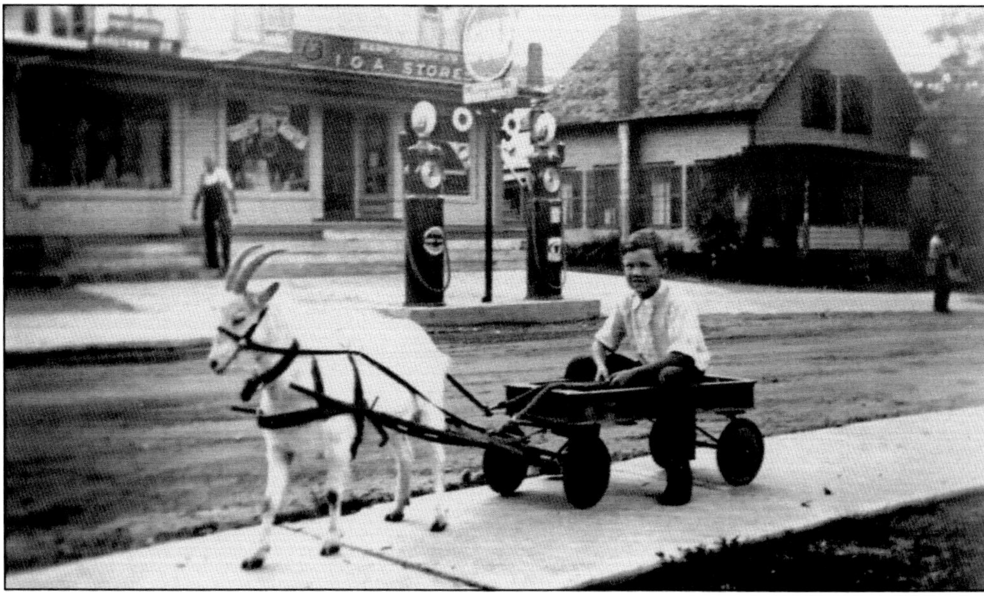

Pictured here, Wilmer White plays giddy-up with a goat owned by William Blair, who lived on the site of the present-day town clerk's office in Moretown. In the background is Herbert Ward, longtime town clerk of Moretown, who is standing in front of Ward's Upper Store. The house at right is the parsonage of the Methodist church. (Courtesy of Moretown Historical Society.)

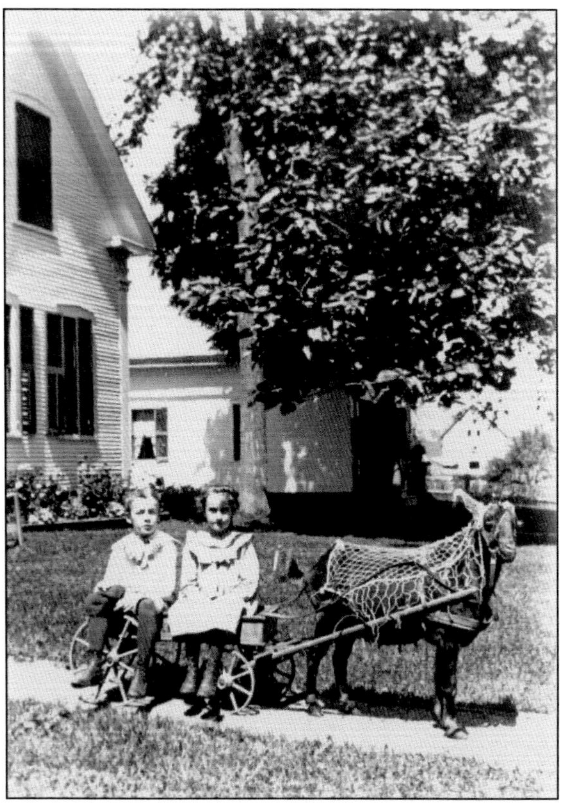

Shown in this goat-powered child's wagon are Alice Billings (left) and her friend Alice Smith. Childhood pastimes were kept simple in those days, but were luxuriant in terms of the vast amount of open space the kids enjoyed and the presence of friendly, caring neighbors to watch over the young ones. The valley has been a magical place to raise children and continues to be. (Courtesy of Waitsfield Historical Society.)

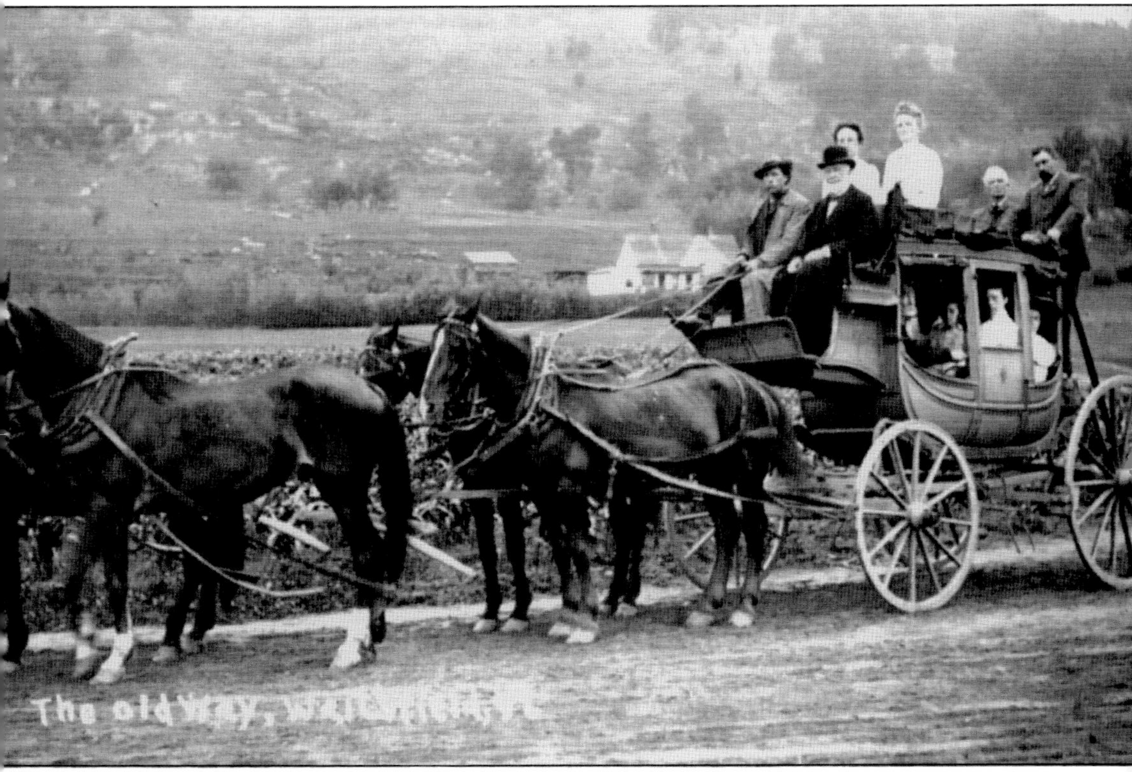

By the 1880s, this stagecoach, owned and operated by J. J. Kelty (in the driver's seat), ran from Waitsfield to Middlesex, where the railroad was, and charged 75¢ for a one-way fare. By this time, Waitsfield Village had about a dozen merchants, a hotel, a gristmill and sawmill, three church buildings (Congregational, Methodist, and Universalist), a school system, three doctors, one lawyer, one photographer, and many mechanics. The original coach, which had been obtained by the Henry Ford Museum in Dearborn, Michigan, is now owned by Eleanor Haskin of Waitsfield and Champlain Valley Telecom. The Kelty coach was one of the original Concord coaches built in Concord, New Hampshire, beginning in 1813, by Lewis Downing, a wheelwright by trade. The styles of coach were revised and improved as years passed, from heavy and cumbersome to light and durable, and were noticeably smooth-riding by 19th-century standards. (Courtesy of Waitsfield Historical Society.)

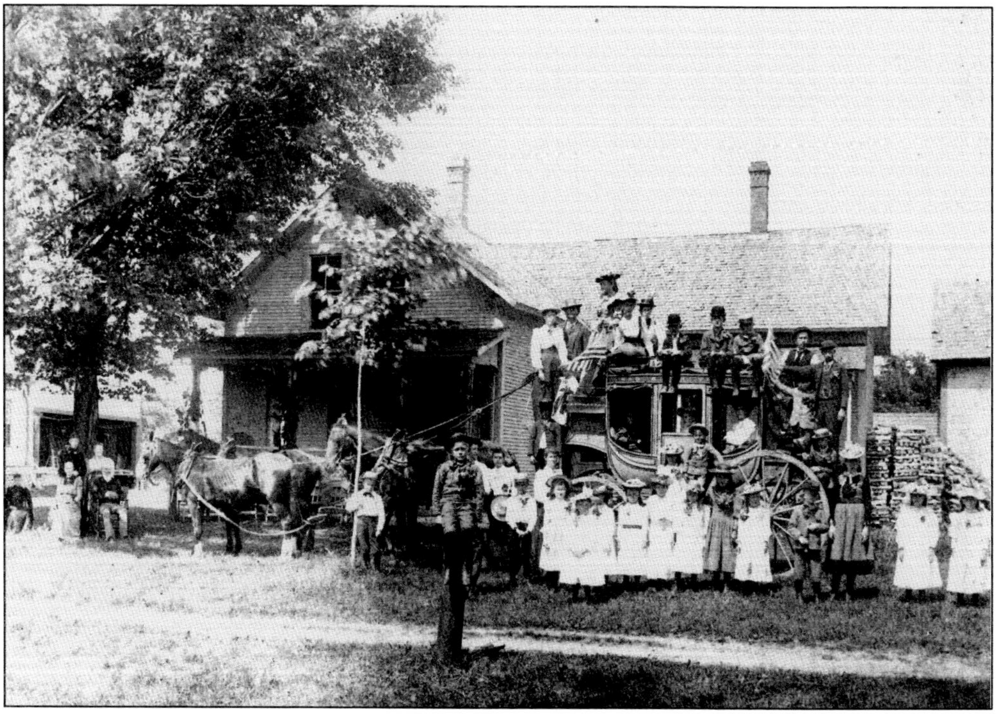

The Kelty coach is parked in front of the Marble House on Bridge Street in Waitsfield. Kelty was originally from Passco, Rhode Island, but attempted to overcome that by marrying a valley girl named Marietta E. Thayer. (Courtesy of Waitsfield Historical Society.)

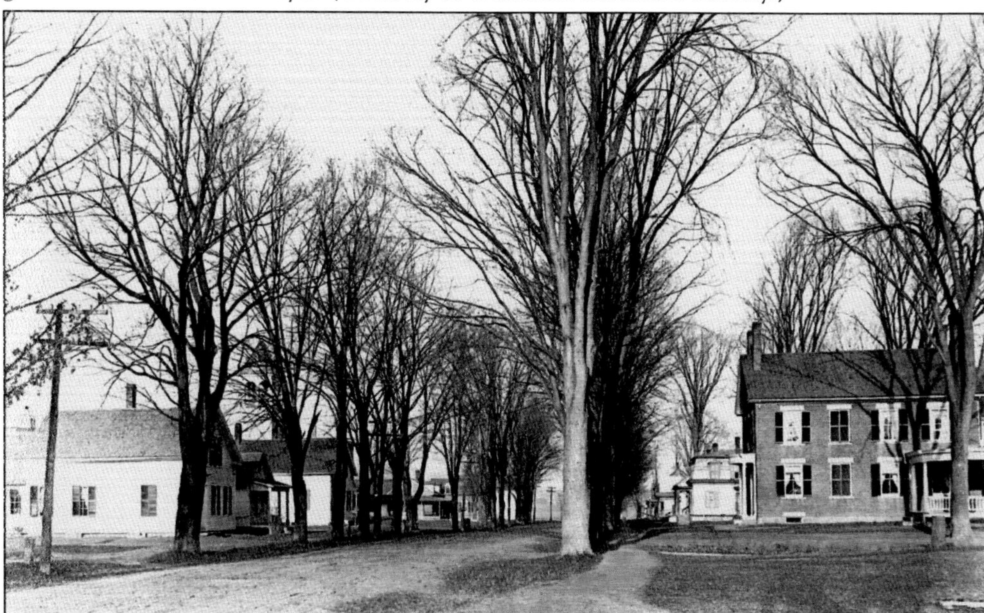

This is a view of Main Street in Waitsfield, looking north, c. 1900. Many of the Waitsfield buildings still standing in the nationally certified historic district were erected between 1796 and 1894. Roderick Richardson, along with Gen. Benjamin Wait, is given credit for the development of the present location of the village. (Courtesy of Waitsfield Historical Society.)

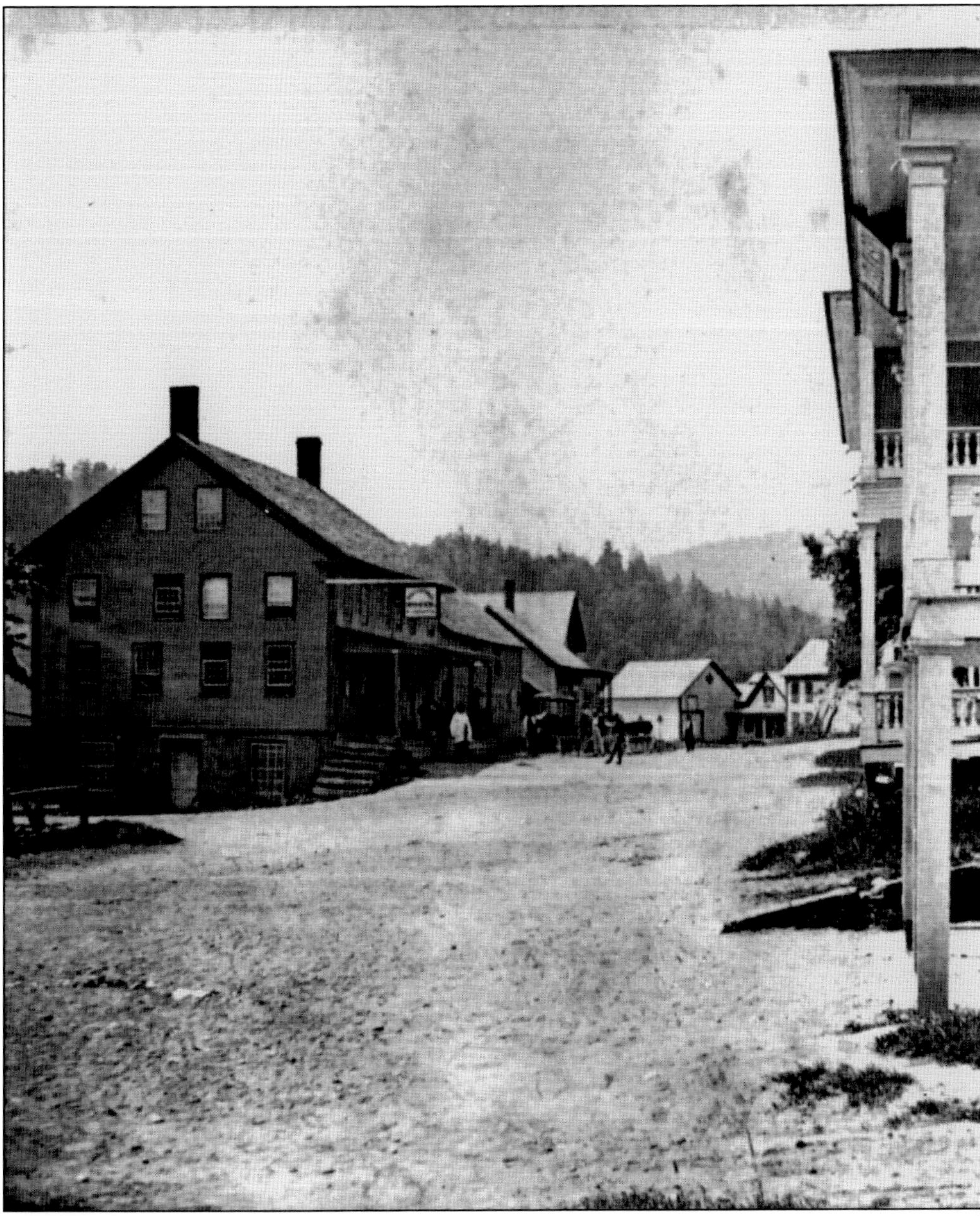

The Waitsfield House Hotel, seen on the left in this southward view, appears today much like it does in this photograph taken before Waitsfield's Main Street was paved. The village center, its covered bridge on Bridge Street, the white steepled Congregational church, and several 18th- and 19th-century single homes and shops have put the neighborhood on the National Register of Historic Places. The hotel was moved to its present site in 1851 from its original location at the foot of the Dugway, Routes 100 and 17, in Irasville. Twelve teams of oxen carried out the massive engineering and logistics effort. Testimony to the viability of the town center is that businesses continue to thrive there, serving locals and tourists alike through the town office and library, restaurants, gift shops, village grocery, bakery, Christmas shop, computer services companies, and marketing firms. (Courtesy of Waitsfield Historical Society.)

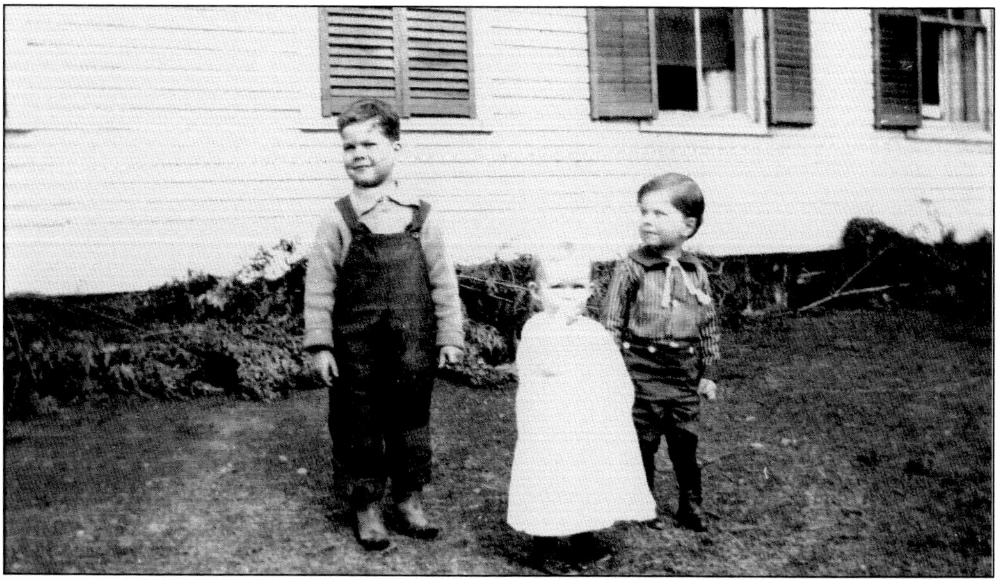

Latter-day members of the durable Joslin family are represented in this c. 1916 photograph. From left to right are Riford, cousin Rebecca, and Fletcher. Riford operated the family feed store, which was located just east of the Village Bridge, where the Miramar Ski Club is today. Fletcher is a retired lawyer. The family's presence in the Mad River Valley dates from the original settlement. (Courtesy of Stephen Joslin.)

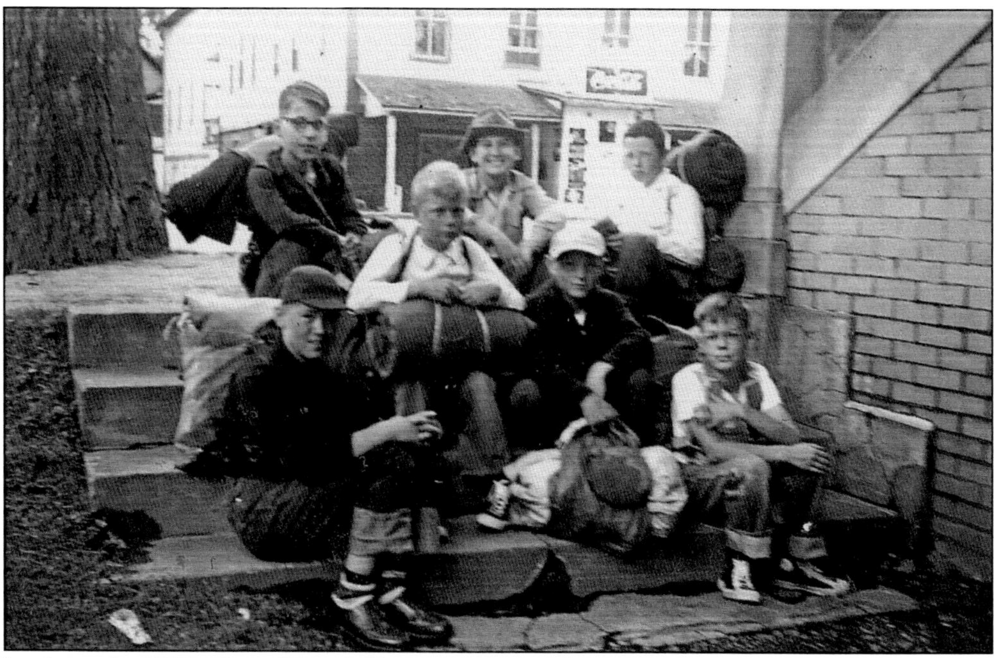

In the early 1950s, these Waitsfield Boy Scouts made ready to go on a camping trip to the Appalachian Gap, on what is now Route 17. Among those pictured are Buddy Jones, Tom Tucker, Roger Stafford, Jerry Tucker, Kenney Ketchum, and Stephen Joslin. (Courtesy of Stephen Joslin.)

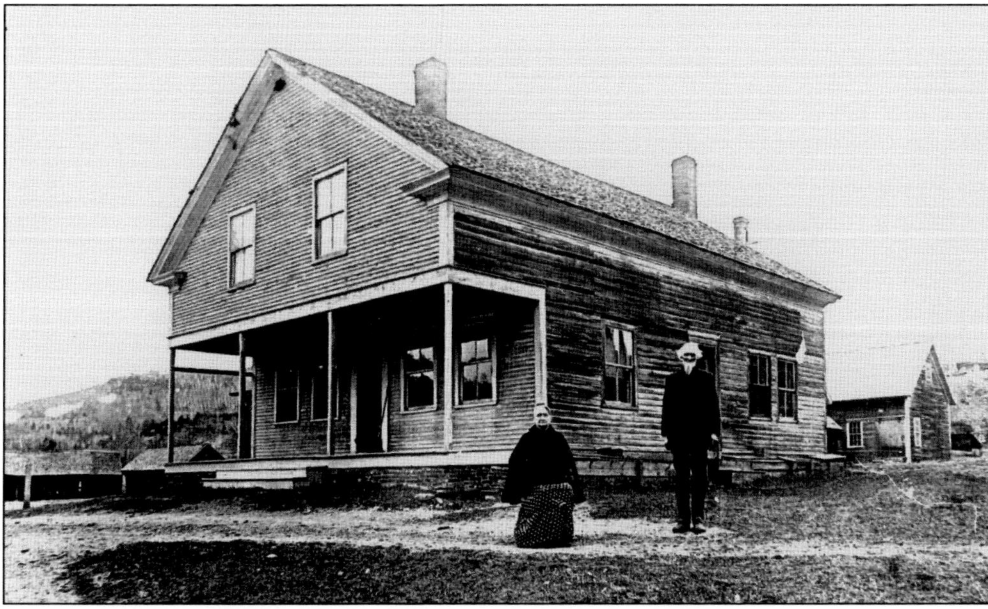

The Blair House in Warren is shown here with David and Lucy Blair in the front yard in 1900. It was one of the first houses—if not the first in Warren Village—to be built between the town hall and the church on Main Street. By the time of this photograph, 120 years after the awarding of the original land grants, Warren Village had become fairly well defined. (Courtesy of Katherine Hartshorn.)

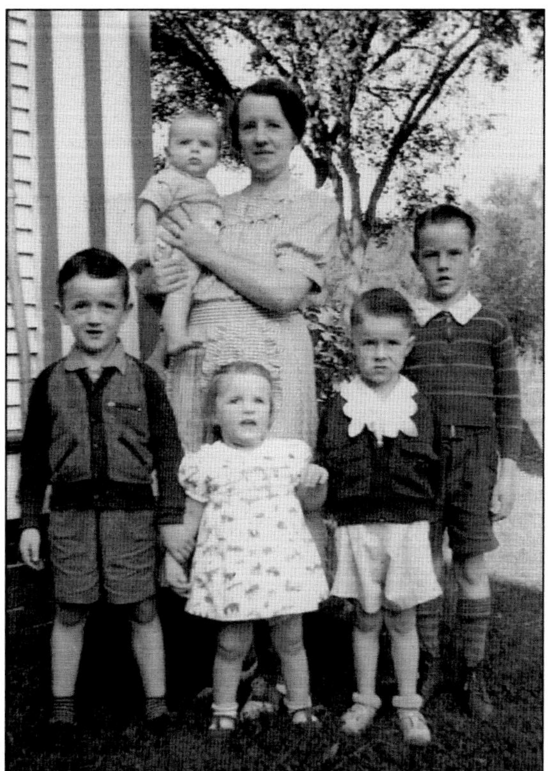

Members of the Ferris family pictured in this pre–World War I photograph in Moretown are Mrs. Melba Ferris and baby Eldon, and from left to right, Howard, Barbara, Stuart, and Horton Ferris. (Courtesy of Howard Ferris.)

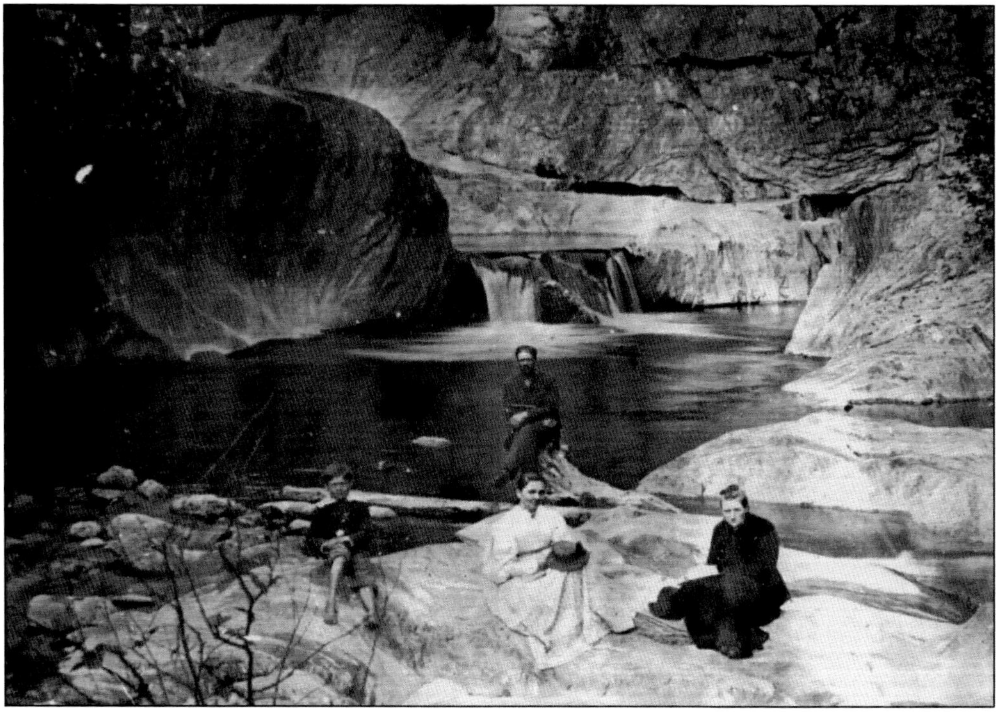

Warren Falls, popular through the years as a spot for cooling off from the summer warmth, is near the headwaters of the Mad River as one approaches Granville Forest on Route 100. Back when this photograph was taken, the area was known as Carleton Falls. (Courtesy of Katherine Hartshorn.)

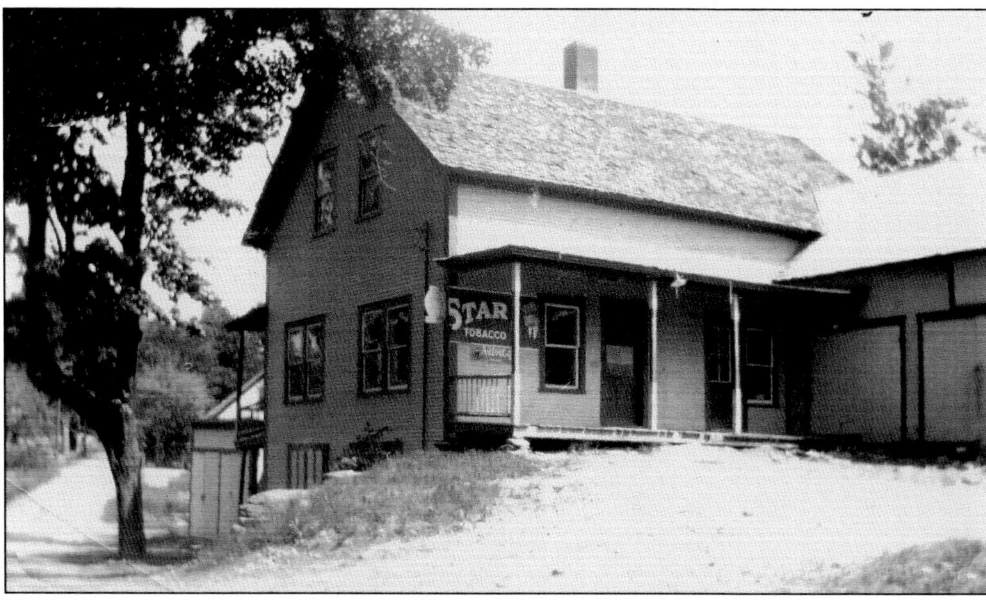

The International Order of the Odd Fellows Hall in Warren was also occupied by the Brooks store. At one time it was a tenement house and it also once housed the library in its basement. Later, the upstairs was made into a meeting hall, lodge room, and dance hall. Clarence Hartshorn showed movies on the first floor of the Odd Fellows Hall. Eventually, the lodge was disbanded and the building was sold by the Grand Lodge of Vermont. (Courtesy of Katherine Hartshorn.)

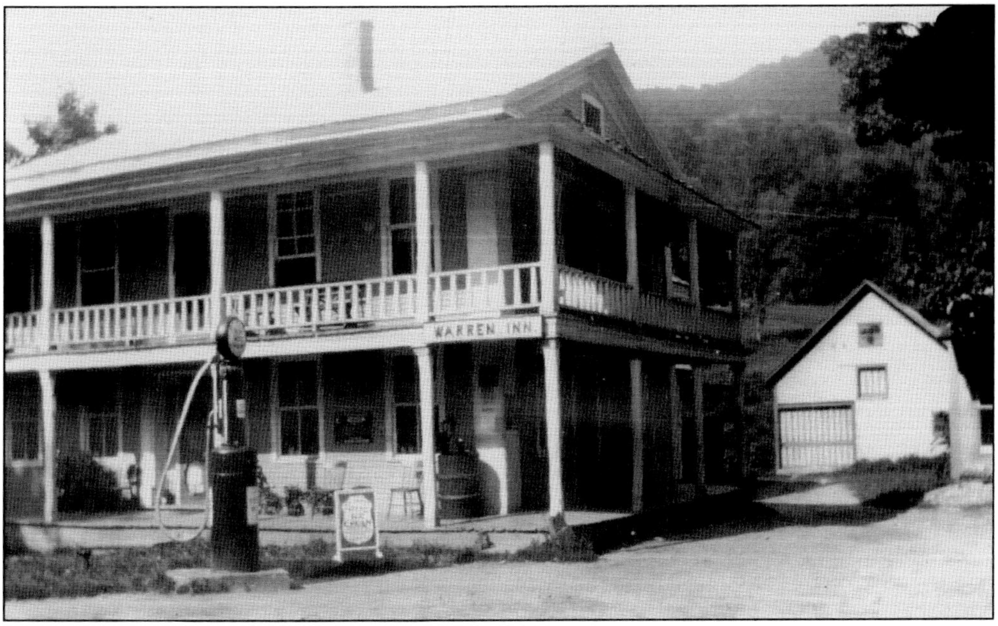

First known as the Warren House, this famous landmark was bought by Horace Lyford in 1861, and was operated as a hotel until the death of Rubin Downer in 1927, when ownership passed to his son-in-law Roy E. Long. Now home to the Warren Store, the former inn has had many uses, including a stagecoach stop, a meat market, and a car and wagon repair shop. (Courtesy of Katherine Hartshorn.)

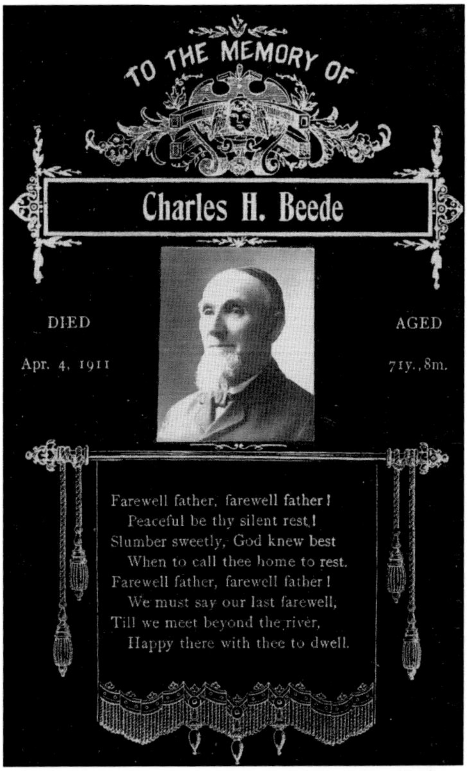

This card is dedicated to the memory of Charles H. Beede, who died in 1911. Funeral cards like this one were a carry-over from Victorian times, serving as a convenient way to remember the deceased. (Courtesy of Warren Library.)

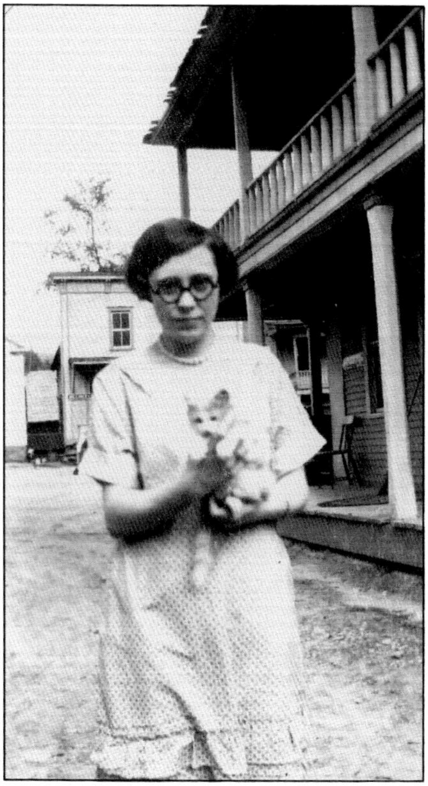

Mildred Downer's father operated the Warren House and passed ownership to his son-in-law Roy Long, who was Mildred's husband. The store is in the center of the Warren historic district, which contains 75 buildings. Warren Village itself was founded in the 1820s to take advantage of the water power from the Mad River. (Courtesy of Katherine Hartshorn.)

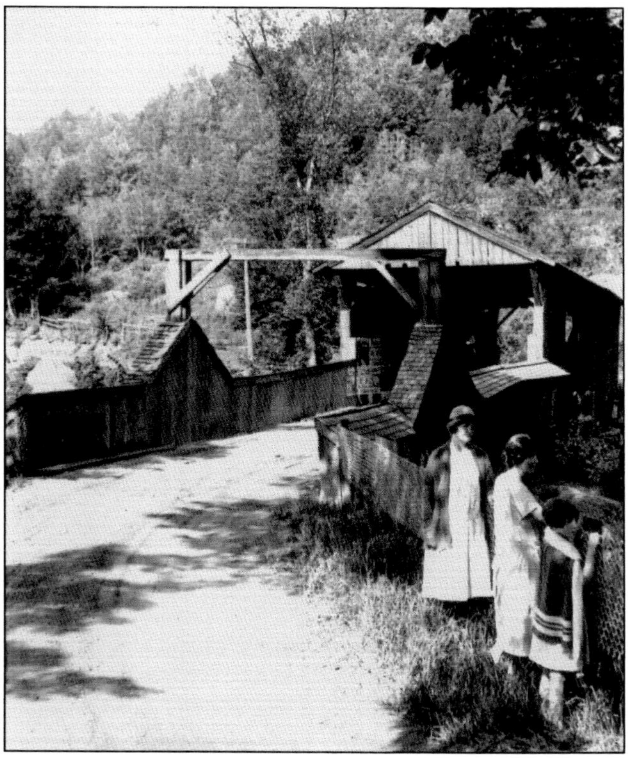

The Ford Covered Bridge, which stood near where the Golden Lion Motel is now, was replaced by the iron Kingsbury Bridge, still found on Route 100. Note that half of the Ford bridge was covered. The exposed part is of king post construction. Also note how sharp the turn was between the bridge and what is now Volkstown Road. (Courtesy of Katherine Hartshorn.)

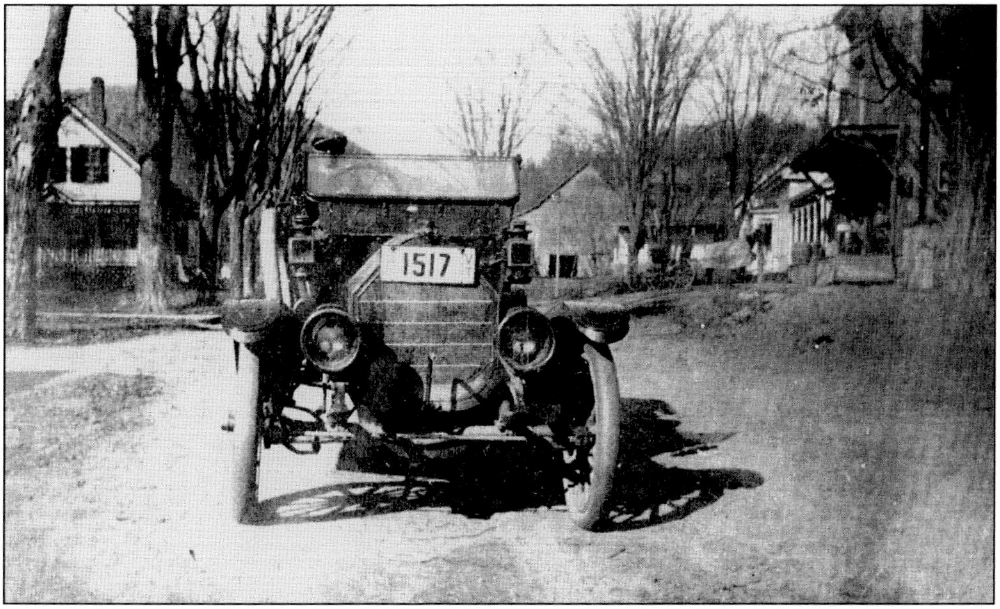

The snow and mud of winter and spring slowed the introduction of the mechanically testy horseless carriage to the Mad River Valley. Hand cranks and carriage lights distinguished the early vehicles *c.* 1905. Eventually, the automobile became the quickest connection to the outside world; it was especially welcome after the failure of many attempts between 1875 and 1910 to bring a railroad to the valley. (Courtesy of Katherine Hartshorn.)

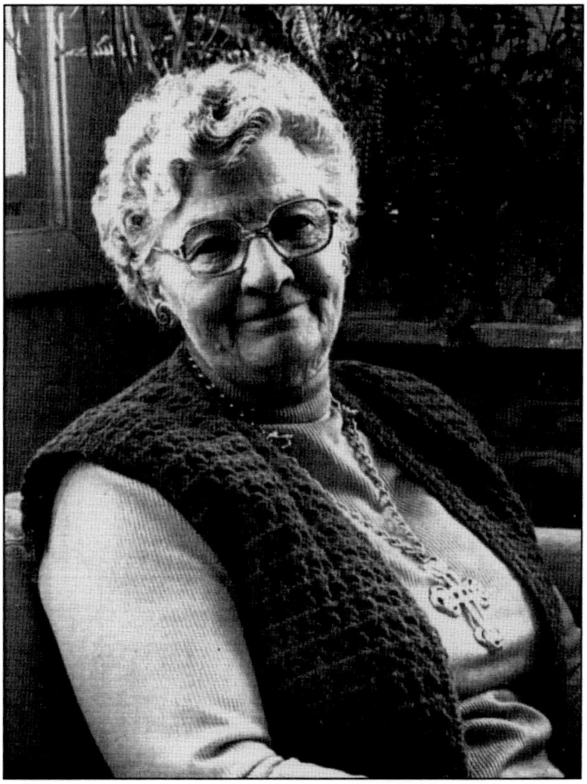

Emma Robinson Ford, wife of Lawrence Ford, was a real-estate agent, a longtime town clerk, and a dedicated member of the United Church of Warren, on Main Street. The most recent addition to the church was dedicated in 1941 in her honor. The church, built in 1838, was ecumenical in that it served the congregations of Free Will Baptists, Universalists, Congregationalists, and Methodists. (Courtesy of Katherine Hartshorn.)

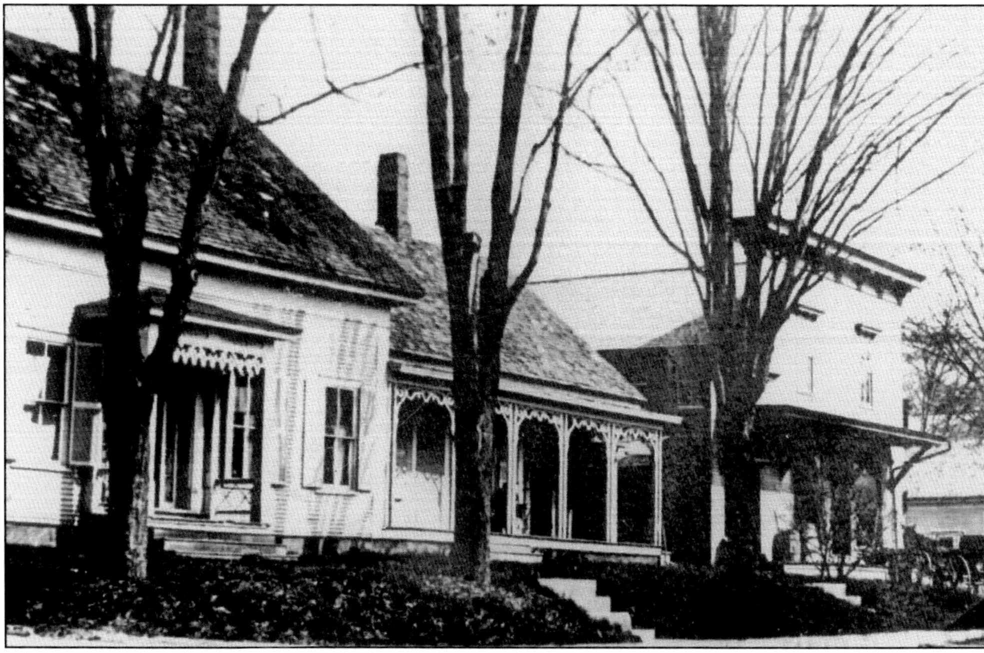

The Warren home of James Cardell, on Main Street, was photographed in 1865, about the time the Civil War ended. Records show that 87 men from Warren served in the Civil War. Next door to the Cardell home is the Spaulding store (right). (Courtesy of Katherine Hartshorn.)

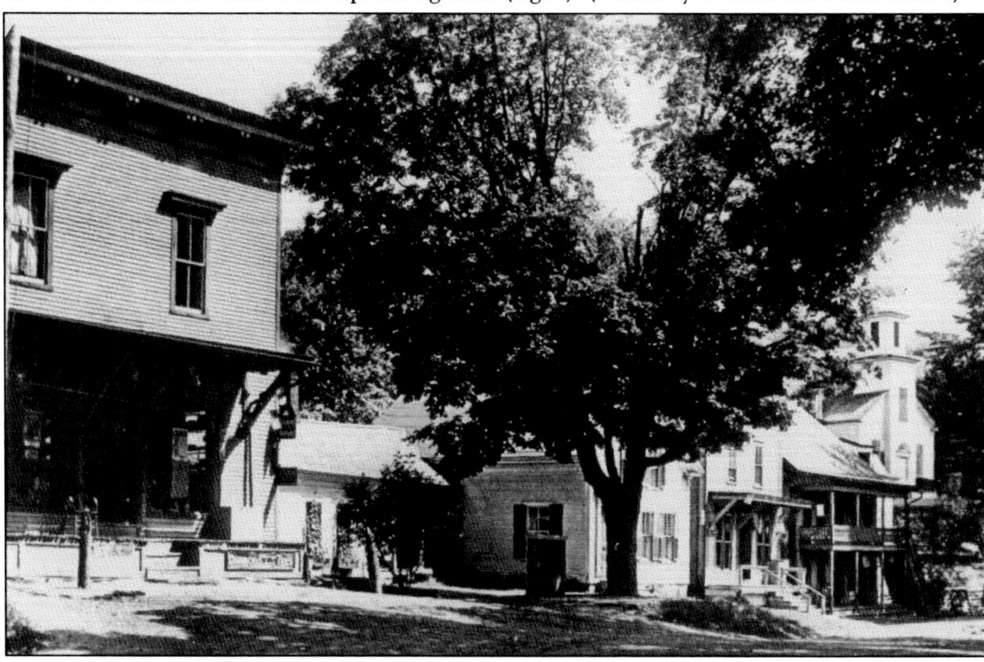

At the site of the present-day Pitcher Inn, on Main Street in Warren, this *c.* 1915 scene features Spaulding's store, the Bragg-Drew Home, and Bragg's store, which had a scale for weighing produce. Warner Moore's hardware store is at far right. The original Pitcher Inn dates to 1850. The main streets of Vermont villages were the foci of outdoor social life in many villages. (Courtesy of Katherine Hartshorn.)

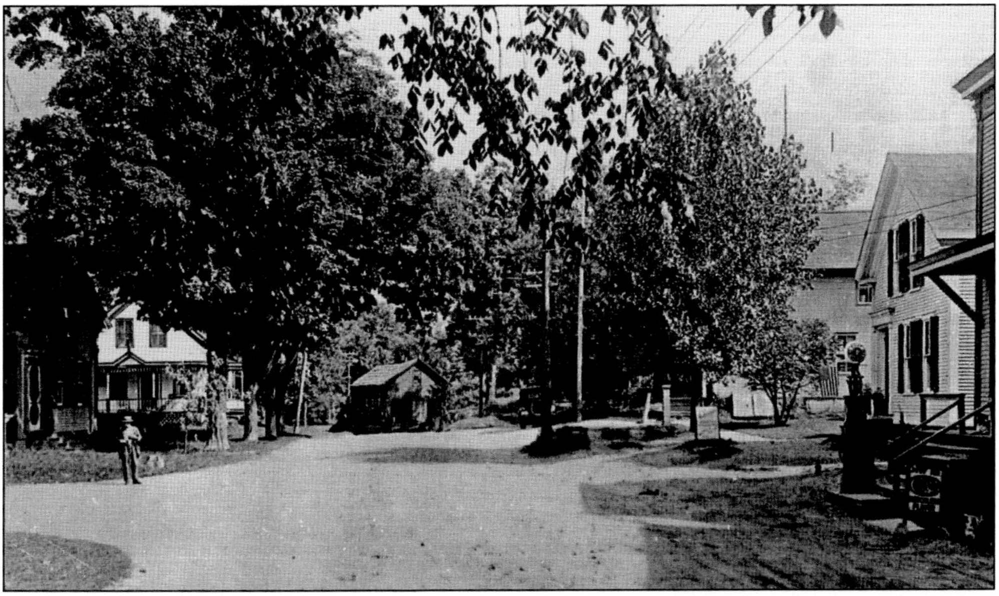

This northward view of Warren Village's Main Street, photographed sometime after World War I, shows the blacksmith shop and gas pump. Farmers brought their produce to be weighed on a scale platform in front of the store. To the left, but outside the view of the photograph, is the present location of the Warren Store. The town's civic complex includes the United church (1838), village cemetery (1826), town hall (1872), and the municipal building and library (1867), which was formerly a schoolhouse. (Courtesy of Katherine Hartshorn.)

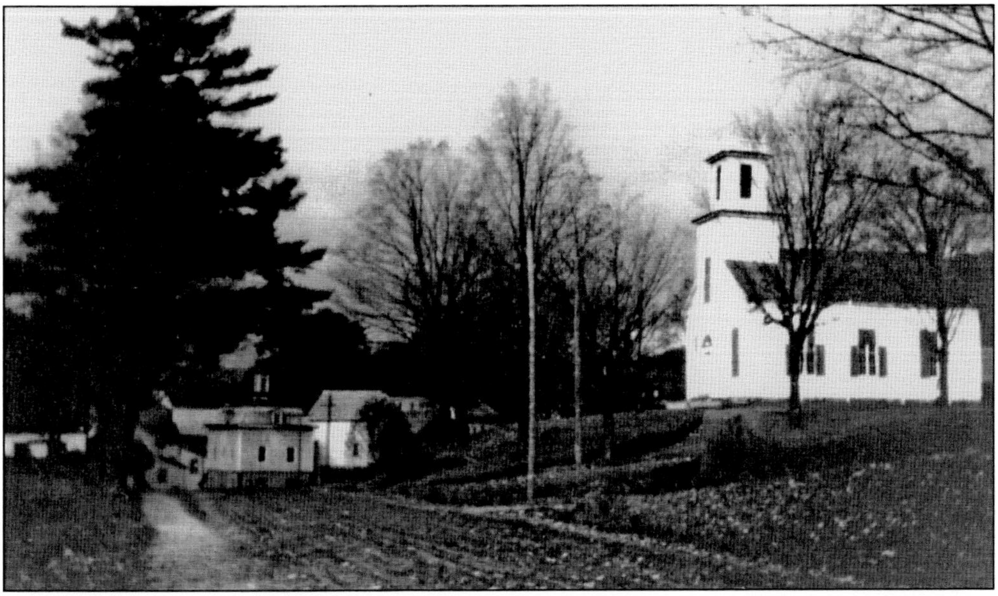

On March 6, 1838, David Ralph deeded part of his property as a site for the construction of the United Church of Warren. The meetinghouse was built by the Warren Meeting Society and was completed in 1839. The society was composed of Free Will Baptists, Universalists, Congregationalists, and Methodists. Horse sheds were built in back of the building. A chapel was added in 1941, and stained-glass windows were installed in 1926. (Courtesy of Katherine Hartshorn.)

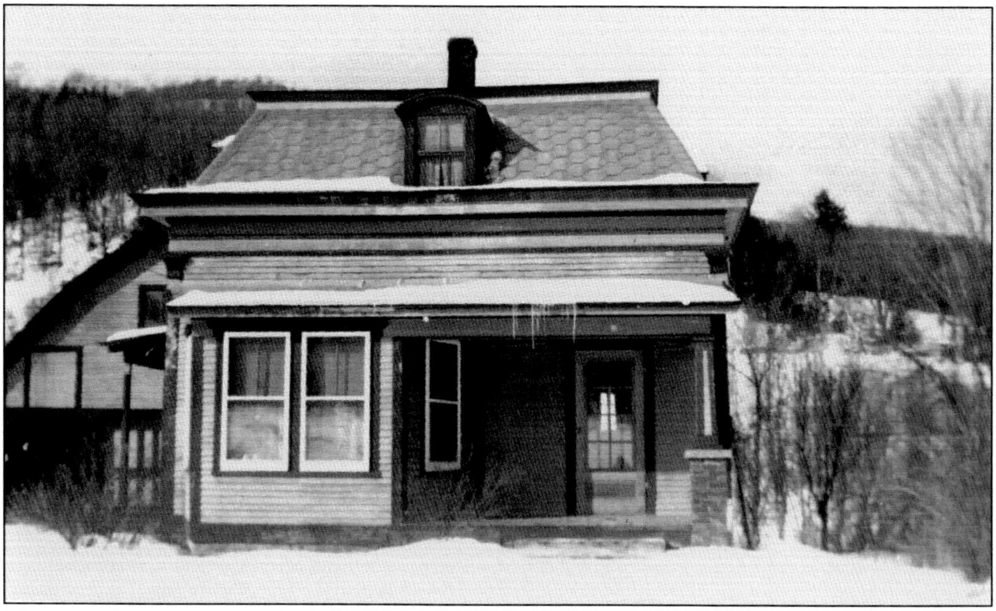

The Jesse Cota home was built by Gary Campbell from a barn in front of the Freeman Store. Most post-and-beam barns constructed in the 19th century were built to last. Their floorboards, rafters, and bar tops may be found in more than one modern home in the valley. (Courtesy of Katherine Hartshorn.)

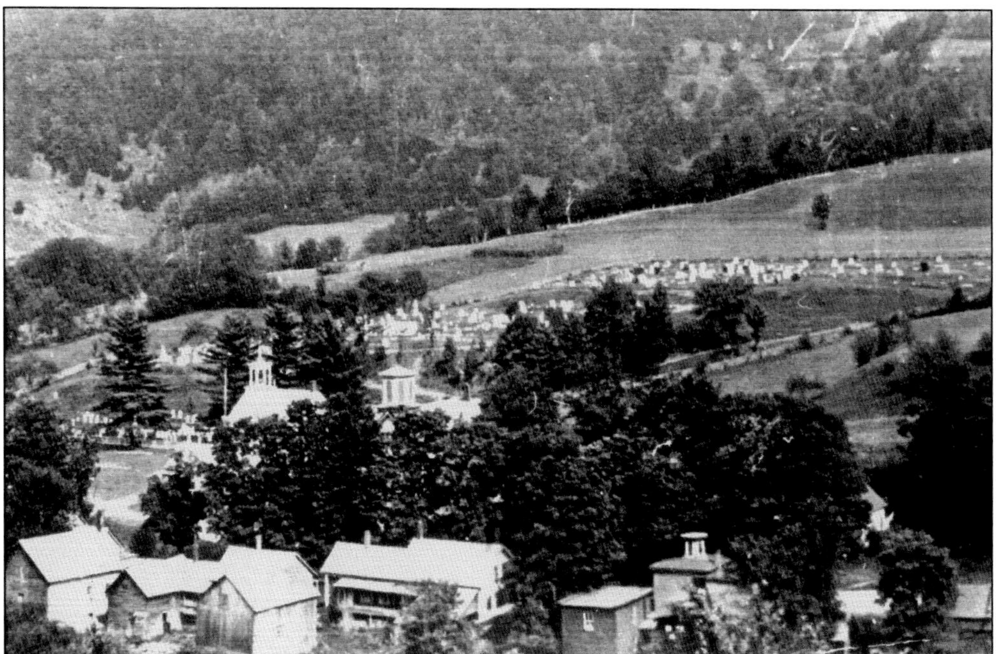

The buildings in the foreground of this Warren Village photograph burned in 1936. Water to fight the fire was drawn from the Mad River in buckets, tubs, and anything else that was handy. Houses constructed of clapboard burned often and swiftly. The menace of house fires did not abate until well into the 20th century, when pumper trucks became available. (Courtesy of Katherine Hartshorn.)

Lucy Thayer, wife of Will Thayer, a mill owner on Lincoln Gap, poses in a formal portrait style popular during the Victorian era. Sitting still for a photograph in the 19th century demanded a strong back, resolute concentration, and superb muscle control. The frozen, serious expressions seen in many portraits of those days were necessitated by the terribly long exposure time required by the early cameras and film. (Courtesy of Katherine Hartshorn.)

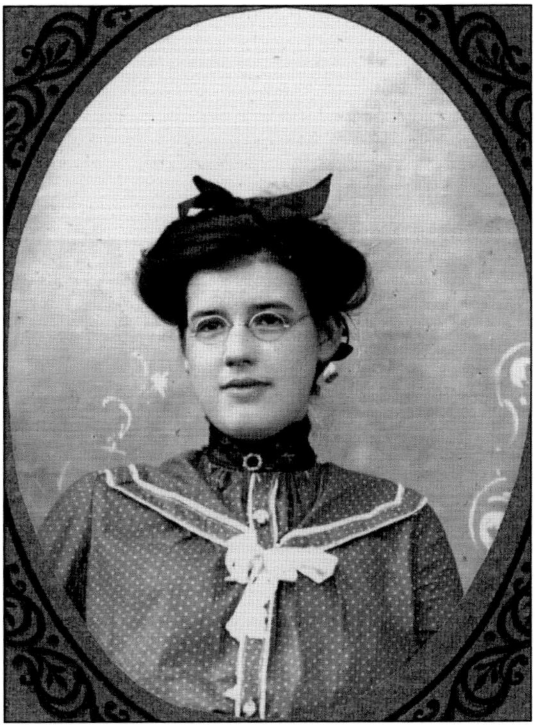

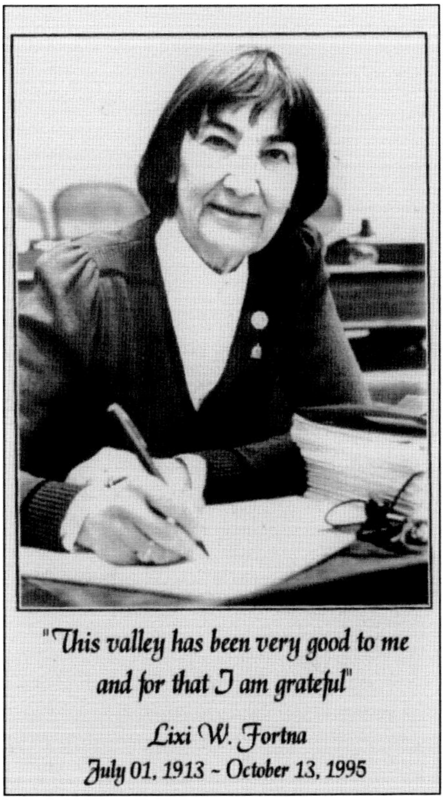

Lixi W. Fortna's home was located off Sugarbush Access Road. She was a state representative and a selectwoman, but was perhaps better known as the do-it-all office manager of the Sugarbush Resort when it first opened in the 1950s. (Courtesy of Katherine Hartshorn.)

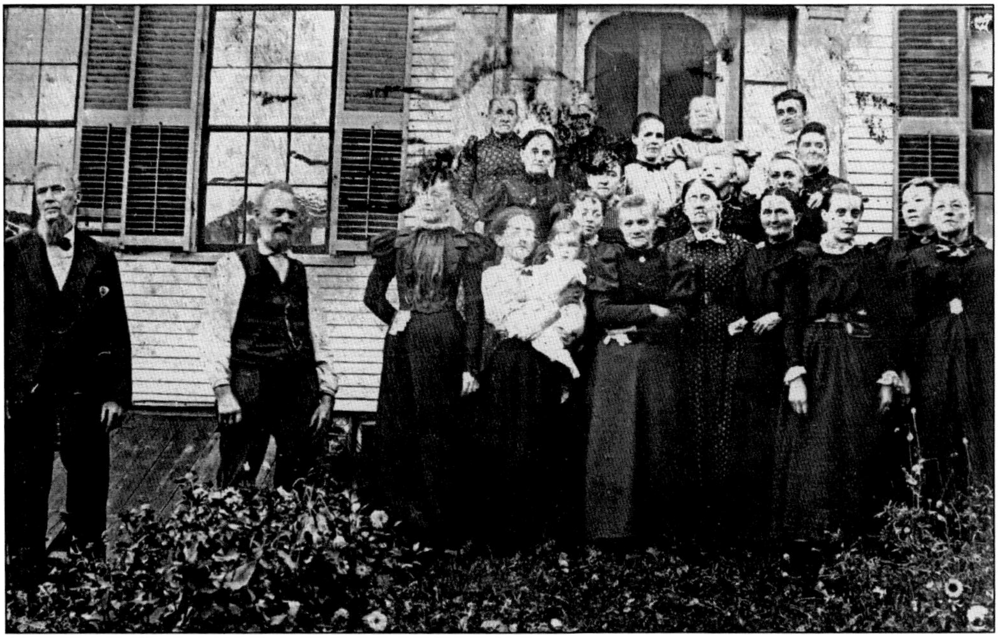

The Warren Ladies Aid Society is pictured here in 1912. Some of those identified in this image include Dan James, ? Van Deusen, ? Moore, May Daniels' baby, Anna May, Rachel Hartshorn, Anna Hartshorn,? Schyler, ? Pike, and ? Heath. (Courtesy of Katherine Hartshorn.)

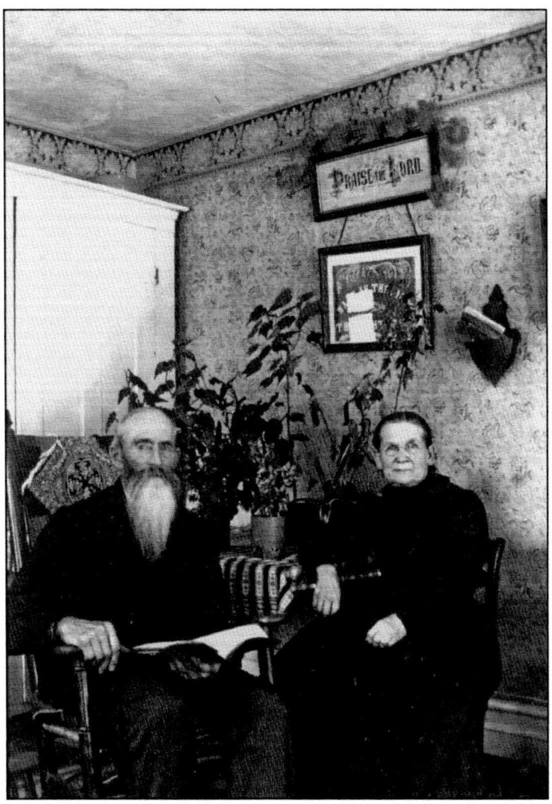

Leander and Lorraine Brigham are pictured here. Leander was the preacher at the Christian Advent Church in Warren Village. Until 1833, when the Methodist church was built on Old Stage Coach Road, religious services were held in private homes. At one time, four congregations met in the Warren River Meetinghouse, which later became the United Church of Warren. (Courtesy of Katherine Hartshorn.)

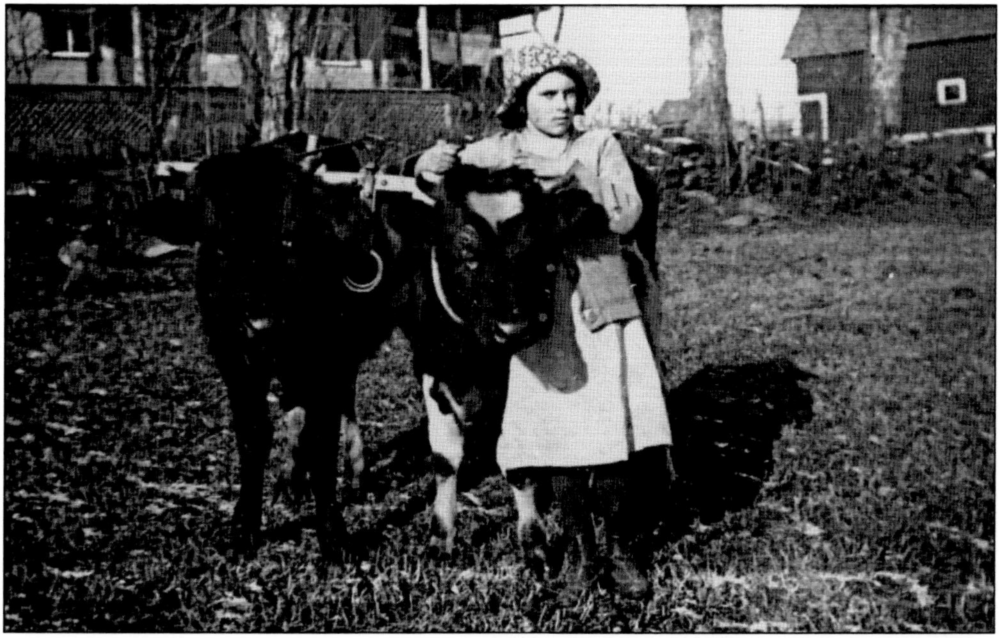

Josie Trask is shown here with her bulls. Among the towns of the Mad River Valley, Warren had a reputation as having the most-fertile farmlands in the area. (Courtesy of Warren Library.)

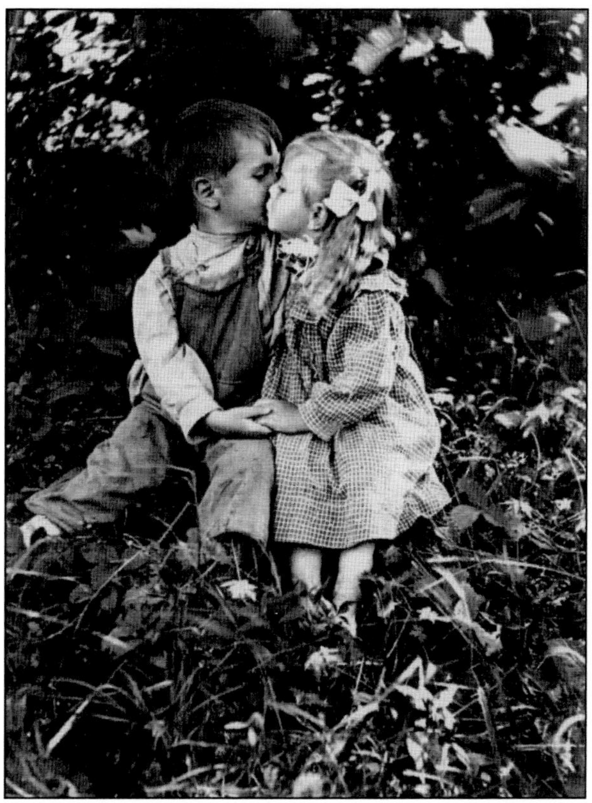

All evidence would suggest that Homer La Morder and Carrie Mobus were caught during an unguarded moment on a summer day. However, the story handed down through the years was that the scene was set up by the photographer. (Courtesy of Warren Library.)

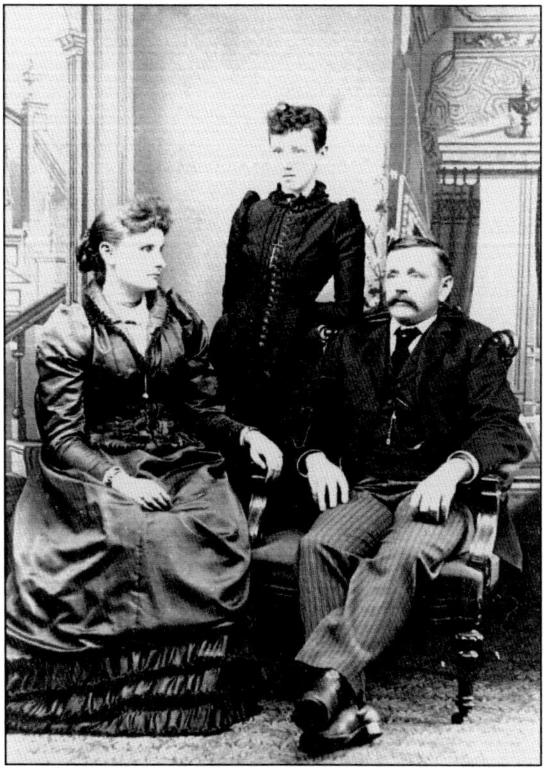

The Parker family lived in relative Victorian elegance when this photograph was taken in 1888. Pictured from left to right are Laura Parker, her daughter Jennie (who later married O. M. Jones), and Plyne Parker, a prosperous mill owner in Warren. Over the years, Mr. Parker owned three mills in town. (Courtesy of Warren Library.)

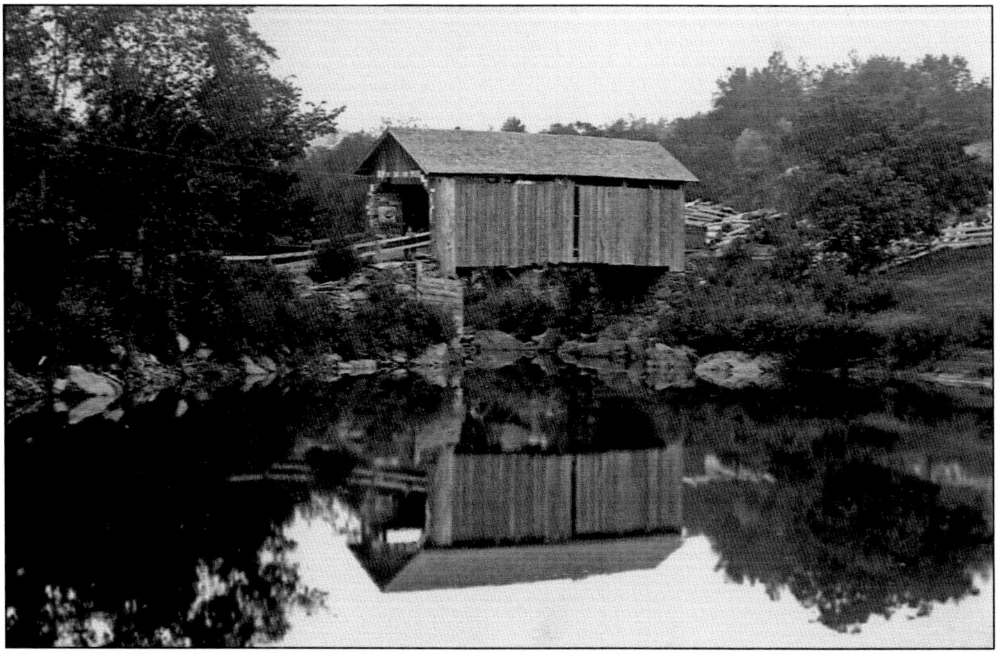

The Upper Covered Bridge in Moretown was destroyed by the flood of 1927. This view is looking north. At the right are stacks of lumber at the Ward Upper Mill, which was destroyed by fire in 1961. It had survived the 1927 flood, one of the few mills in the valley that remained standing in that flood's wake. (Courtesy of Moretown Historical Society.)

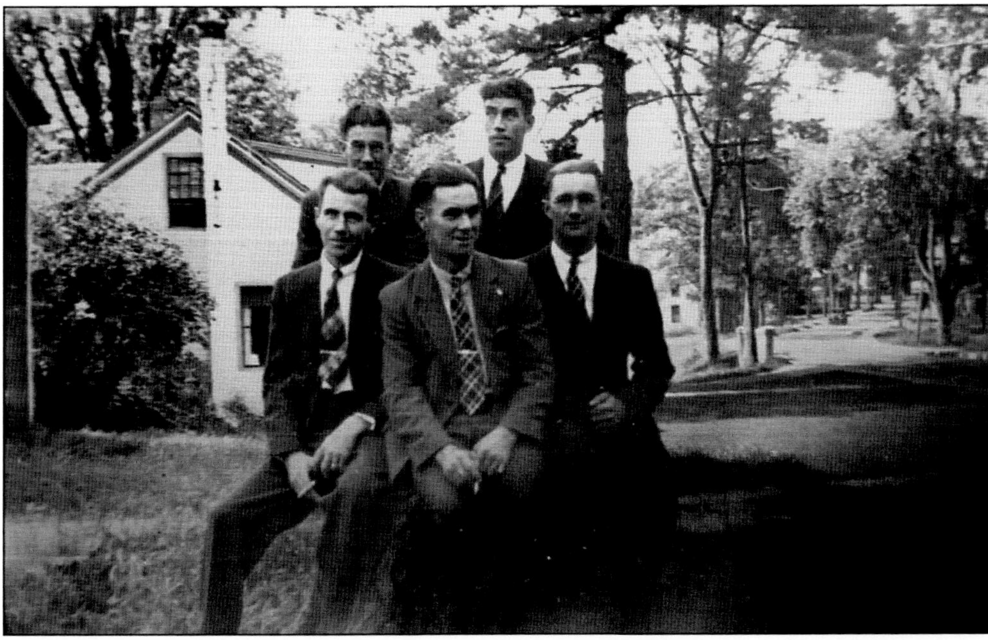

The five Reagan brothers are, from left to right, Raymond, Merrill, Francis, Leo, and Walter, shown here prior to World War II. They descended from Irish immigrants who came to Vermont in the mid-1850s. Many of the Irish worked on the Central Vermont Railway, and settled in the South Hill section of Moretown known as Paddy Hill. (Courtesy of Moretown Historical Society.)

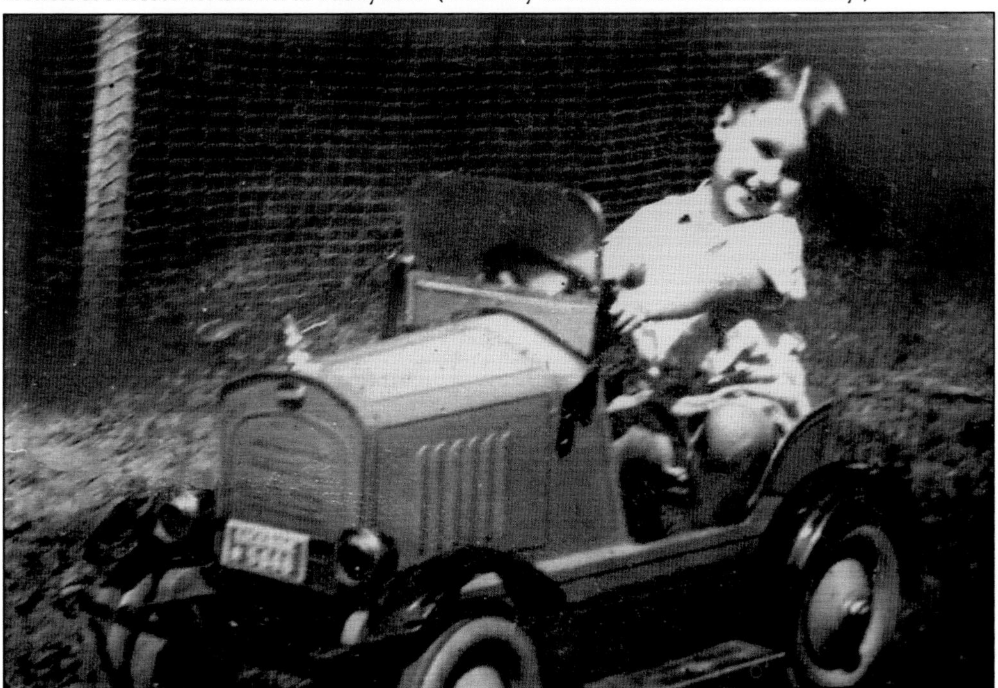

Cedric Reagan, the son of Merrill Reagan and Ruth Cutler Reagan, drives his toy car in 1932. Next to the British, the Irish and the French made up the largest immigrant groups in the early days of settlement in the Mad River Valley. (Courtesy of Moretown Historical Society.)

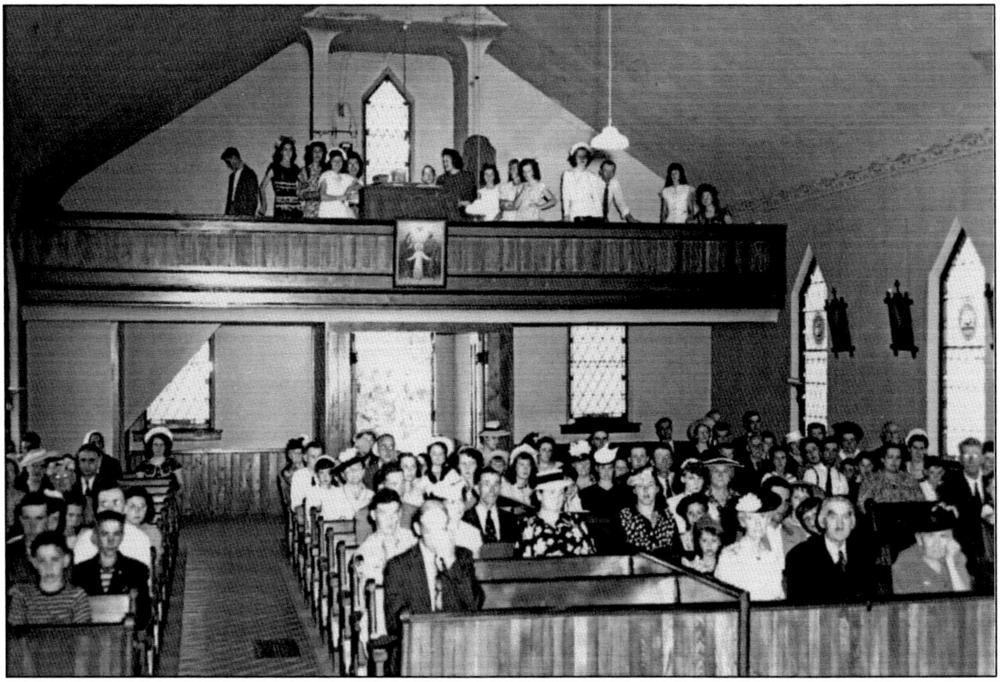

St. Patrick's Church has served the Catholic community of the Mad River Valley at its present location in Moretown Village since 1882. Before then, the church was located on South Hill Road, where the old parish cemetery exists now. This photograph was taken in 1944. (Courtesy of Moretown Historical Society.)

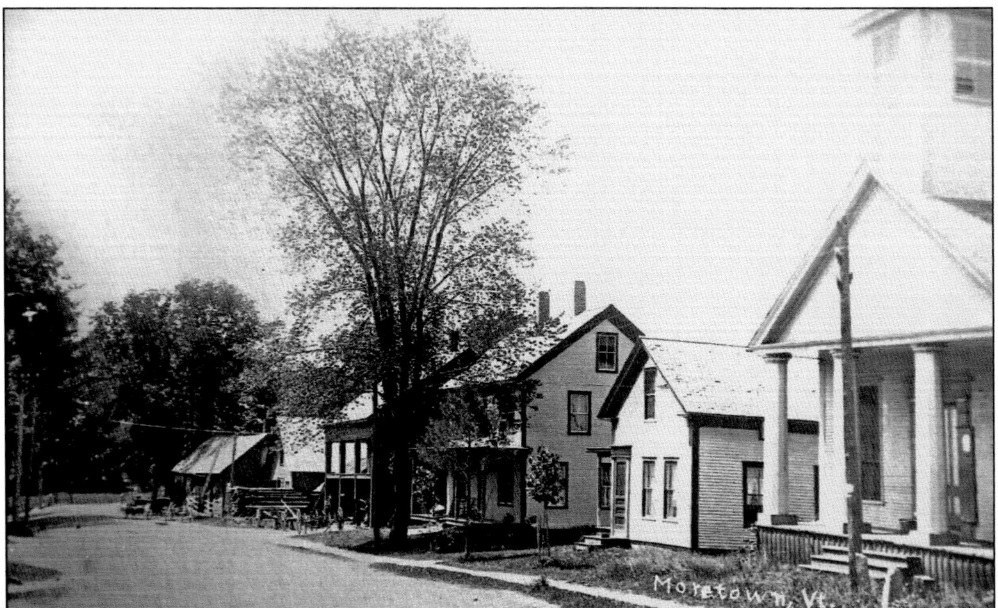

Main Street in Moretown is shown here in the early 1900s. The town hall, built in 1835, is at the far right. The Goss home is to the right of the tree, and beyond it, where the present-day post office is located, were a blacksmith and a carriage house. (Courtesy of Moretown Historical Society.)

J. J. Towle was one of a few professional photographers who captured quality images of people and things in and around the Mad River Valley, particularly in the years from 1893 to 1896. (Courtesy of Moretown Historical Society.)

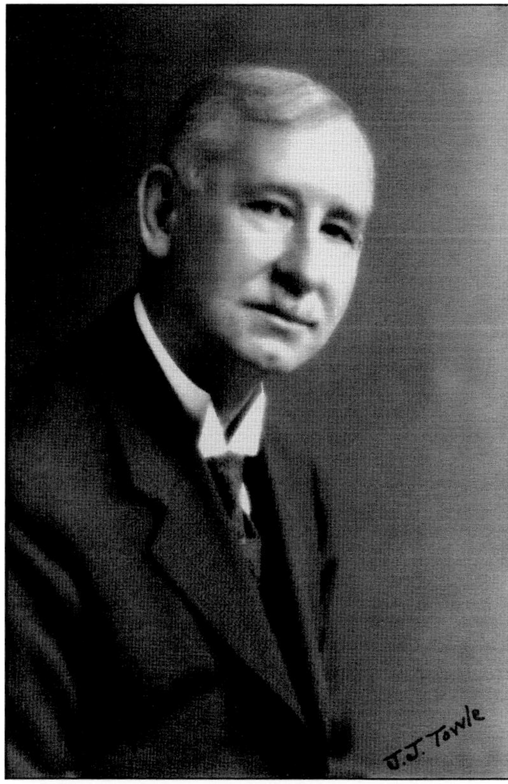

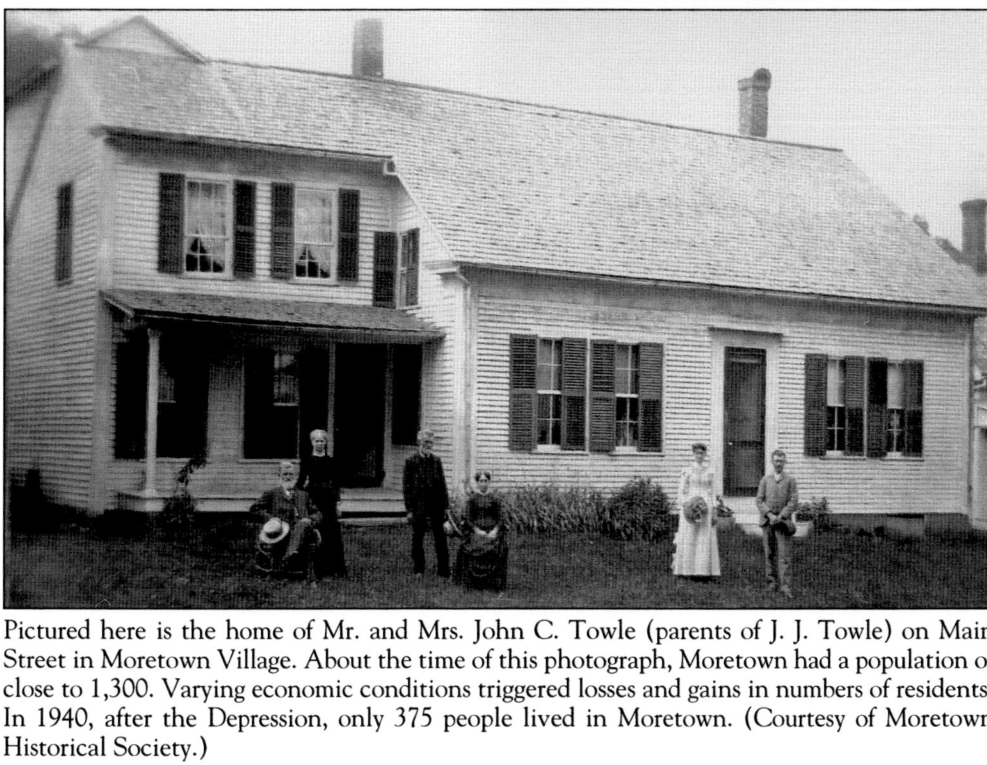

Pictured here is the home of Mr. and Mrs. John C. Towle (parents of J. J. Towle) on Main Street in Moretown Village. About the time of this photograph, Moretown had a population of close to 1,300. Varying economic conditions triggered losses and gains in numbers of residents. In 1940, after the Depression, only 375 people lived in Moretown. (Courtesy of Moretown Historical Society.)

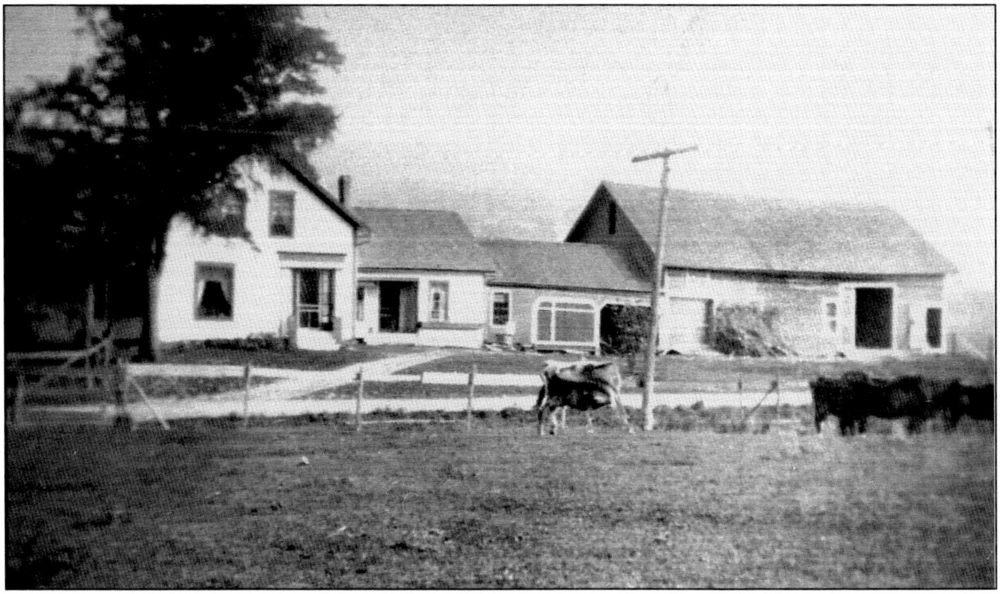

The farmhouse and barn of Wilma and Jerry Maynard still stand south of Moretown Village on what is now Route 100B. This photograph was taken from the site where Maynard's Snack Bar, a popular summertime food stand, is located. In 1935, someone counted 339 farms in the Mad River Valley (not including Duxbury). The most, 108, were in Moretown; there were 52 in Fayston, 86 in Waitsfield, and 93 in Warren. (Courtesy of Moretown Historical Society.)

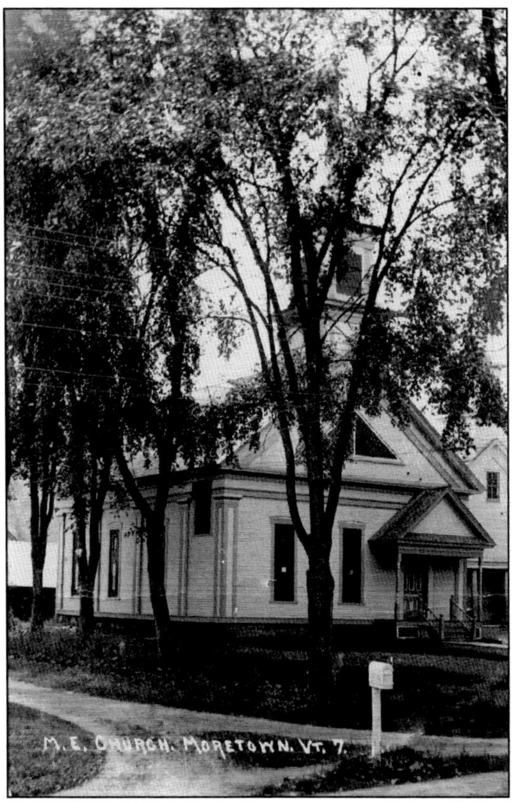

The Moretown Methodist Church was built in 1853 and renovated in 1922. It was the second Methodist church in town; the first was on the common and it was built in 1832. St. Patrick's Catholic Church stands a block away on Main Street and dates from 1882. (Courtesy of Moretown Historical Society.)

This plate, featuring a photograph by Ellie Hilferty, commemorates the 150th anniversary of the Moretown Methodist Church. Other Methodist churches were located in Waitsfield, on Main Street, where the Cabin Fever store is now, and in Warren, when it was one of three congregations that used the present United church. (Courtesy of Ellie Hilferty.)

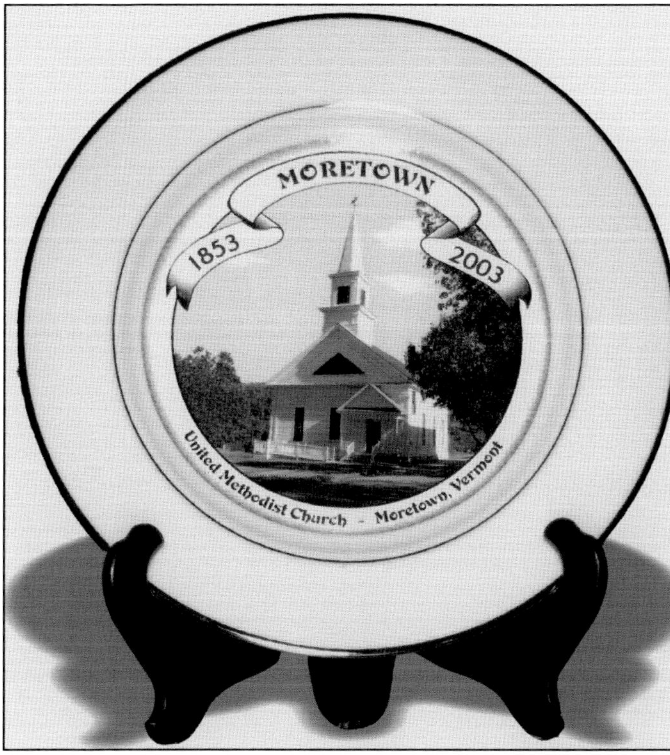

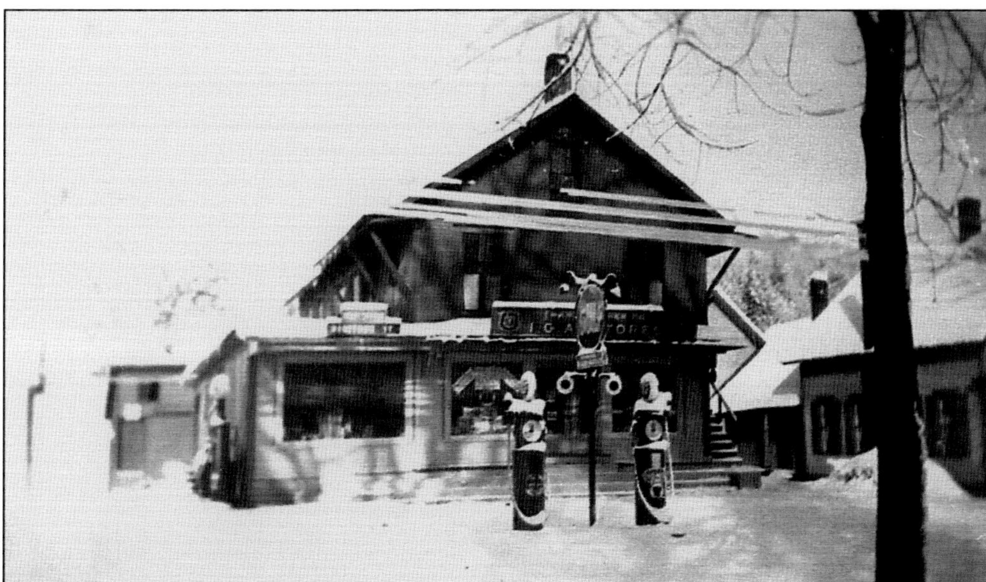

Moretown's Upper Store burned in 1952 and was never rebuilt. Small country stores are a legacy in Vermont, selling everything from bag balm to lip balm, and from farm implements to auto parts. Such stores typify the independence and self-reliance that make up a truly unique Vermont character. (Courtesy of Moretown Historical Society.)

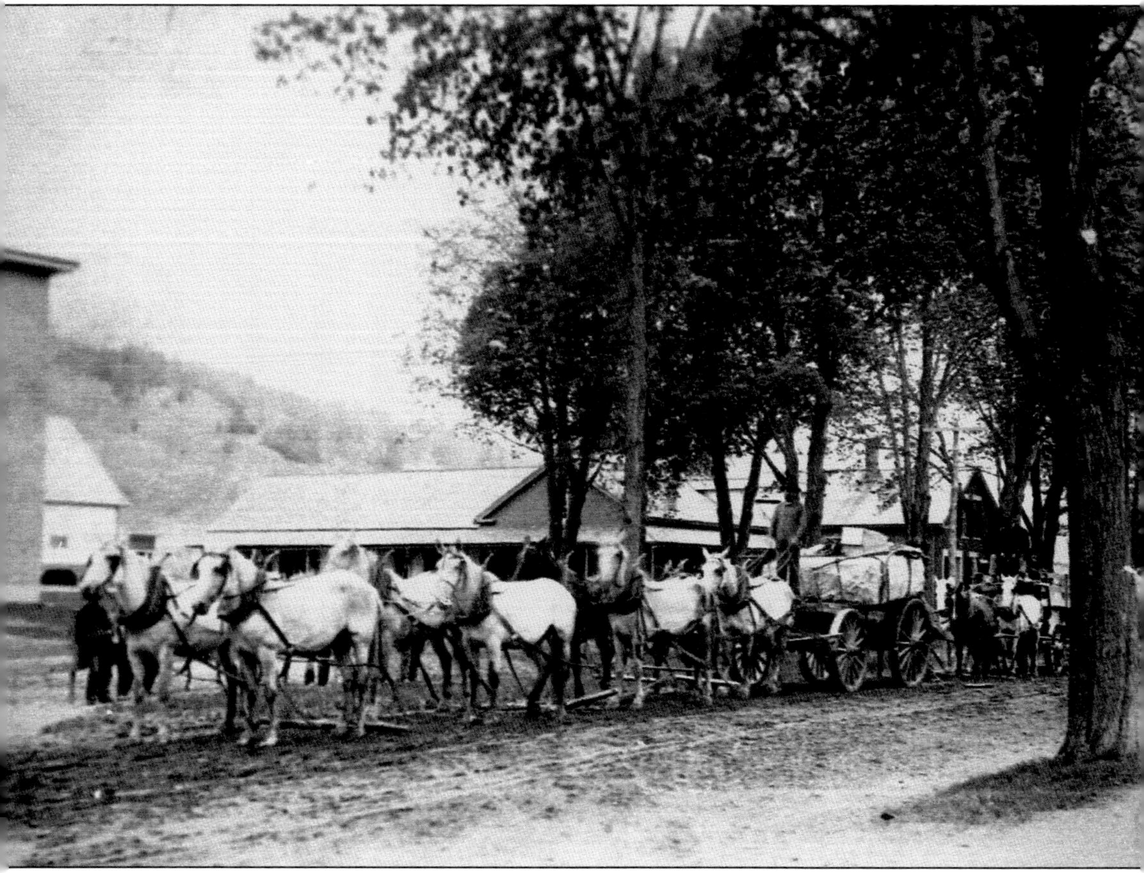

Waitsfield's Civil War monument, listing those who served in the great conflict, arrives via a wagon train pulled by eight horses. It is visible today on Main Street. The numbers of young men who served in the War between the States was phenomenal, in relation to their overall populations: Moretown, 122; Fayston, 64; and Waitsfield and Warren, 87 each. Poignant histories about this war are preserved in the form of letters sent home by the soldiers. To his wife in Warren, Willard Thayer, of Company B, Tenth Vermont Infantry, wrote: "Since I went out yesterday morning there has [*sic*] four died in the regiment and one the night before so there has five layed [*sic*] here until this afternoon. Now they have gone to bury three of them . . . This from your affectionate husband and father. Write soon." (Courtesy of Moretown Historical Society.)

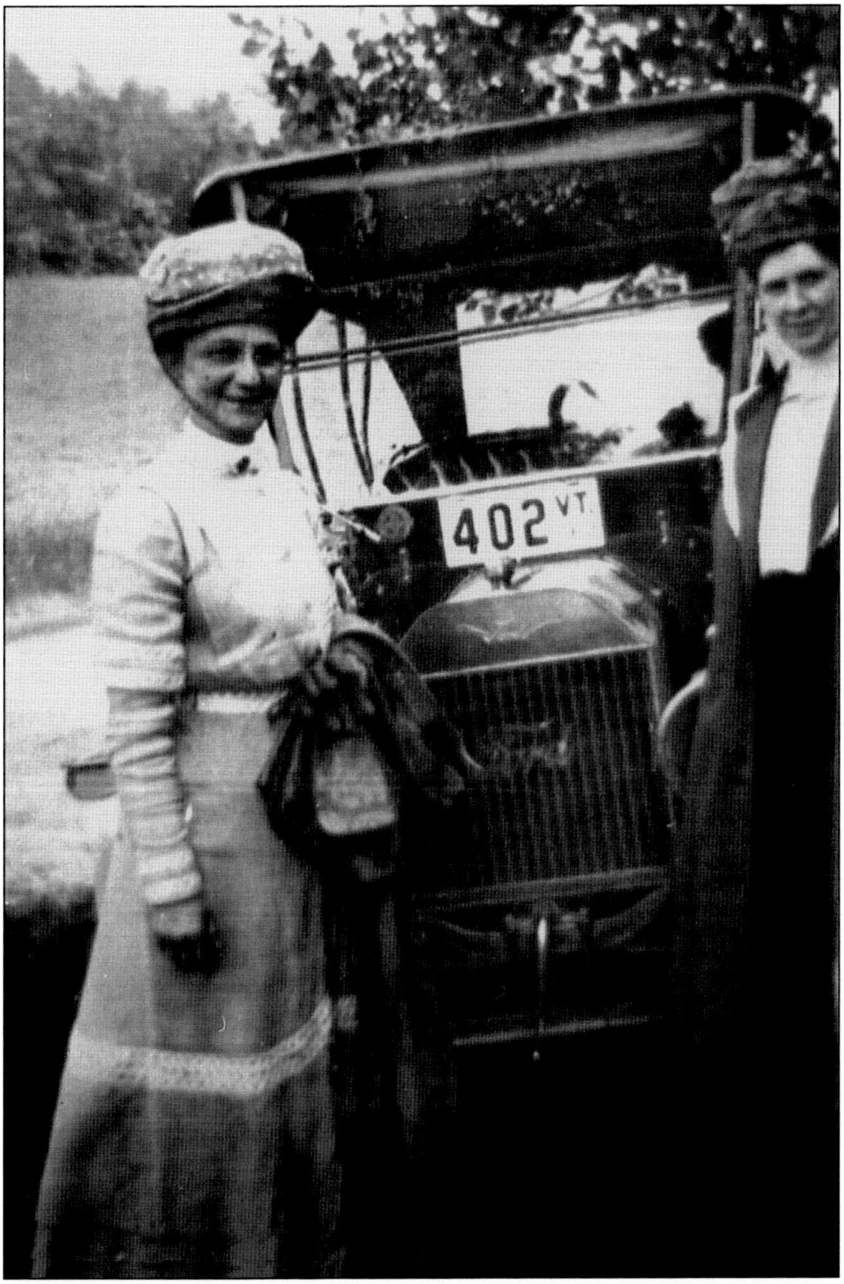

Sisters Addie Sawyer (left) and Harriet Sawyer pose with their new 1912 Ford in Moretown. Vermont winters and springs, deep snow and deep mud, saw to it that the automobile gained prominence over horse-drawn wagons at a much slower pace than in the rest of the country. The arrival of the automobile to the Mad River Valley provided an outlet to the world beyond. With no railroads running through it, the valley was comparatively isolated. There were several attempts to bring a railroad to the area, but all failed, which is a major reason why the valley's villages remained so well preserved. The automobile also brought about the demise of businesses such as carriage makers, livery stables, and blacksmiths. (Courtesy of Moretown Historical Society.)

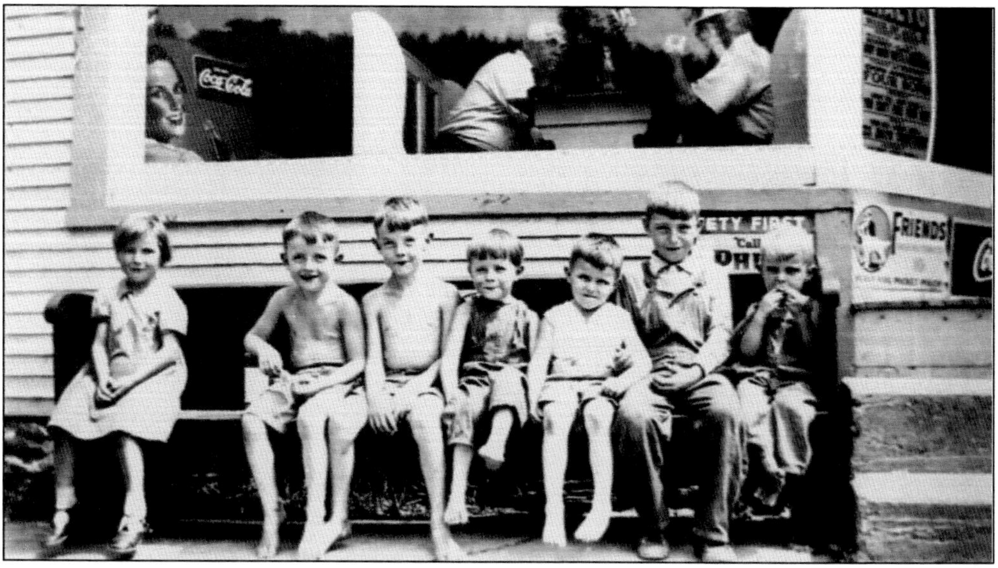

Hanging out on a warm summer day at the Lower Store in Moretown are, from left to right, Marian Fleury, Howard Ferris, his brothers Horton Ferris and Stuart Ferris, Clyde Hutchins, Kenneth Hutchins, and Frederick Fleury. The photograph was taken in the days preceding World War II. (Courtesy of Moretown Historical Society.)

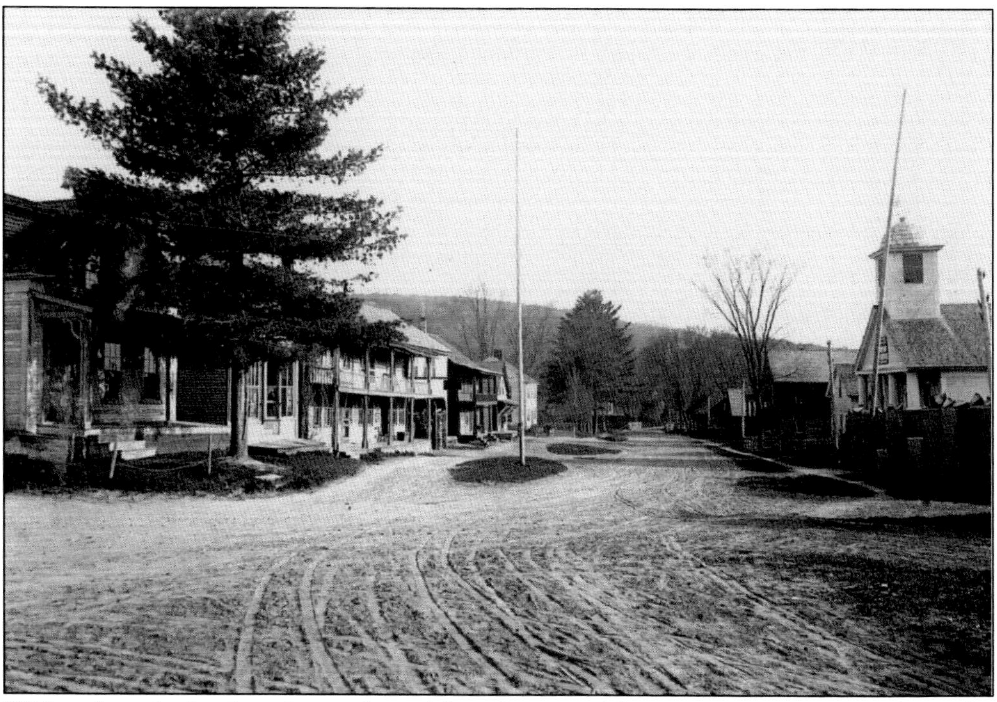

With a flagpole dividing the roadway, Main Street in Moretown at one time took on the appearance of a mini boulevard for north–south traffic. The Moretown Mountain Road appears at the left, and at right is the town hall, built in 1835. (Courtesy of Howard Ferris.)

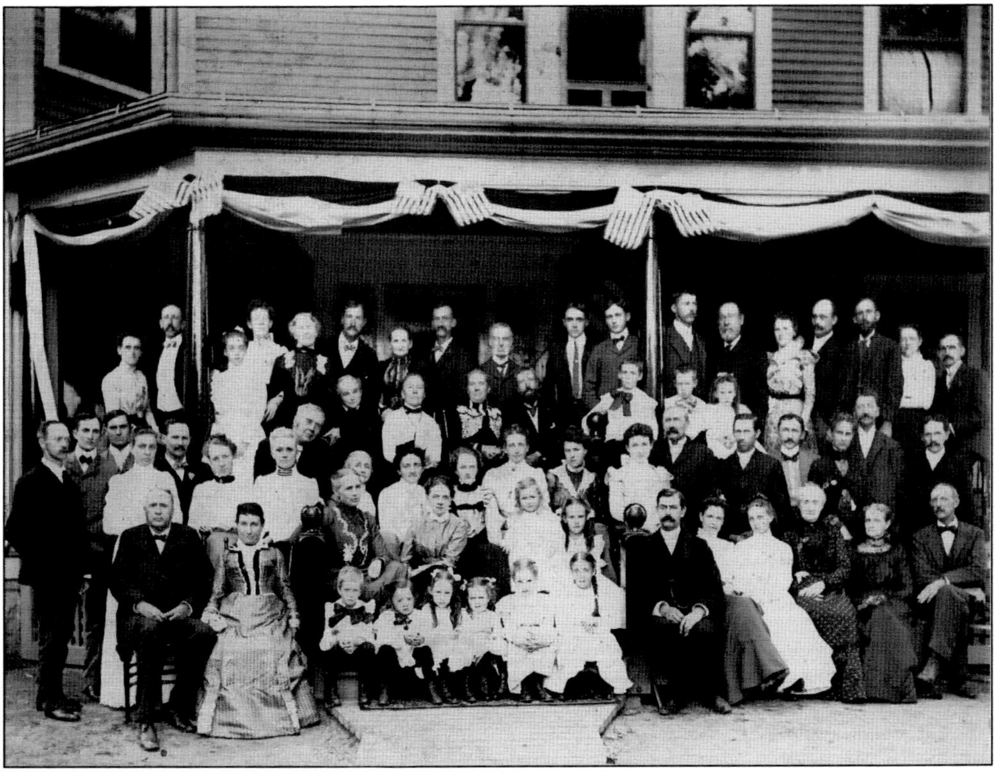

Represented at this large gathering of the Ward family at Big House in Moretown are people named Brown, Bisbee, Munson, Turner, Gilbert, Scott, Parker, Crandell, and many more familiar to the Mad River Valley. Still standing at the highest point on Main Street, the mansion became an overnight refuge for many families in the village when the flood of 1927 struck. (Courtesy of Moretown Historical Society.)

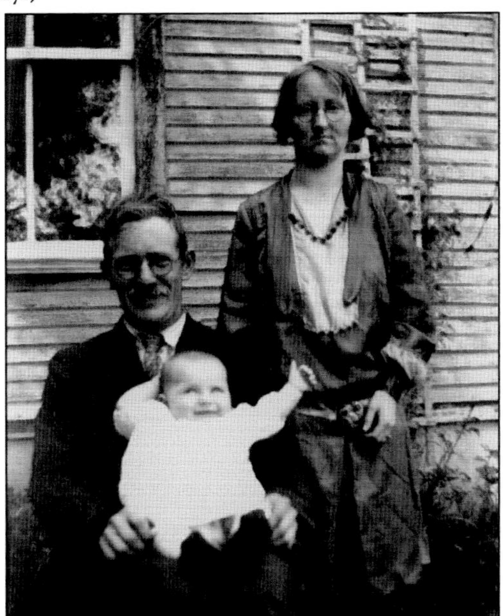

Baby Catherine Kilby cheerfully hails the world in this 1929 photograph with her parents, Elias and Rita Casey Kilby. Her parents are the progenitors of the many members of the Goss family, a particularly civic-minded family in Moretown. (Courtesy of Evelyn Goss.)

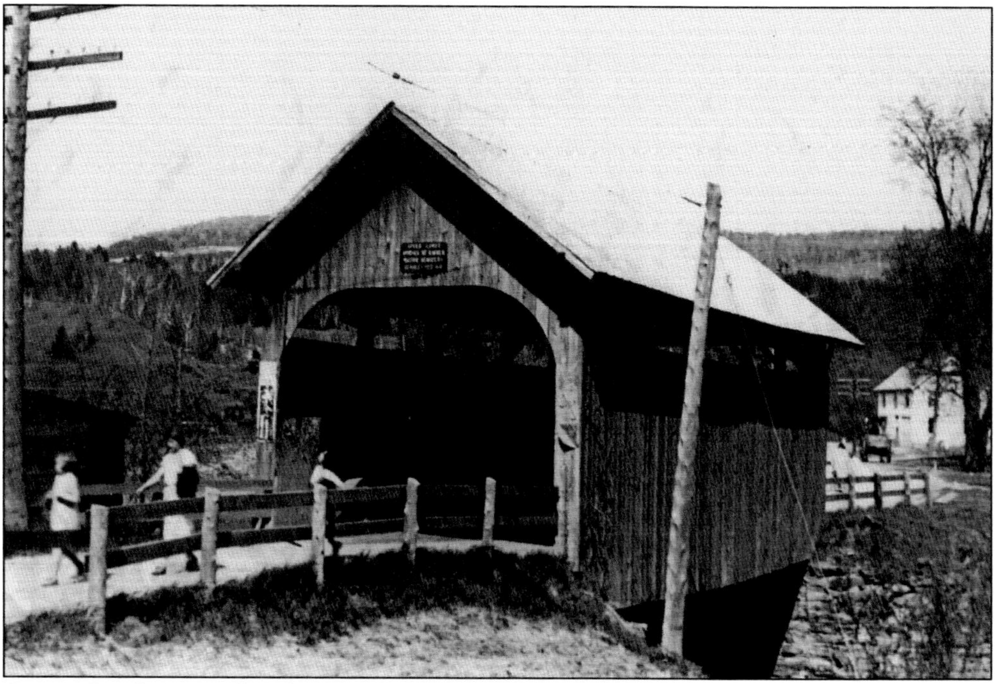

Crosset Brook Covered Bridge on the Moretown Road at Duxbury Corner, like many others in the Mad River Valley, was destroyed by the 1927 flood. "It was a huge lake there in the field when the flood hit," said Duxbury historian Alice DeLong, who was 17 at the time. (Courtesy of Alice DeLong.)

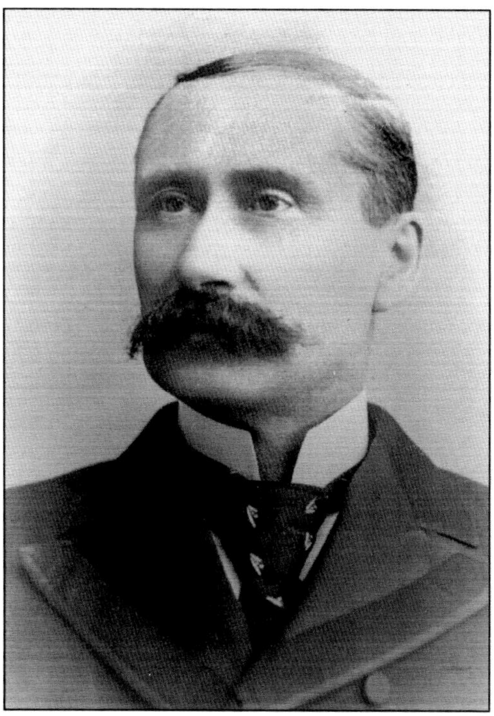

Pictured here, Hiram Owen Ward started the Ward family's vast lumber holdings and sawmill enterprises in the Mad River Valley. The Hiram O. Ward box factory and gristmill were the forerunners of the Ward Lumber Company mills. The Ward Clapboard Mill in Moretown is on the original Ward mill site. (Courtesy of Moretown Historical Society.)

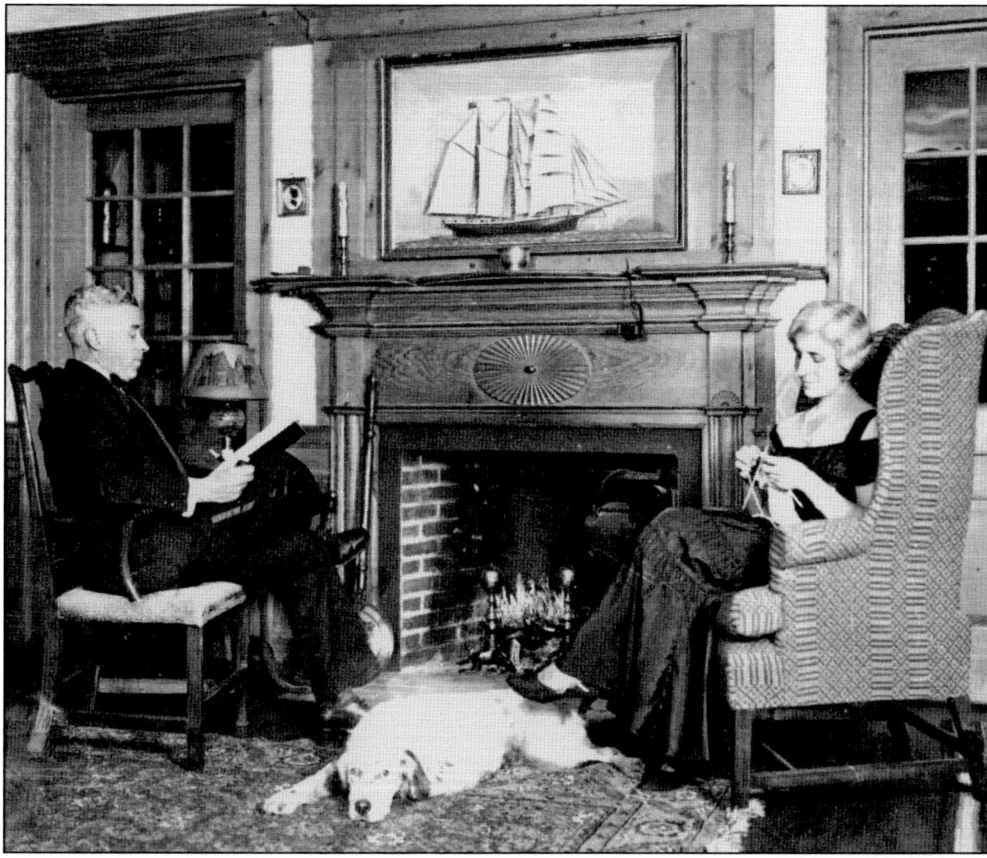

Mr. and Mrs. Alan Towle were prominent residents of Duxbury. The handsome mantelpiece in their living room was originally part of a home built in the 1790s near Bolton Falls. (Courtesy of Alice DeLong.)

Rankin Bridge over Shepard Brook in North Fayston is shown here. This was on Airport Road close to Joseph Marble's mill. Like many of the valley's covered bridges, Rankin was a casualty of time and the weather. Severe storms were recorded in 1824, 1830, 1858, 1869, 1927 ("the great flood"), 1938, and 1998. Local author Anna Bragg wrote of the 1858 storm, "Every bridge between Fayston and Middlesex, but one, was swept away." (Courtesy of Doris Rank Wimble.)

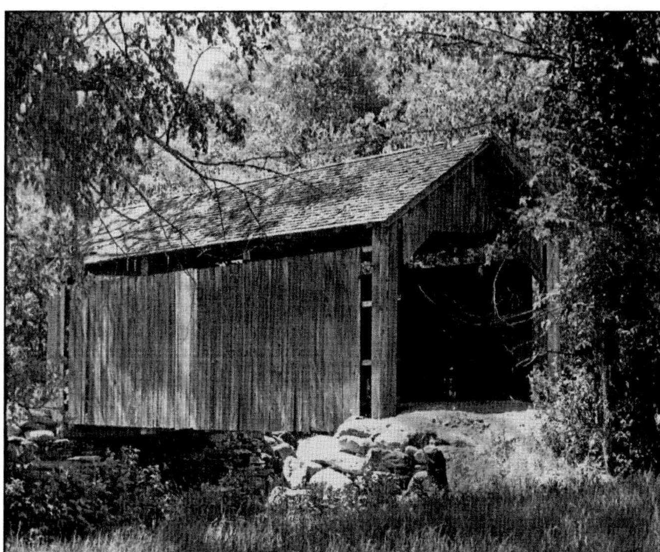

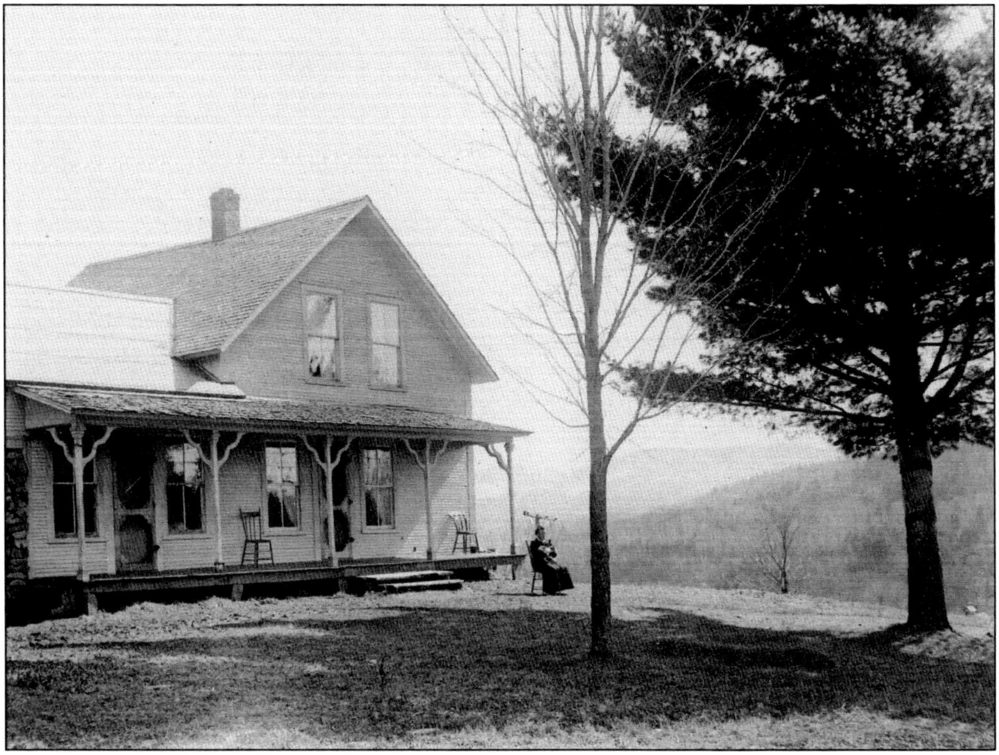

The Bettis House was at the foot of the rock and mud slide that swept away a huge portion of land between Lincoln Peak and Mount Ellen in Fayston. However, this home on German Flats Road was spared. (Courtesy of Fayston Historical Society.)

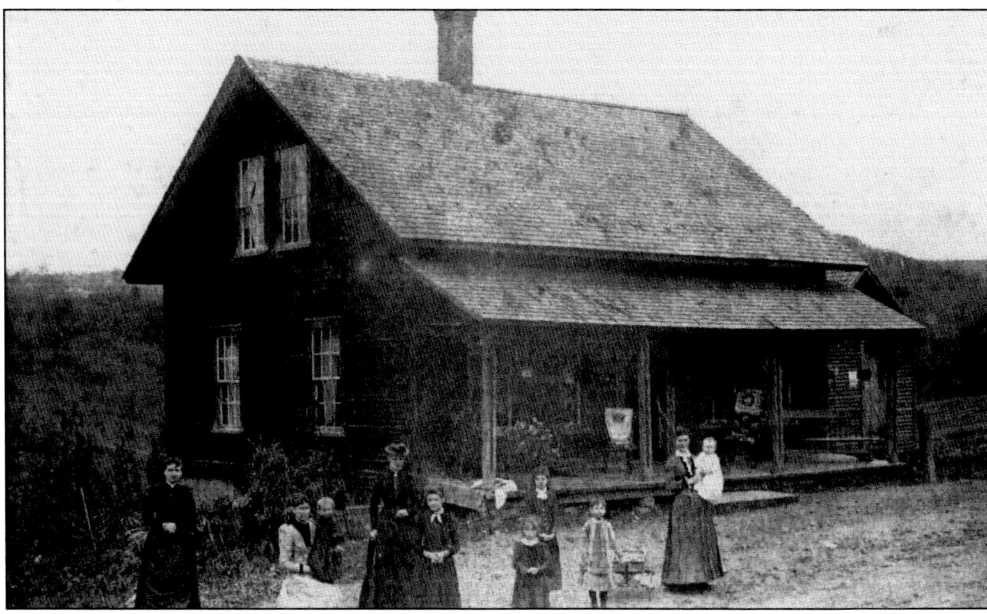

This image of the residence of Daniel and Katherine (Pever) Pasnett was taken in 1891 by local photographer J. J. Towle. A room at the right side of the house formerly served as the post office in Fayston. (Courtesy of Fayston Historical Society.)

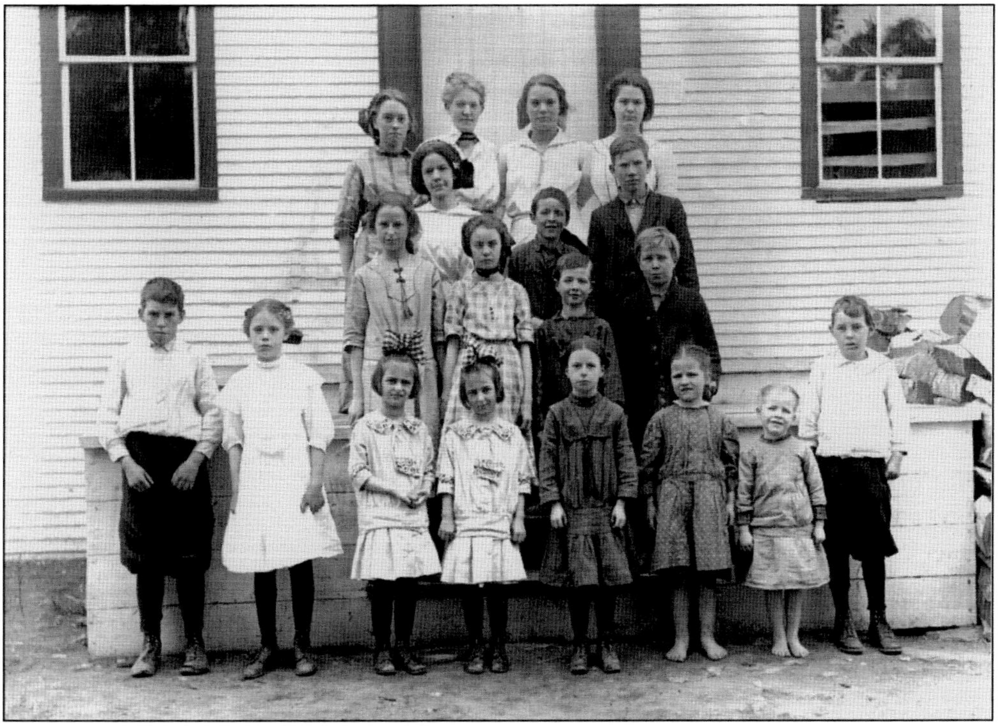

In the 1890s, about three miles west of the present Route 100 on North Fayston Road, there was a complex containing the District No. 4 School, the post office, and town hall. Students from the No. 4 School are pictured here. Many of these little hamlets vanished or were relocated, just as many mountainside farms and homes of sheep farmers were abandoned when the market for wool turned bad in the mid-1800s. (Courtesy of Fayston Historical Society.)

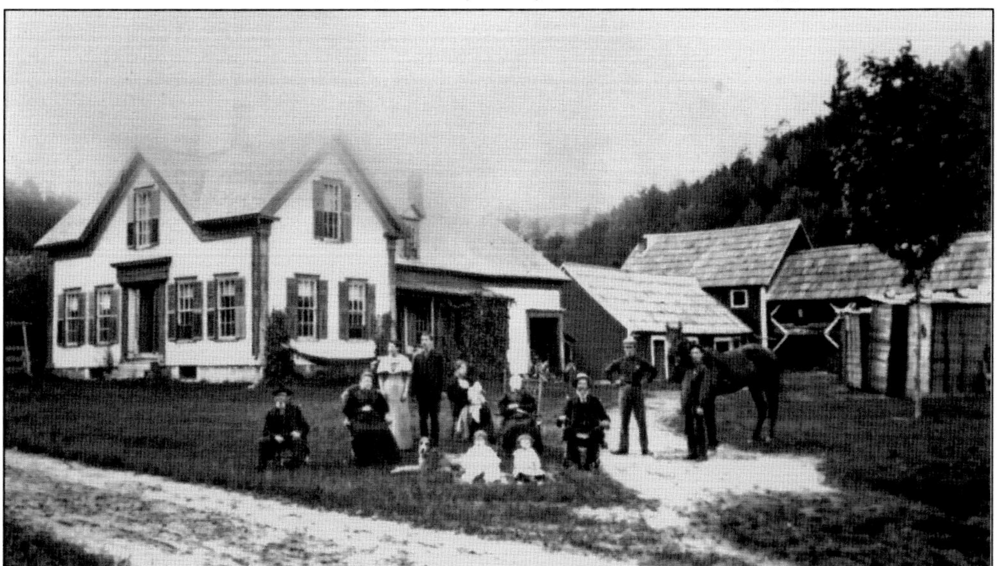

The C. D. Billings Farm is pictured in the late 1800s; it is where the Hyde Away Inn is located today on Route 17. After 1900, many farms were abandoned in Fayston. Beginning in 1920, the population dropped by 116 citizens over 10 years. (Courtesy of Fayston Historical Society.)

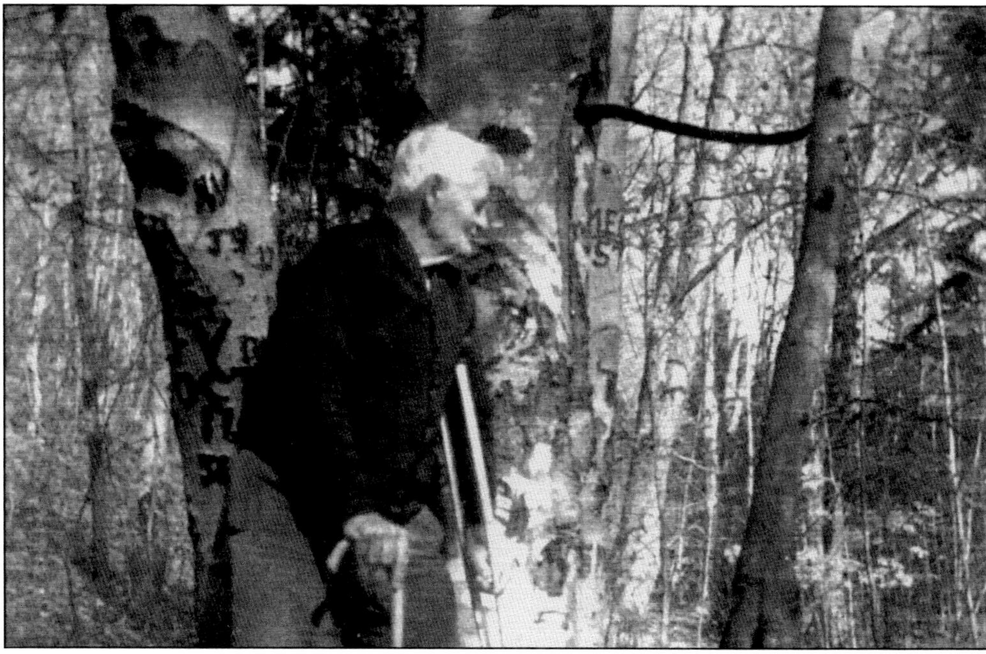

The late Perley Boyce stands next to what became known as the Scythe Tree, on Sharpshooter Road in Fayston. The story is that a young man working in the fields laid his scythe in the crotch of the tree and then left to join the Union Army during the Civil War. The scythe, which remained overgrown by the tree trunk for more than 100 years, is now on display in a chunk of the since-dead tree that is kept in the Fayston Town Hall. (Courtesy of Fayston Historical Society.)

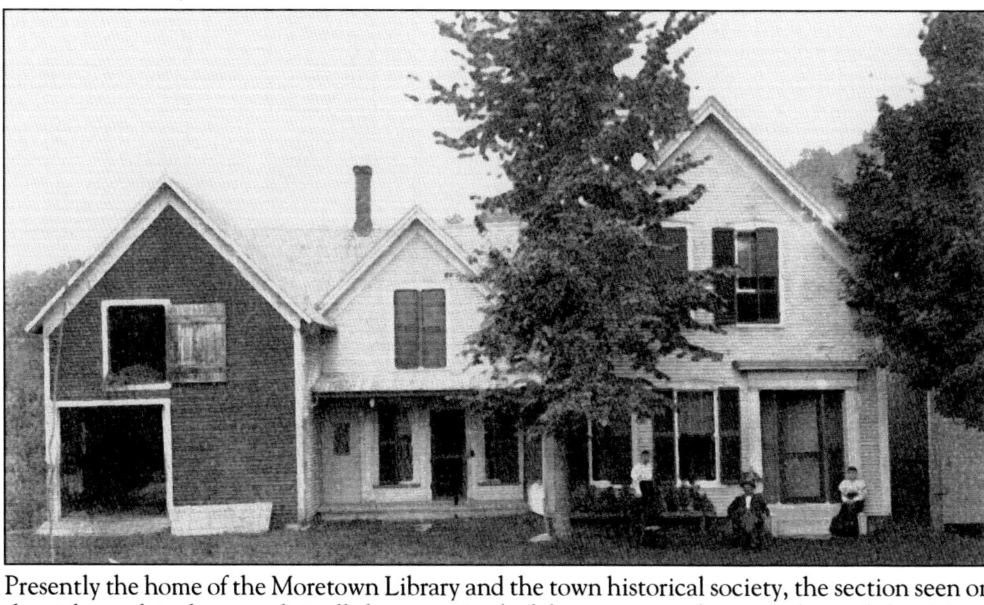

Presently the home of the Moretown Library and the town historical society, the section seen on the right in this photograph is all that remained of the structures that once housed the Palmer family. The other sections were swept away during the flood of 1927. The library company was founded in 1873 by Lilla Buckley Haylett, wife of Dr. James Haylett. (Courtesy of Moretown Historical Society.)

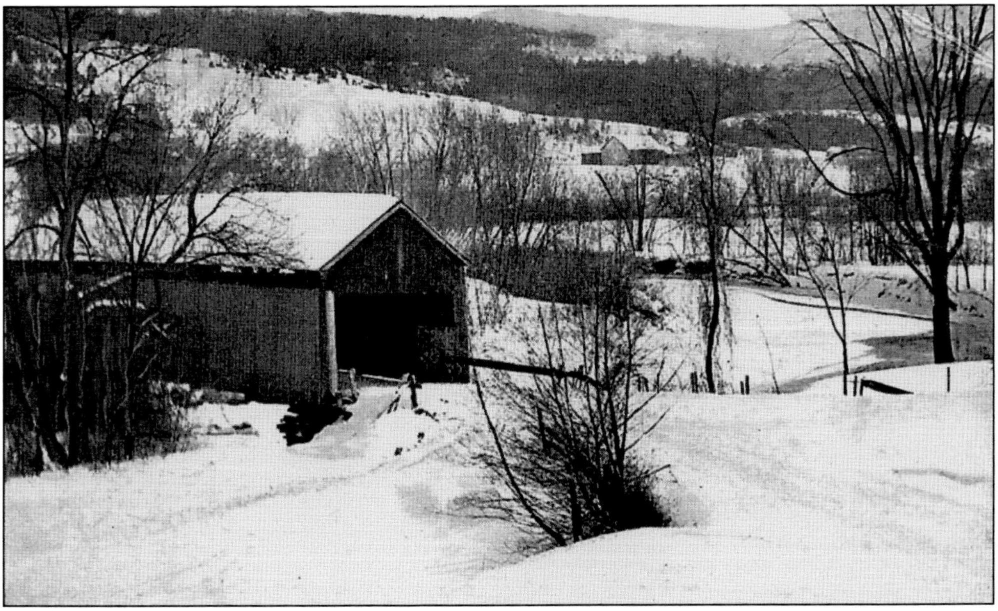

This covered bridge formerly spanned the Mad River on Meadow Road in Waitsfield before being taken out by a truck loaded with logs sometime in the 1950s. A steel and concrete bridge that replaced it overlooks the Mad River Path, a popular trail for jogging, hiking and biking. (Courtesy of Fred Messer.)

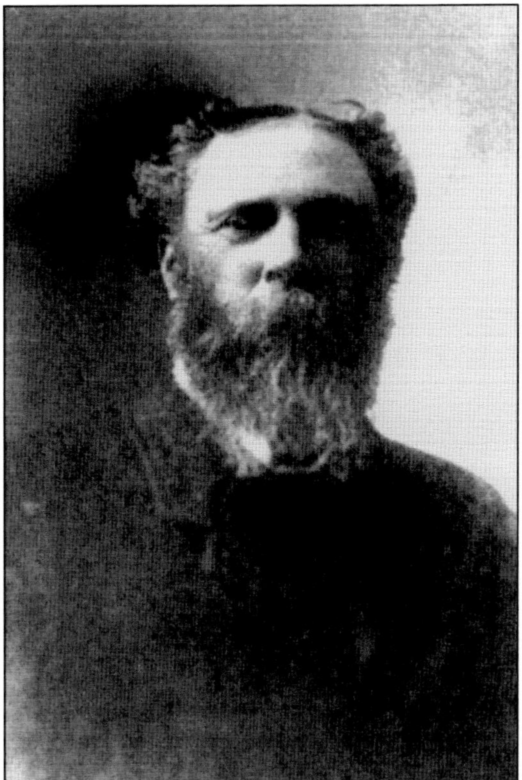

Dr. James Haylett, pictured, continued the tradition in Moretown of the local physician taking on other civic roles in addition to his medical practice. He came to Moretown in 1889, and was a state legislator and town clerk for many years. His predecessor, Dr. Lester Kinsley, settled in Moretown in 1827 and was postmaster, town representative, and town clerk, holding the latter position until his death in 1881. (Courtesy of Moretown Historical Society.)

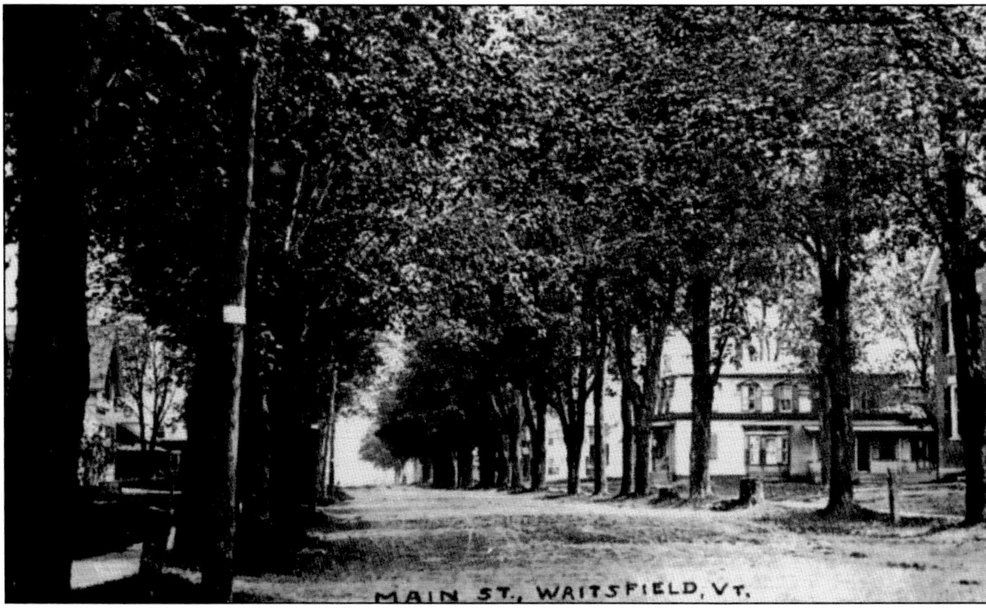

The stately maples that line Main Street in Waitsfield lend a permanence to the thoroughfare, but it was not the main road through town until the 1830s. Prior to that, the major route ran west of the present route, from the Moretown line and into Waitsfield, and according to the town's history written by Matt Bushnell Jones, continued "under the ledges back of the terrace that rises from the square." (Courtesy of Fred Messer.)

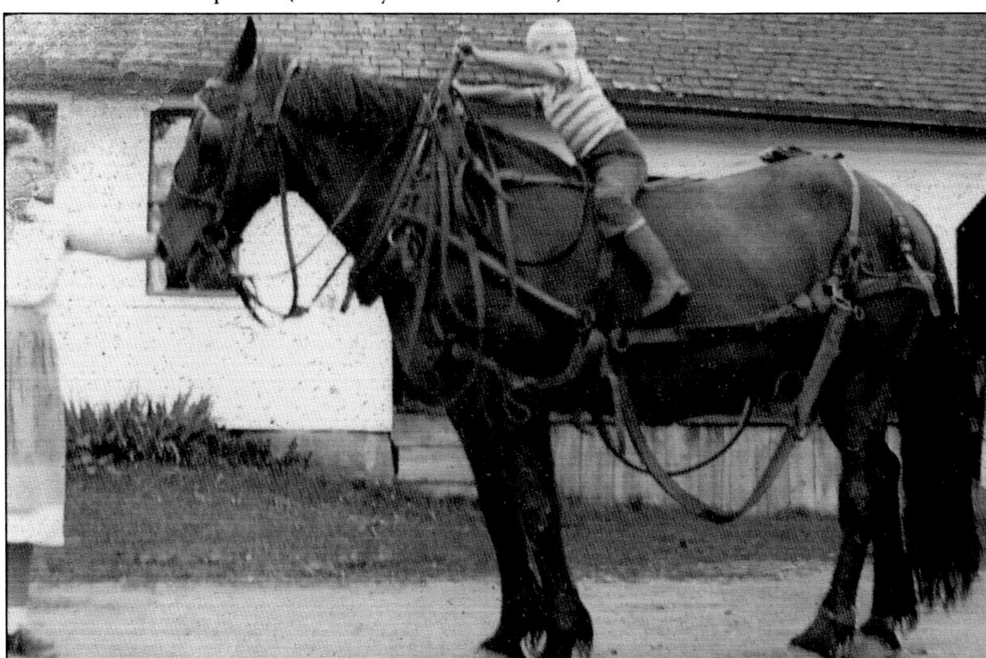

Jennie Palmer Messer and Fred Messer are shown here c. 1953. The Palmer family has been traced back to the 1790s, when the original settlers came to Waitsfield following the lead of the first settler, Gen. Benjamin Wait. Wait's home is now the headquarters of the Sugarbush Chamber of Commerce on Route 100. (Courtesy of Fred Messer.)

Five

Good Times

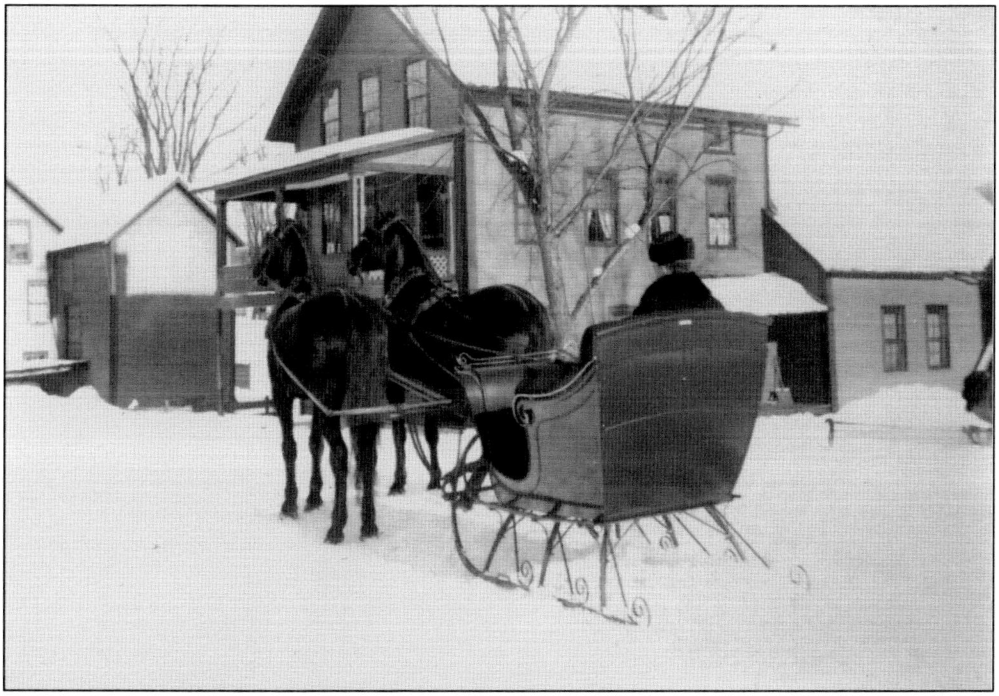

A two-horse open sleigh glides smoothly south on Main Street in Waitsfield. The photograph is reminiscent of the Miller Brewing Company's television commercial that was filmed on Bridge Street and the Pony Farm Road several years ago. The commercial is still seen and admired during the December holiday season. (Courtesy of Waitsfield Historical Society.)

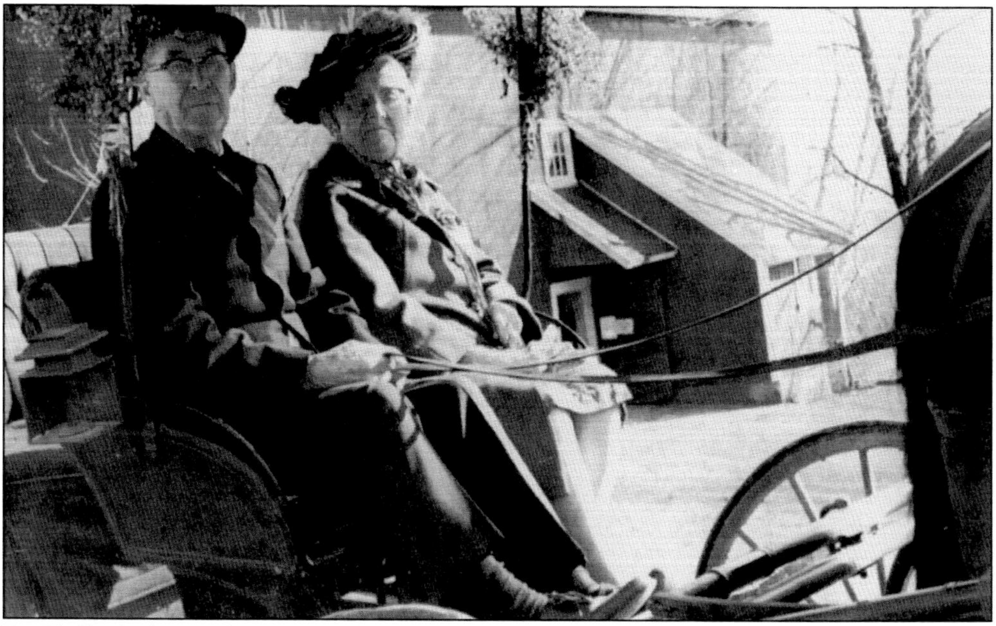

Dr. Phillip Bisbee and Emma Ford re-create a 19th-century Sunday carriage ride at a Fourth of July parade in Warren Village. The parade, held annually since 1948, is a free-swinging potpourri of things American, from the cherry-pit spitting championship to costumed marchers and topical floats. (Courtesy of Katherine Hartshorn.)

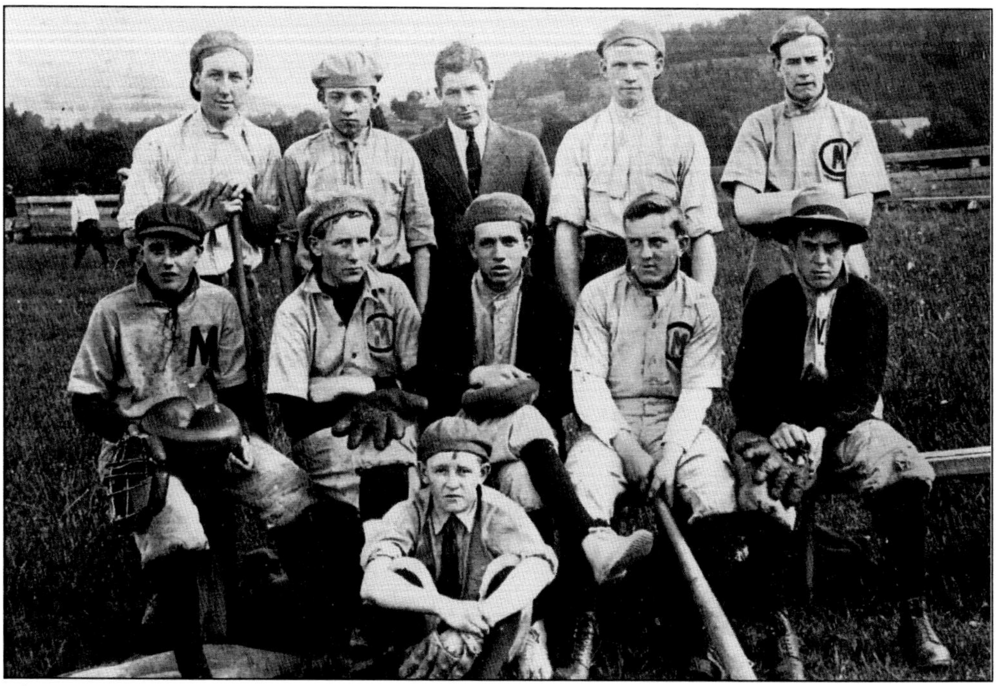

The Warren town baseball team is shown here in the 1920s. From left to right are the following: (seated on ground) ? Newcomb; (first row) unidentified, Harold Greenwood, Ralph Bisbee, Harold Parker, and Lawrence Ford; (second row) two unidentified people, Coach Pitkin, unidentified, and Perle Carpenter. (Courtesy of Katherine Hartshorn.)

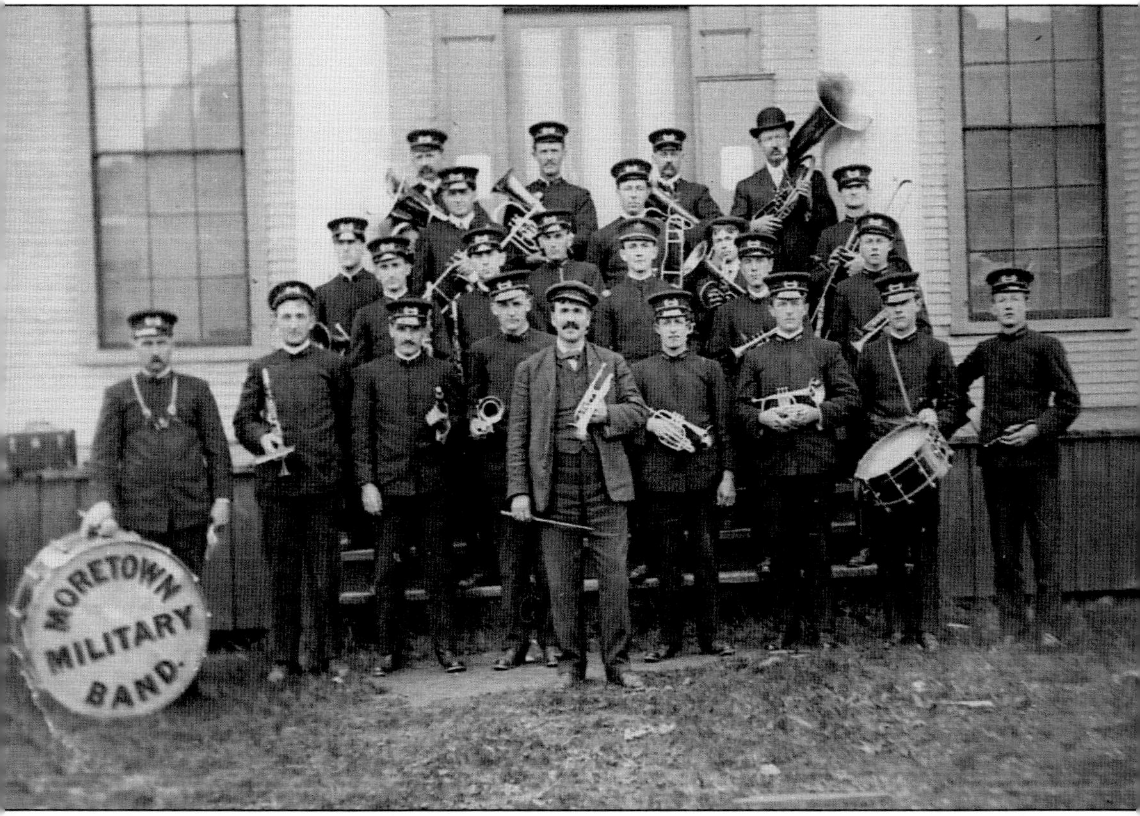

This photograph of the Moretown Military Band was taken by professional photographer J. J. Towle *c.* 1900. The band members are seen standing in front of the town hall. In the early 1900s, the band had at least 24 members, all of whom may not necessarily be pictured here. A historical note identified some of the members as follows: Will Johnson (drummer), Carroll Pierce, Pet J. Griffith, Frank Atkins, Roy Atkins, the Armstrong boys, and Charles Goss. It is a safe guess that marches by John Philip Sousa were tops on the performance chart. The town population was about 1,200 around the time this picture was taken. As the 19th century turned into the 20th, people began to move out, some going west to find more-fertile fields. By 1920, only 930 people lived in town, reducing the population to a low of 375 in 1940. (Courtesy of Moretown Historical Society.)

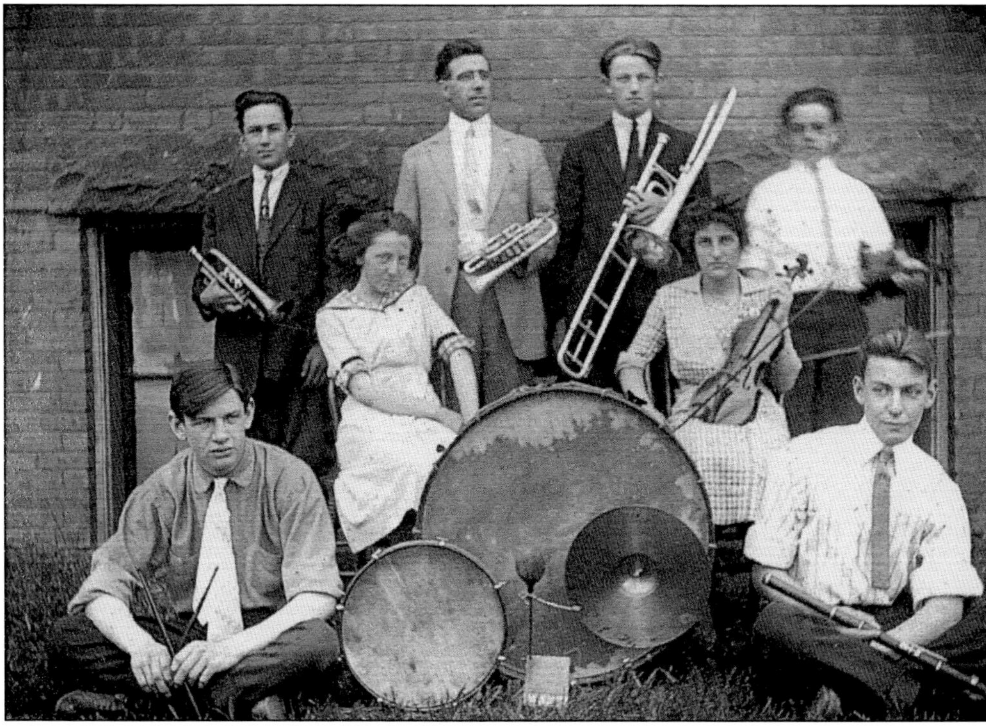

You will not find selections by this group on iTunes. The Warren Band played to live audiences and, in this case, posed prior to a concert near the church on the Warren Village common. Homegrown musical entertainment was an important fixture in a society spared from the influences of television and radio. (Courtesy of Warren Library.)

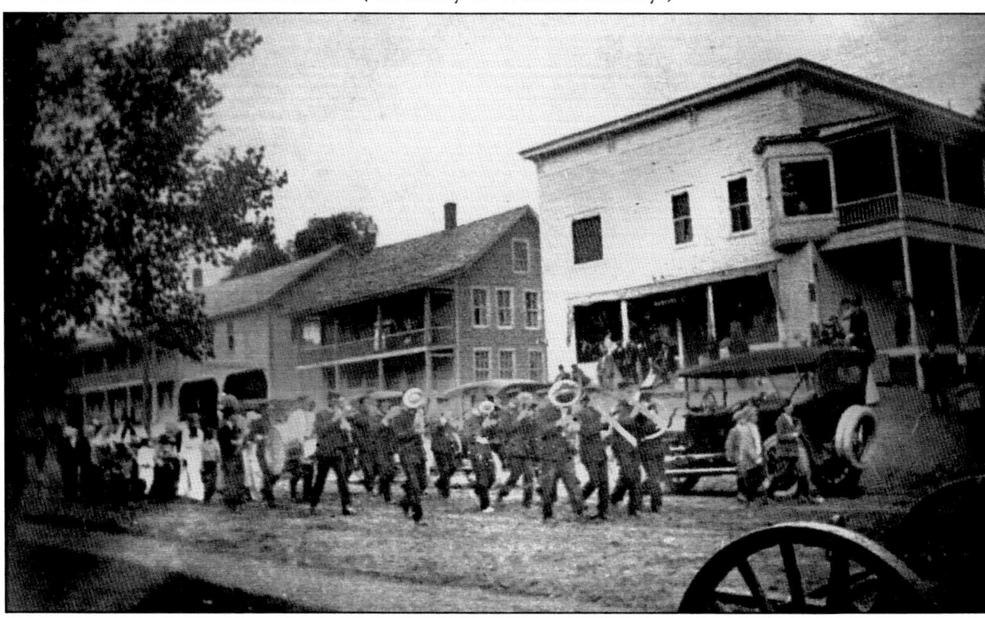

This photograph of a parade in Moretown, taken about 1900, was deemed artistic enough to hang in someone's parlor. The old hotel on the left was consumed by fire on March 15, 1963. (Courtesy of Moretown Historical Society.)

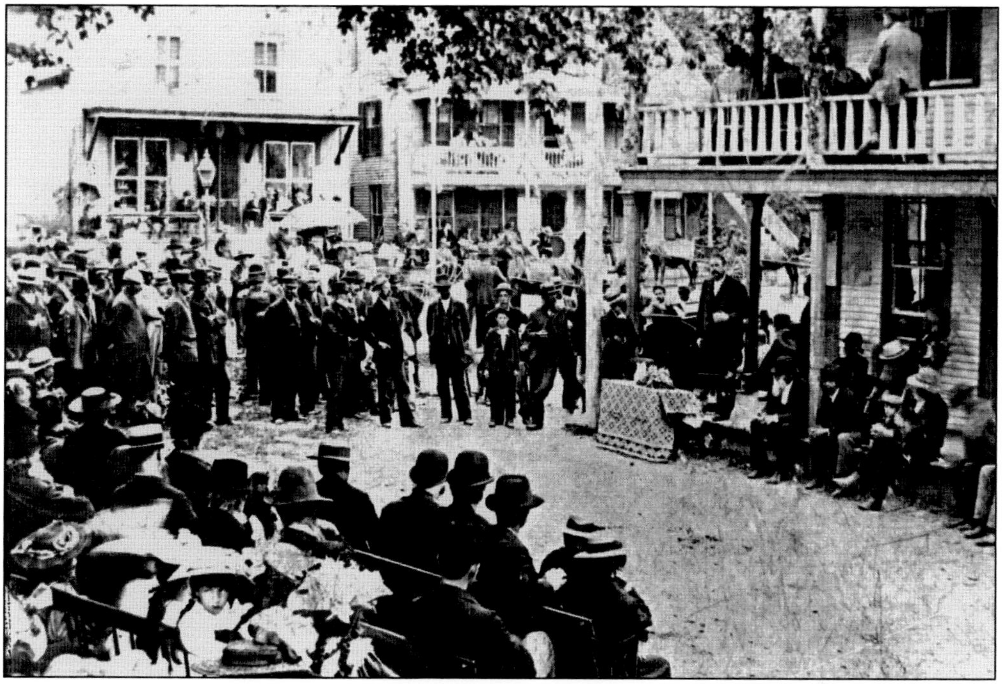

Memorial Day c. 1920 is depicted here in front of Lyford's, now the Warren Store. The speaker was John Senter, a lawyer and state official born and raised in Warren. Viewed on the opposite side of Main Street is the Bragg Millinery Store, which was on the lot where the Pitcher Inn is located today. (Courtesy of Warren Library.)

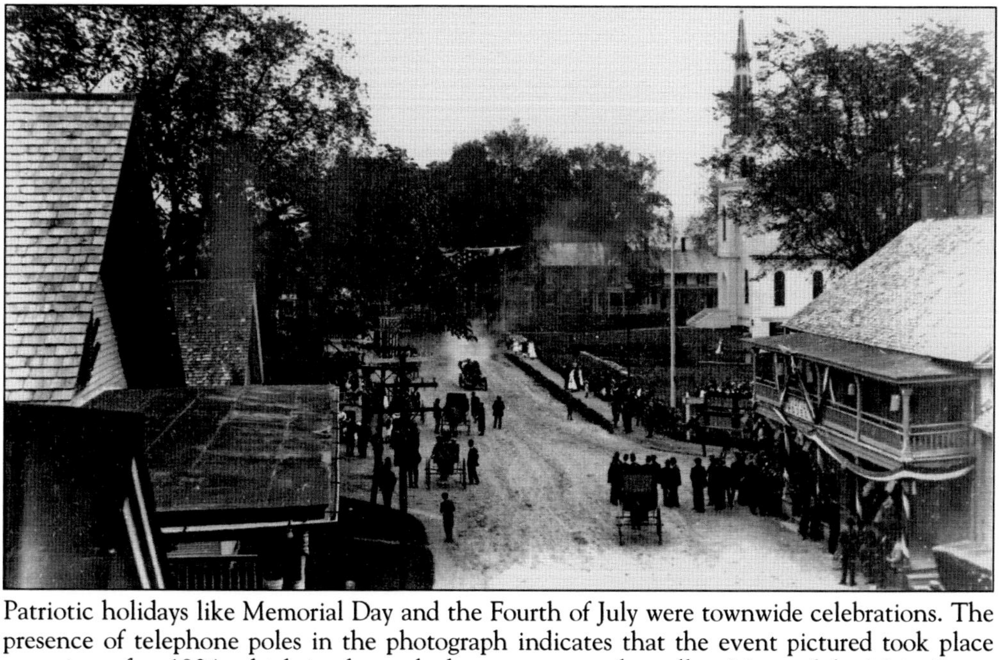

Patriotic holidays like Memorial Day and the Fourth of July were townwide celebrations. The presence of telephone poles in the photograph indicates that the event pictured took place sometime after 1904, which is when telephones came to the valley. Many of the Main Street buildings constructed in the Greek Revival style were built in the 1840s; the United church, at the right, was built in 1875. (Courtesy of Waitsfield Historical Society.)

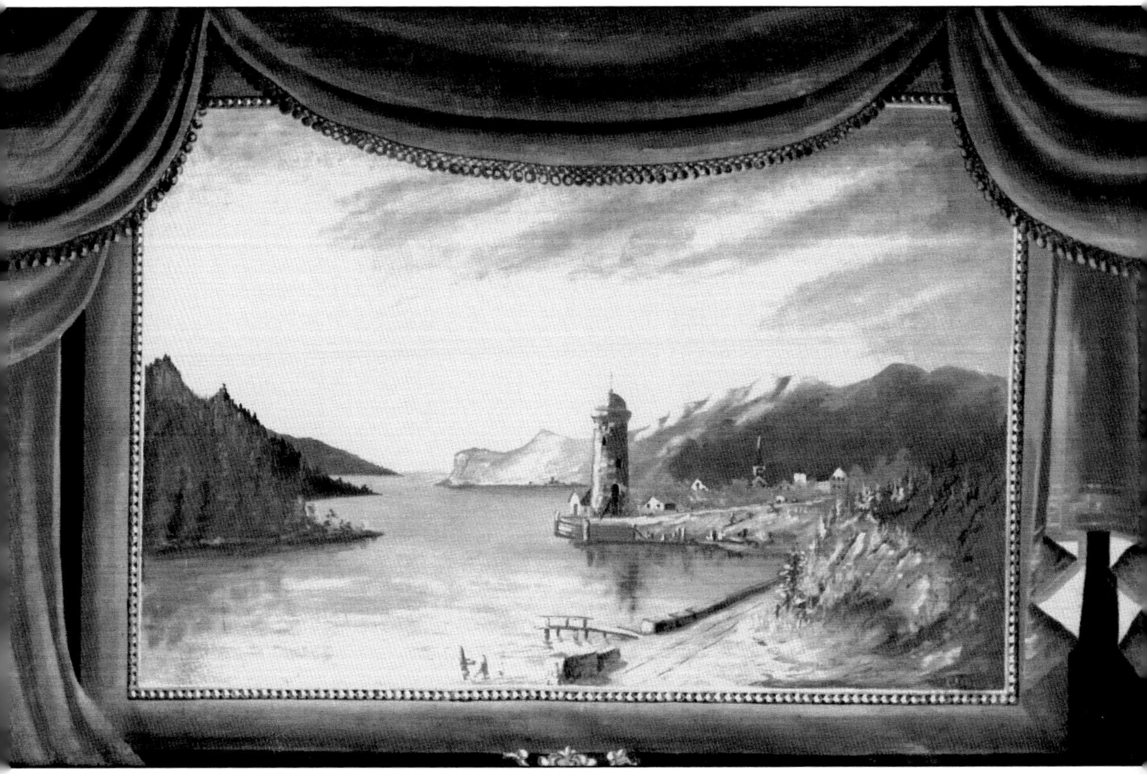

Over a 60-year period beginning in about 1880, itinerant artists traveled around Vermont to paint theater backdrops and curtains in various communities. Shown above is one of five curtains belonging to the town of Moretown that were restored by the Moretown Historical Society with grant assistance provided by Vermont's Painted Theater Curtain Project, a special program of the Vermont Museum and Gallery Alliance. The painted theater curtains in Vermont can be grouped into two styles. One type was designed to serve as scenery in opera houses and performance halls. Most of these scenes were European landscapes or other rural or urban settings to serve as a backdrop for theatrical productions. The other kind of curtain was created for small venues, mostly Grange meeting halls. These often depicted local landscapes and also displayed advertisements for local businesses, which paid for the curtains. (Photograph by Ellie Hilferty.)

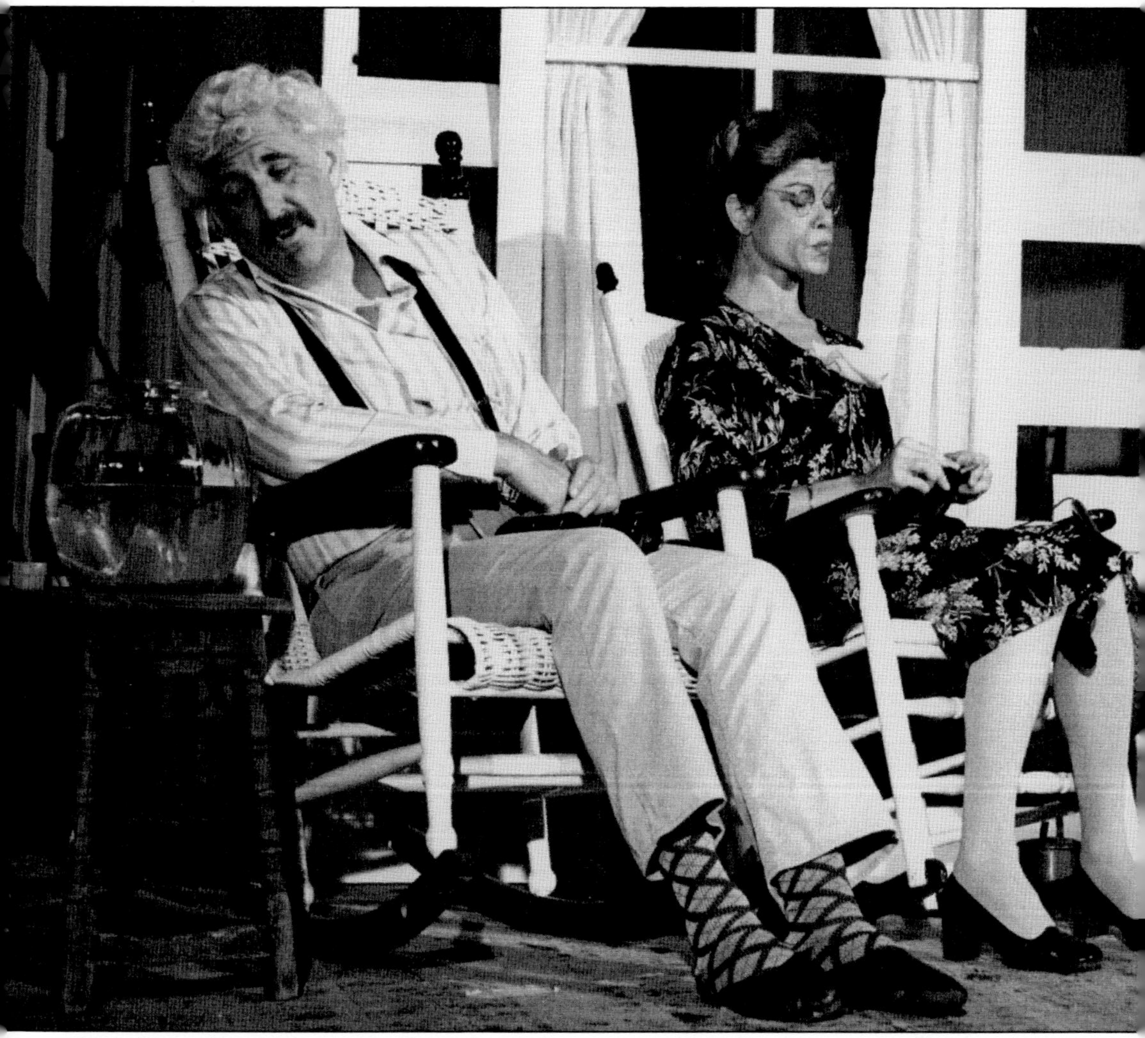

Mitch Kontoff and Nancy Groff are shown here in a 1980 Valley Players production of *I'm Herbert*, which was one of three one-act plays put on by the theater group that year. The Valley Players (VP) have been in the forefront of live dramatic presentations in the valley since 1979. *Harvey* was the Players first production, presented in the Fayston Elementary School. Currently, performances are staged in the theater group's building, the Odd Fellows Hall on Main Street in Waitsfield. The theater company annually presents a Cabin Fever Follies production in the spring, which has grown to become a great comfort to local residents during mud season. The Follies also raise money for charities, including the Vermont Adaptive Ski and Sports, Vermont Children's Aid Society, and the Special Olympics. In 1982, the VP created the Vermont Playwrights Award, providing $1,000 and the possibility of production to a playwright who is the author of the best amateur, full-length play. (Courtesy of Valley Players.)

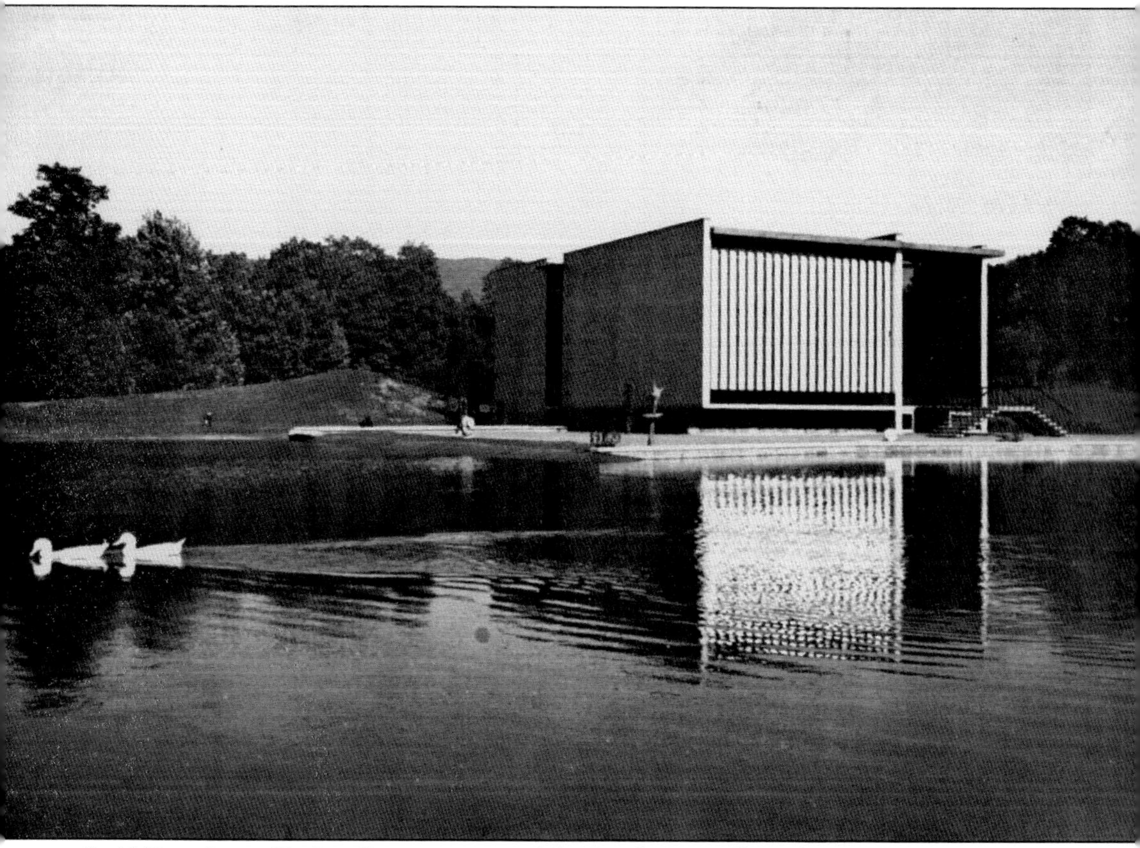

In 1962, architect Harlow Carpenter opened the Bundy Art Gallery, designed as a contemporary country museum on a high plateau off of Route 100 in Waitsfield. Carpenter fulfilled a goal of creating an arts complex "where art and nature could co-exist," providing urban sophistication within a natural setting. The modern building, which is typical of the Bauhaus school of design, was constructed next to an old cellar hole on the former site of the Lizzie Long farmhouse. The complex exists today as the Bundy Center for the Arts and is managed as a music and arts center by the Mad River Chorale. The site is one of many in the Mad River Valley that is a popular setting for Vermont country weddings, allowing views of the Sugarbush Resort and the Green Mountains. (Courtesy of the Bundy Center for the Arts.)

Small-town amateur theatricals, more often than not, have presented comedies where laughs were guaranteed more by the mere stage presence of friends and neighbors than by the quality of the play itself. The 1937 production of *Cheerio, My Deario* in Moretown (right) would have been a definite respite from both mud season and the rigors of the Great Depression. (Courtesy of Moretown Historical Society.)

CHEERIO, MY DEARIO

A Comedy In Three Acts
Presented By

MORETOWN P. T. A.

Directed by Mrs. Merlin Ward
Assisted by Mr. Harold Hewitt

Friday, March 12, '37

8:00 P. M.
Town Hall

Characters

Sue Grahame	Mary Hewitt
Melchizedek	Melvin Ward
Desdemona	Nettie Kingsbury
Dick Grahame	Merrill Griffith
Cherry Holt	Alice Clark
Sophronia Spatchett	Katherine Hayes
Fifi	Arlene Avery
Tommy Tarrant	Robert Fulton
Mrs. T. Jefferson Johns	Mrs. T. McGowan
Gwenneth Johns	Bernardette McGowan
Lord Cuthbert Twillingham	Albert K. Ferris
Snodsbury	Adrian K. Ferris

Candy Sold by J. V. 4-H Girls

Admission 25c and 15c

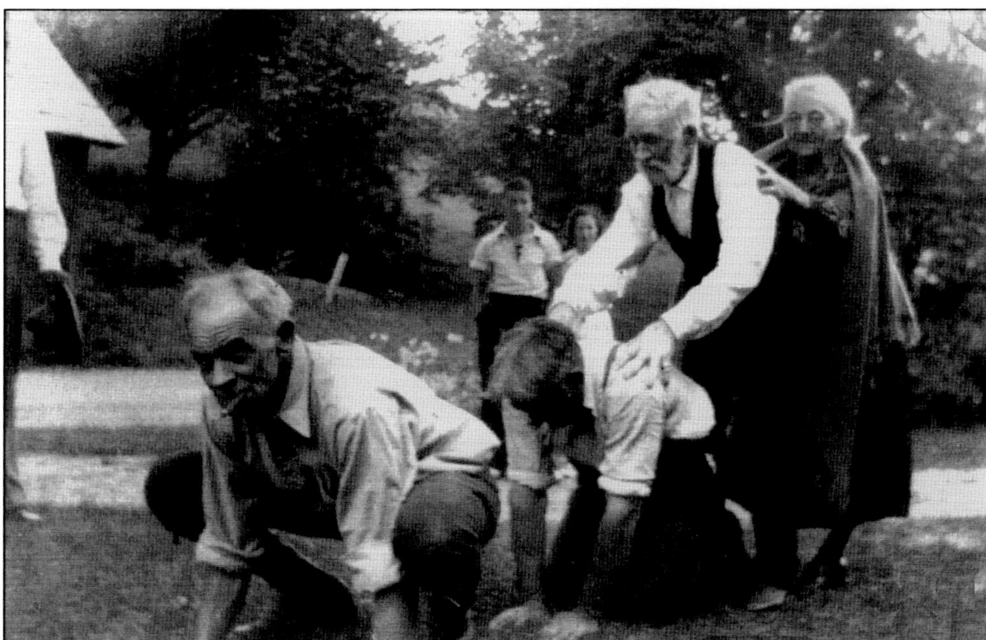

You are never so old as you look, because inside every aged soul lurks a youngster eager to get out, as evidenced by this lively but obviously simulated game of leapfrog enjoyed by Will and Myra Carleton (standing on right) at their 60th wedding anniversary celebration, with their sons, Ira (left) and Frank. (Courtesy of Warren Library.)

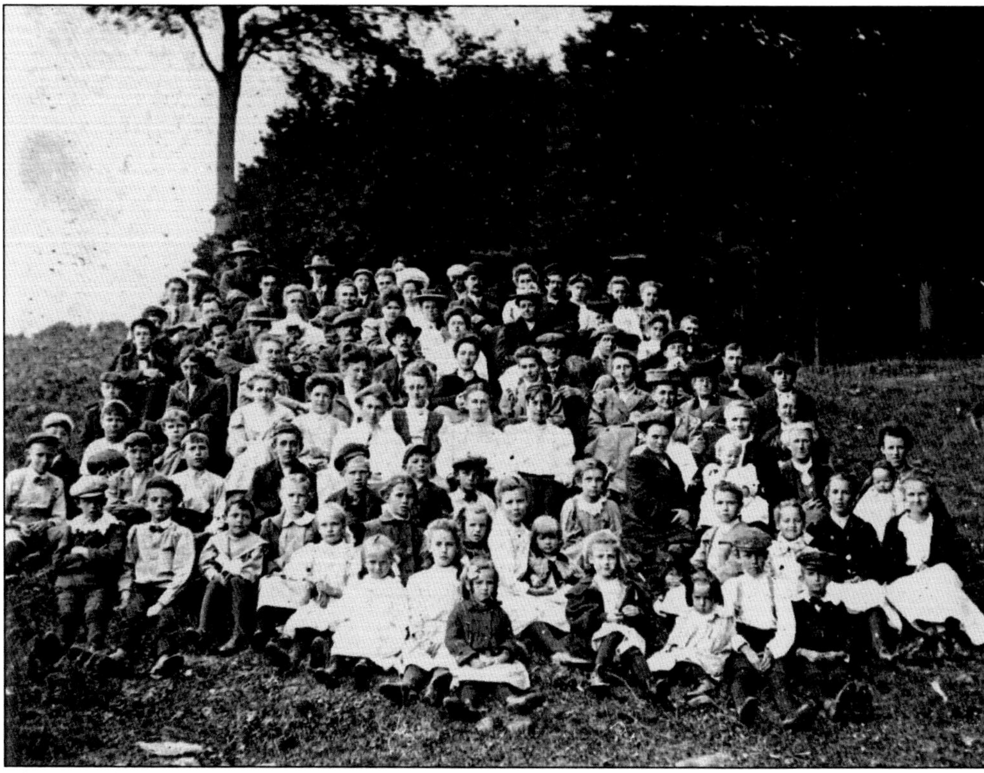

The size of the crowd at this Sunday school picnic in Warren provides an indication of the influence of the Bible and its Scriptures on the daily lives of local citizens. Almost every home had a Bible in the parlor, and the study of and reverence for Scripture was practiced daily. (Courtesy of Warren Library.)

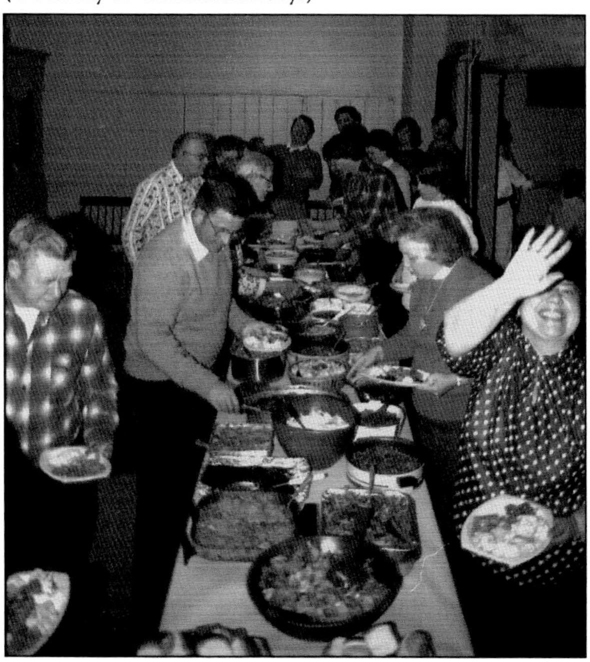

A typical town supper brings Vermont residents together on any occasion deemed necessary, but especially at harvest time. This particular gathering, however, was held during the celebration of the 150th anniversary of the town hall in Moretown in 1984. (Courtesy of Moretown Historical Society.)

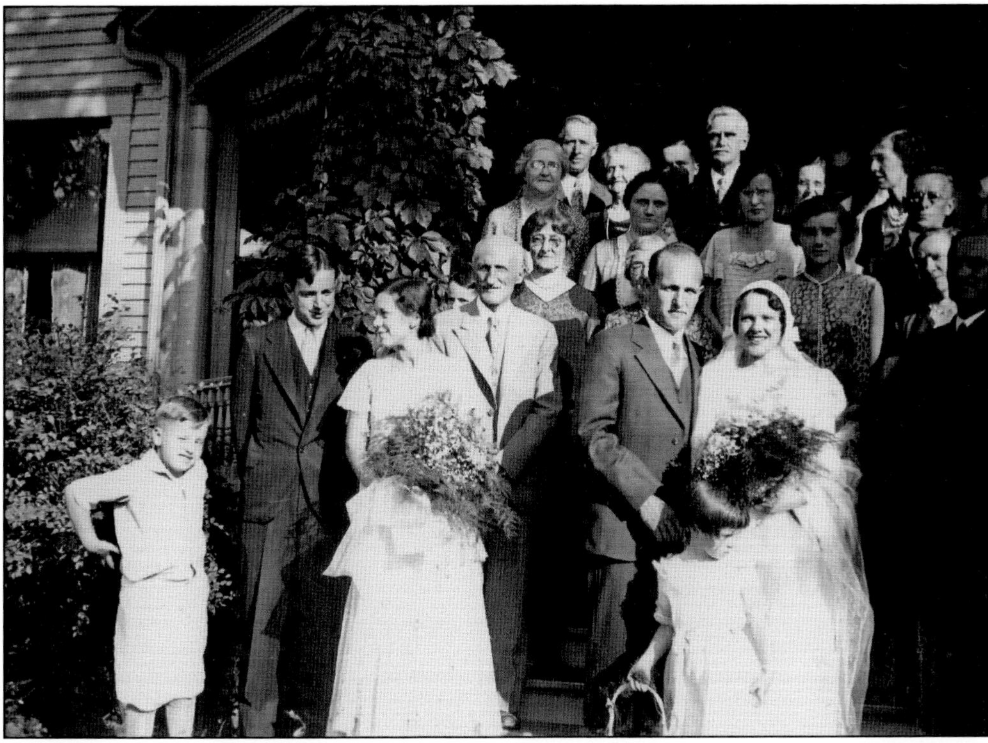

At Big House, the Ward family's Moretown mansion, the wedding of local residents Marian Lena Ward and Roland Tweedie (couple on right) was a major social event. (Courtesy of Moretown Historical Society.)

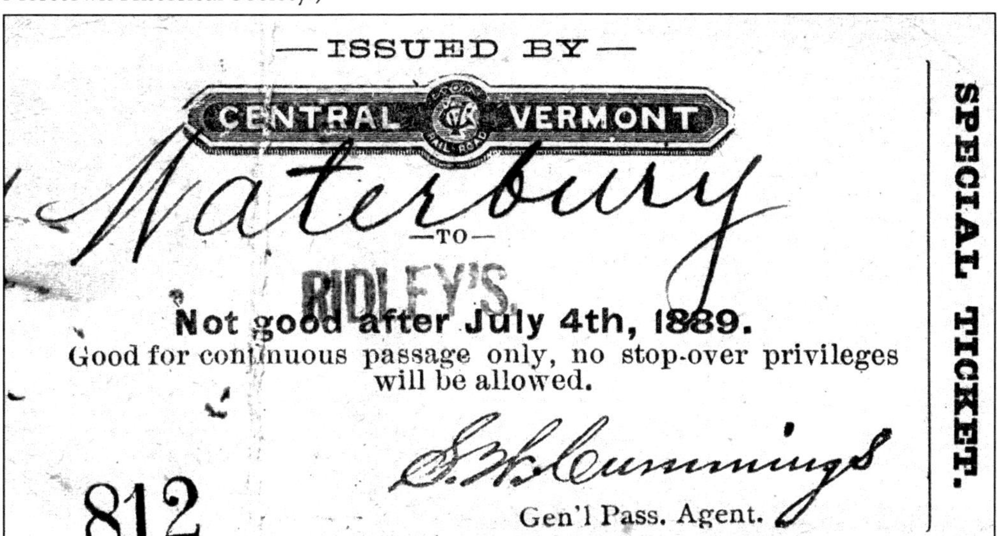

This train ticket to Waterbury expired in 1889. It may have been used by a tourist anxious to ride to near the top of Camel's Hump in Sam Ridley's stagecoach, which met travelers at the no-longer existing Duxbury Station, and then drove up the Carriage Road to a point three miles from the summit. Passengers rode the last leg of the trip on the back of the "Hump Horse" on the bridlepath to the Summit House. The building burned in 1877. (Courtesy of Alice DeLong.)

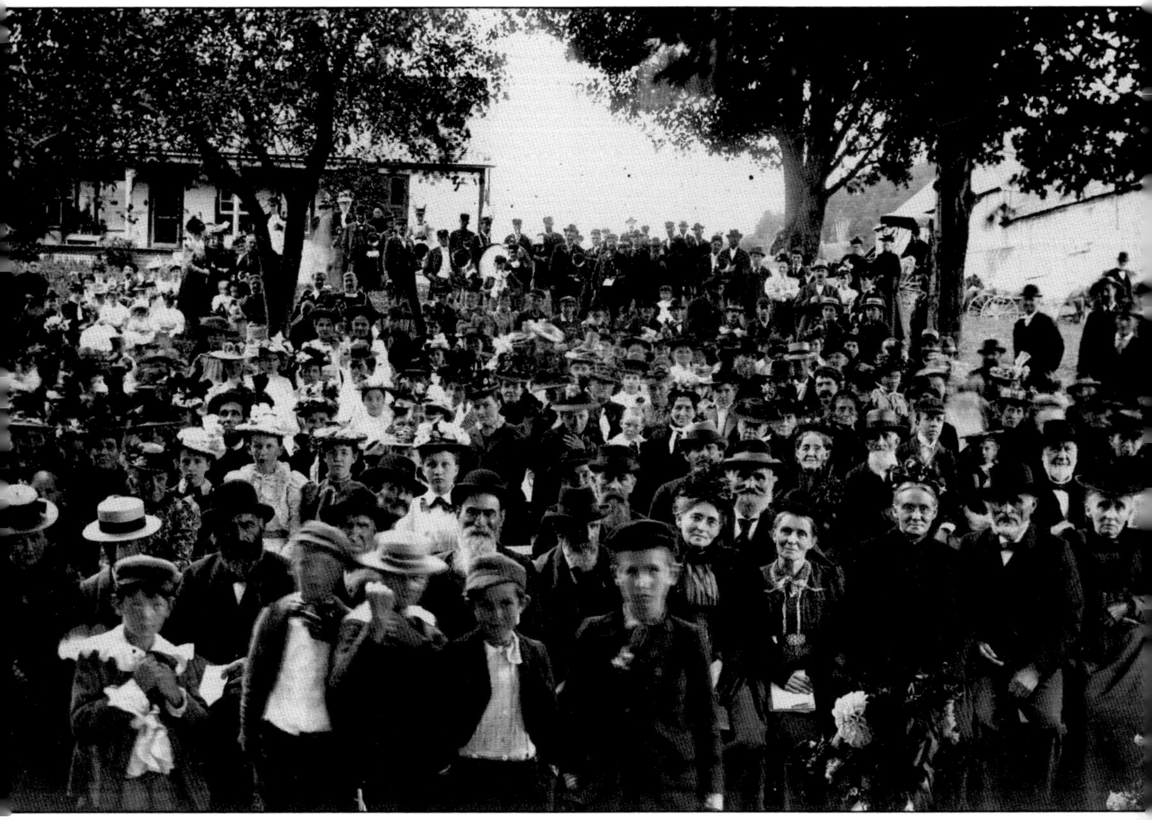

Conditions were fairly prosperous in Fayston in 1898 when the town's centennial celebration—at which this photograph was made—was held at the John Thompson Farm. During that decade, there were seven lumbermills and a cooper shop in town, all powered by water, mostly along the Shepard and Mill Brooks. Workers often stayed overnight at the mills in camps that were set up there. Over the years, Fayston's population shifted according to the economic climate. Someone wrote that the population increase in Fayston of more than 100 persons between 1850 and 1860 was due to unemployed persons, many of them Irish railroad workers who sought brighter lives in Fayston. The 1860 census showed that one-third of the heads of households in Fayston traced Irish roots. In addition to the lumbermills, Fayston also had gristmills and mills that made cider, clapboard, clothespins, and butter tubs. (Courtesy of Fayston Historical Society.)

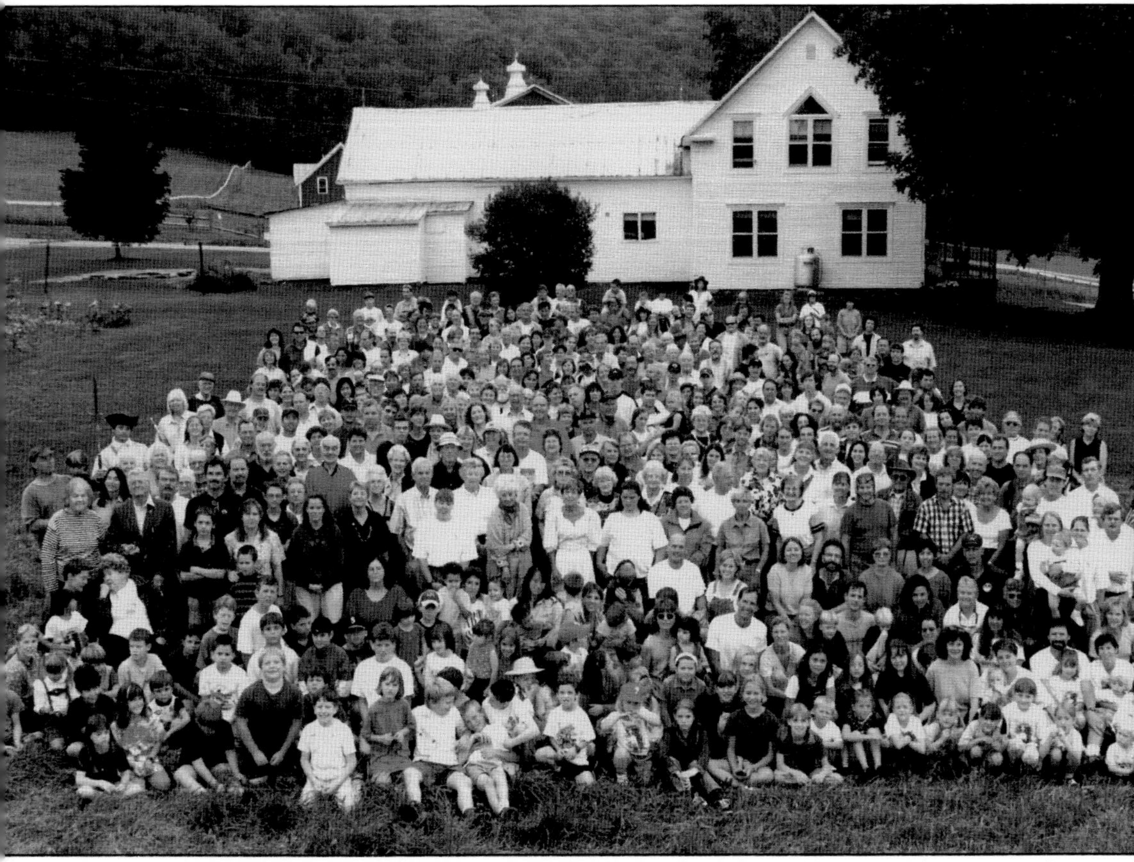

Can anyone guess how many of the Fayston residents seen here during the town's bicentennial in 1998 were descended from the folks pictured one hundred years prior? Probably few if any. The town's makeup today may be credited to the influx of owners of second homes and other "flatlanders" who sought a better way of life in rural Vermont. It is also a good guess that they found that better life. The arrival of electricity to the town in 1946 and the startup of the Mad River Glen ski resort in 1948, followed by Sugarbush 10 years later, and Glen Ellen in 1963, transformed Fayston from basically a logging and farming community to one centered on recreation. However, the town's population sagged to 158 persons by 1960. Though still sparsely settled by any standards, Fayston's population has since boomed by comparison to 1,142 by 2000. (Courtesy of Fayston Historical Society.)

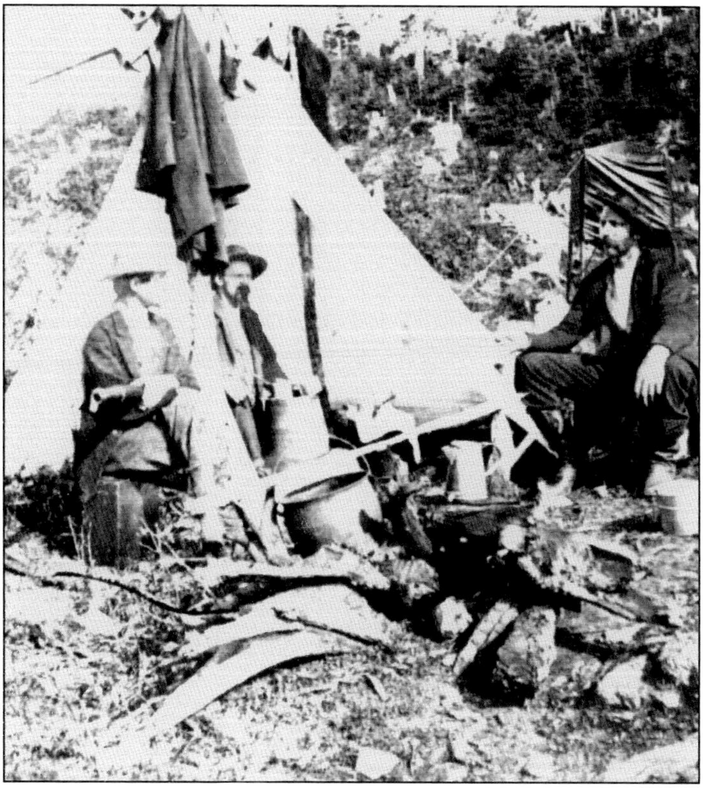

Camping on Camel's Hump has been popular for hikers before and since the Long Trail was laid down over its summit. The mountain has the distinction of being the highest undeveloped mountain in Vermont. The Vermont quarter, the fourth quarter in the 2001 series issued by the U.S. Mint, features Camel's Hump Mountain with an image of maple trees and sap buckets in the foreground. (Courtesy of Alice DeLong.)

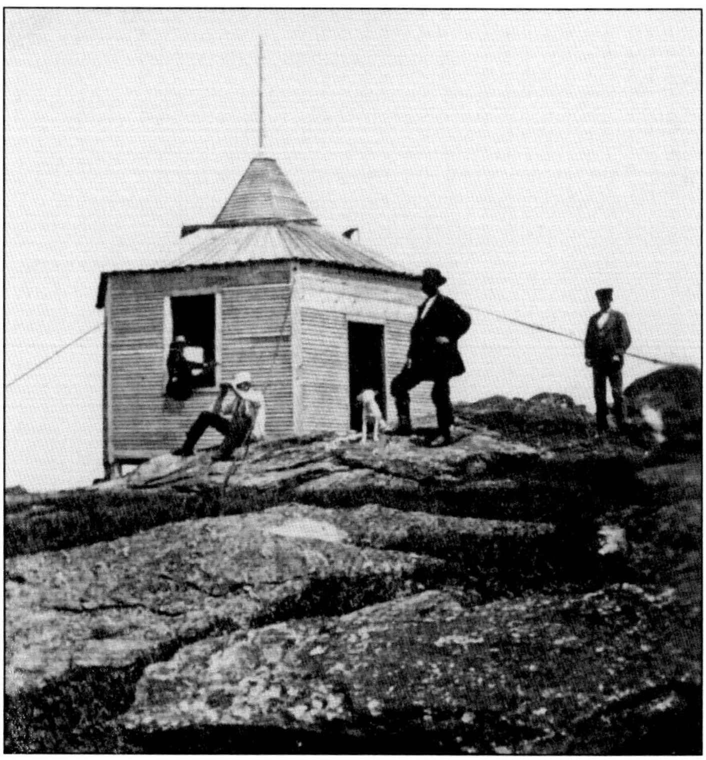

Pictured in the late 1800s, this observation tower at Camel's Hump is no longer present. Visible are cables holding the structure fast against high winds. Also gone from the mountain is another 19th-century fixture: the Summit House, a small hostel that hosted adventure seekers who either hiked or rode by horseback up the mountain. (Courtesy of Alice DeLong.)

As early as 1910, the Green Mountain Club began protecting the Long Trail, which marks the western boundary of the Mad River Valley. (Courtesy of Warren Library.)

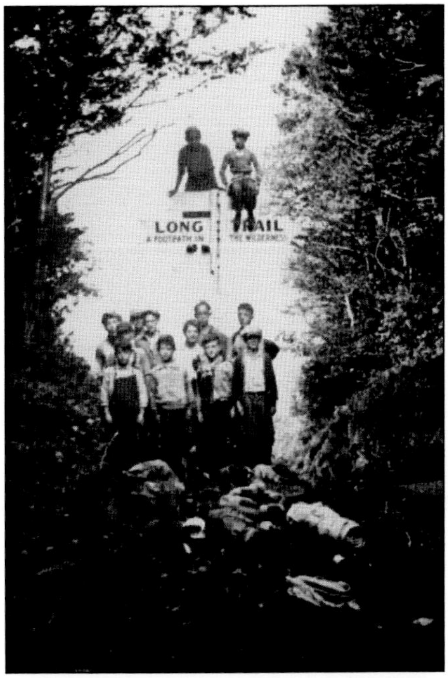

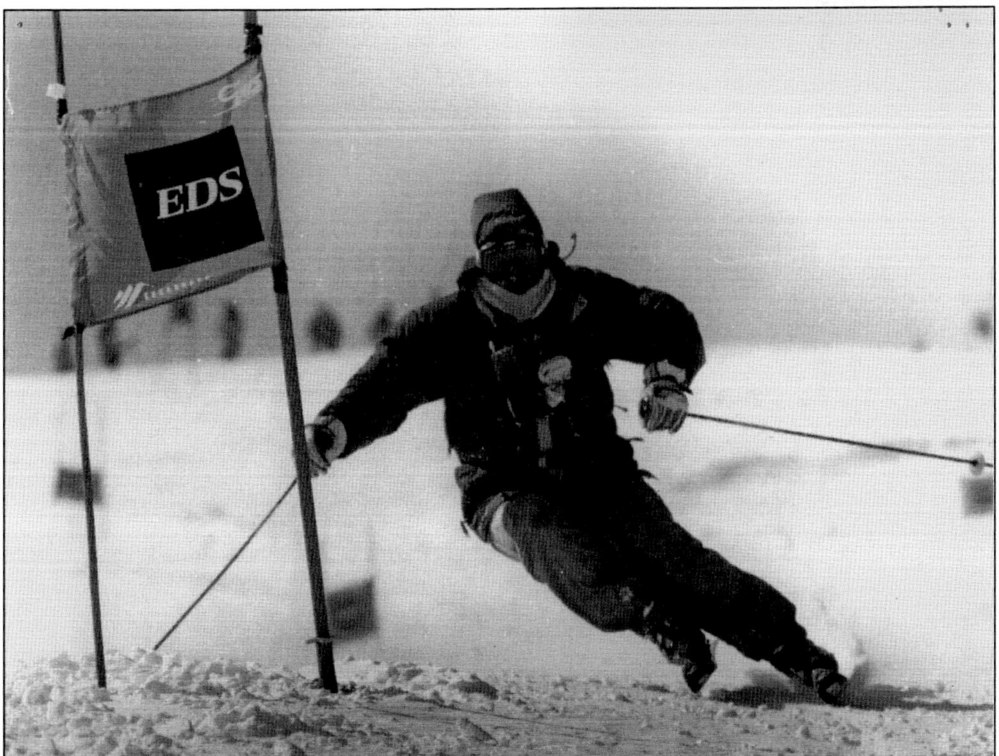

Al Hobart, founder of the Green Mountain Valley School, is shown as a front-runner in a race at Sugarbush. The GMVS is a ski racing academy with a double-edged creed of strict academics combined with the development of elite young ski racers. (Courtesy of Green Mountain Valley School.)

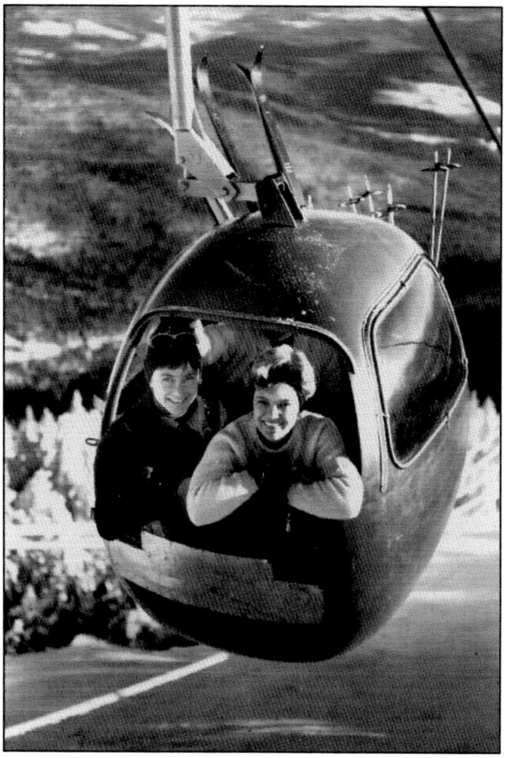

The new gondola installed at Sugarbush Resort when it opened in 1958 might as well have been designed by Fabergé. The three-person, weather-protected egg, which traveled 9,300 feet up a vertical rise of 2,400 feet, helped launch skiing from a simplistic cow pasture and towrope image to that of a playland for the rich and famous. (Courtesy of Sugarbush Resort.)

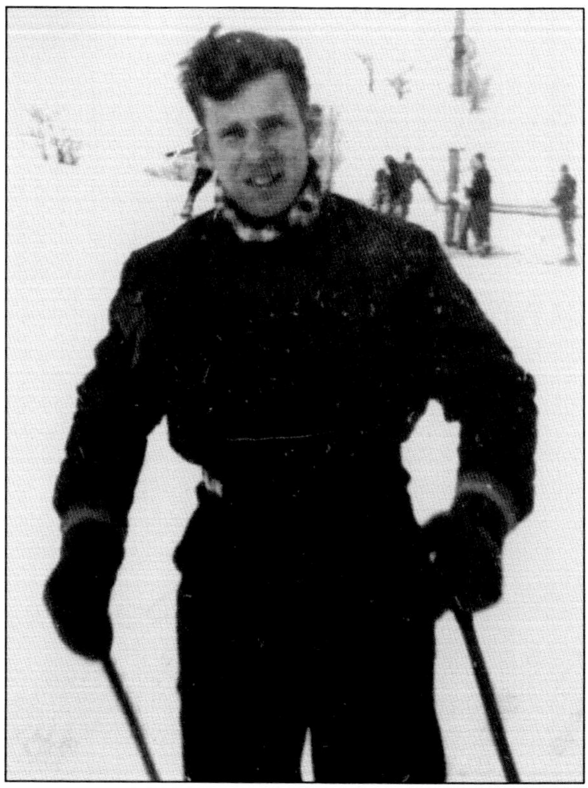

Willis Bragg stands at the Warren Outing Club ski tow, the first tow in the valley, at the Austin Farm on present-day Route 100. It was one of many backyard operations in Vermont that prefaced the rise of skiing into a recreational industry that transformed the Mad River Valley economy. (Courtesy of Katherine Hartshorn.)

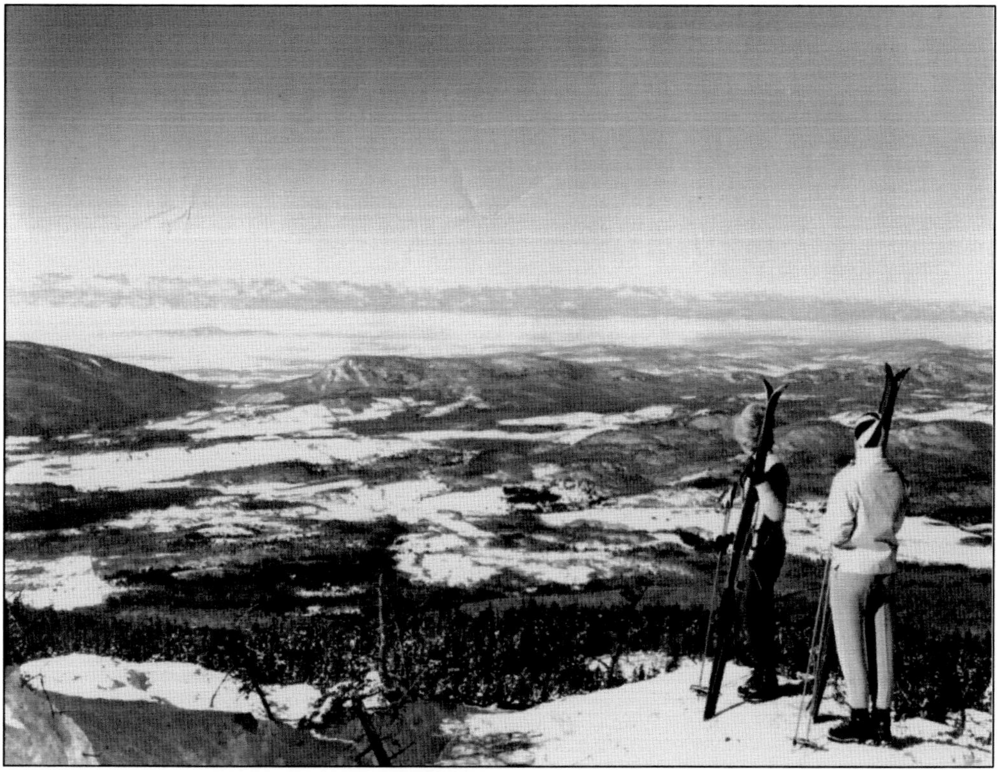

Some things never change. From the top of the Panorama Trail at Sugarbush's Mount Ellen, the view west is of the Adirondacks and Whiteface Mountain, and in between, Lake Champlain and the rolling fields and farms of its valley. (Courtesy of Sugarbush Resort.)

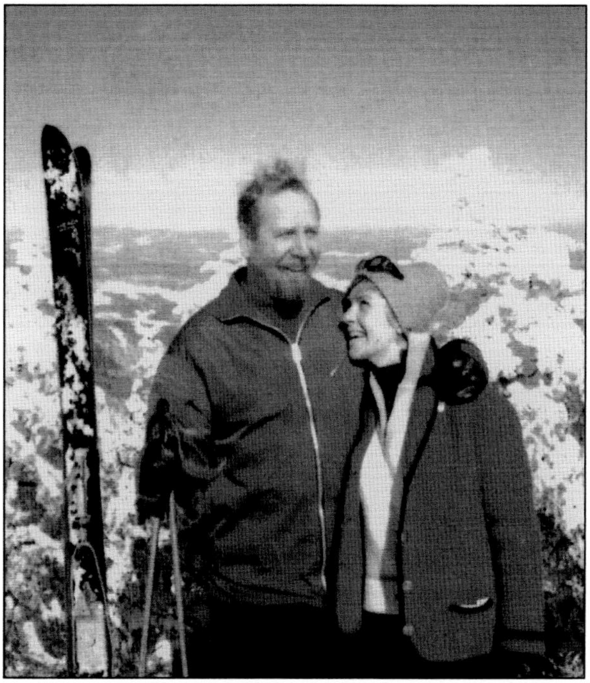

Skitch Henderson, shown atop Sugarbush with his wife, Ruth, was an omnipresent bandleader and a TV personality perhaps best known for his *Tonight Show* run with Steve Allen and Johnny Carson. Henderson helped put Sugarbush at the forefront of swank winter resorts by leading a contingent of TV and movie stars to the Vermont resort in the 1960s. (Courtesy of Sugarbush Resort.)

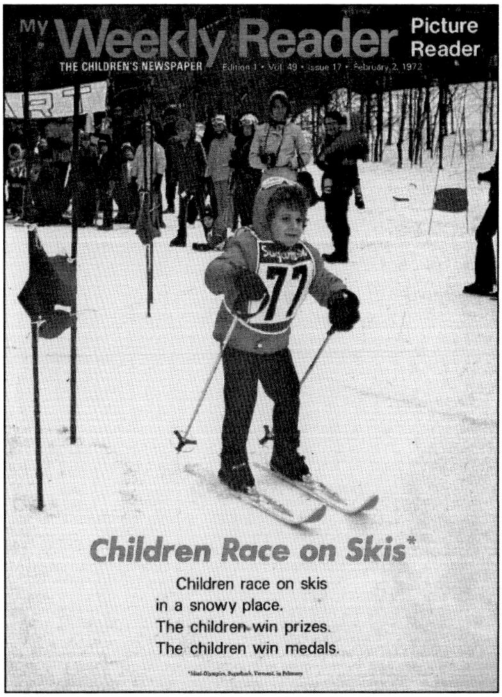

My Weekly Reader Picture Reader
THE CHILDREN'S NEWSPAPER Edition 1 • Vol. 49 • Issue 17 • February 2, 1972

Children Race on Skis*

Children race on skis
in a snowy place.
The children win prizes.
The children win medals.

Shown here is a 1972 issue of *My Weekly Reader* magazine for children that featured a story on the Sugarbush Ski School for kids. Founded by Damon and Sarah Gadd, along with their friend Jack Murphy, Sugarbush was sold in 1977 to Roy Cohen, who sold it to ARA Services of Philadelphia in 1983. Subsequent owners have been Claniel Enterprises and the American Skiing Company. The resort is presently owned by Summit Venture, a locally held company owned by Adam Greshin, Win Smith, and Bob Ackland. (Courtesy of Sugarbush Resort.)

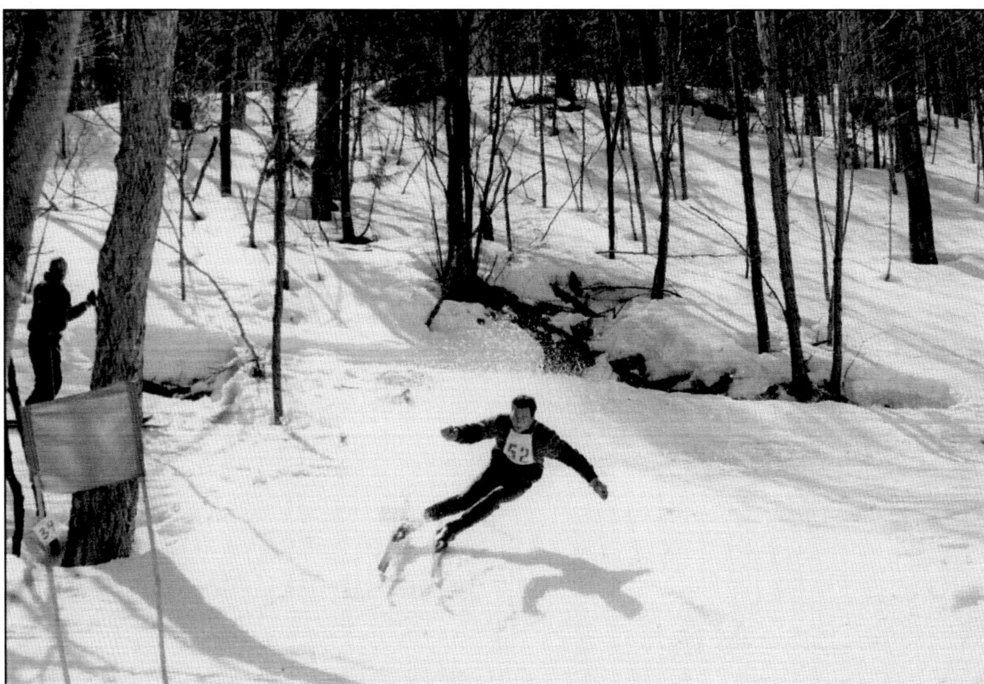

Jean Guy Brunet masters the World Cup New England Kandahar race held at Mad River Glen on March 25, 1956. The race is named for the Kandahar Ski Club, which had derived its name from the city of Kandahar in Afghanistan. British forces, led by Lord Roberts, fought over that city several times in the 19th century. Roberts later became an officer of a ski club named after Kandahar. (Courtesy of Mad River Glen.)

Sewall Williams owned the Ulla Lodge, which rented accommodations to skiers. Sewall and is wife, Ann, converted the lodge from an old farmhouse that occupied the grounds of the present-day Hyde Away Inn on Route 17. (Courtesy of Mad River Glen.)

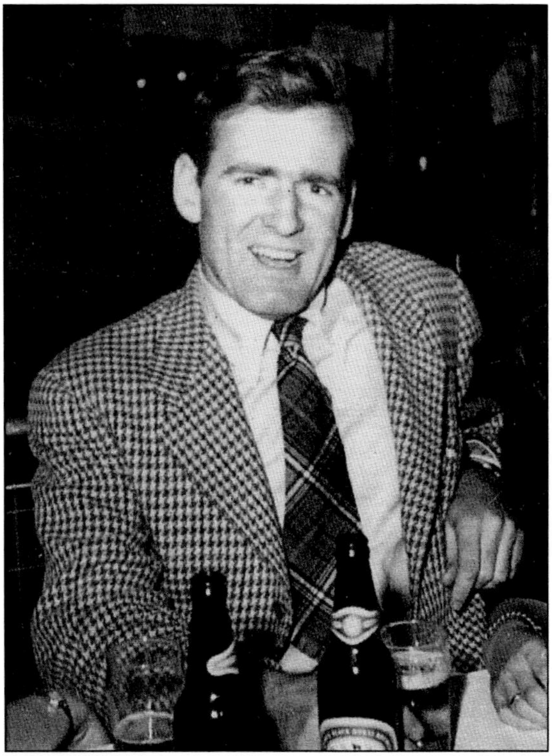

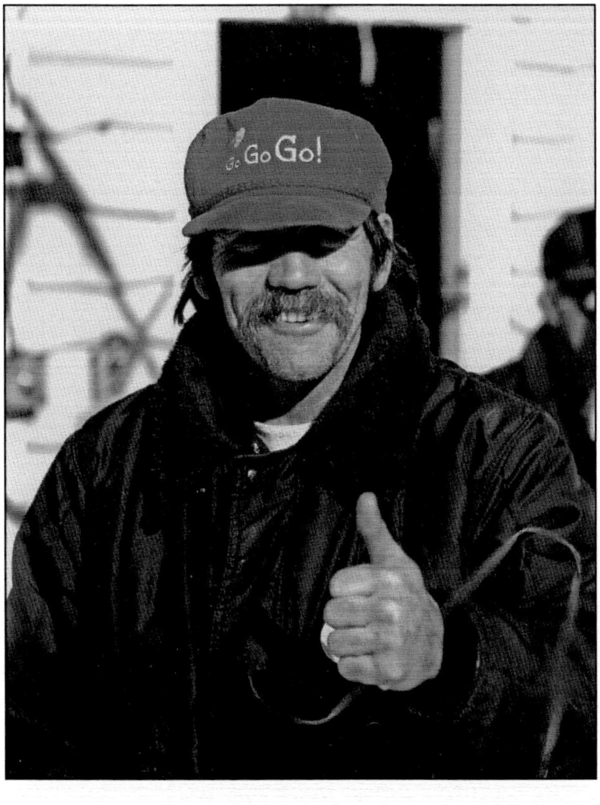

The late Bill Lawrence, for many years the operator of the Mad River Single Chair, believed that sending skiers to the summit required the heartiest of send-offs. It is printed on his cap. (Courtesy of Mad River Glen.)

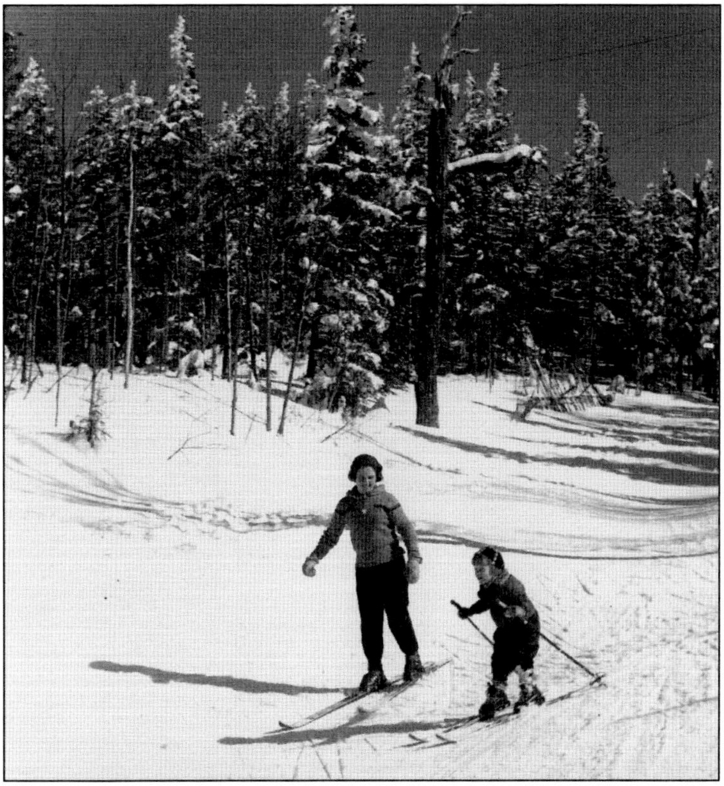

Mad River Glen's worldwide reputation is that of a challenging, ungroomed mountain, but to its longtime local devotees it is a part of their family, many of whom are now teaching third- and fourth-generation skiers to master its gnarly slopes. Pictured in 1957 are Marilyn Hilly and daughter Meg, who was only three years old at the time. (Courtesy of Mad River Glen.)

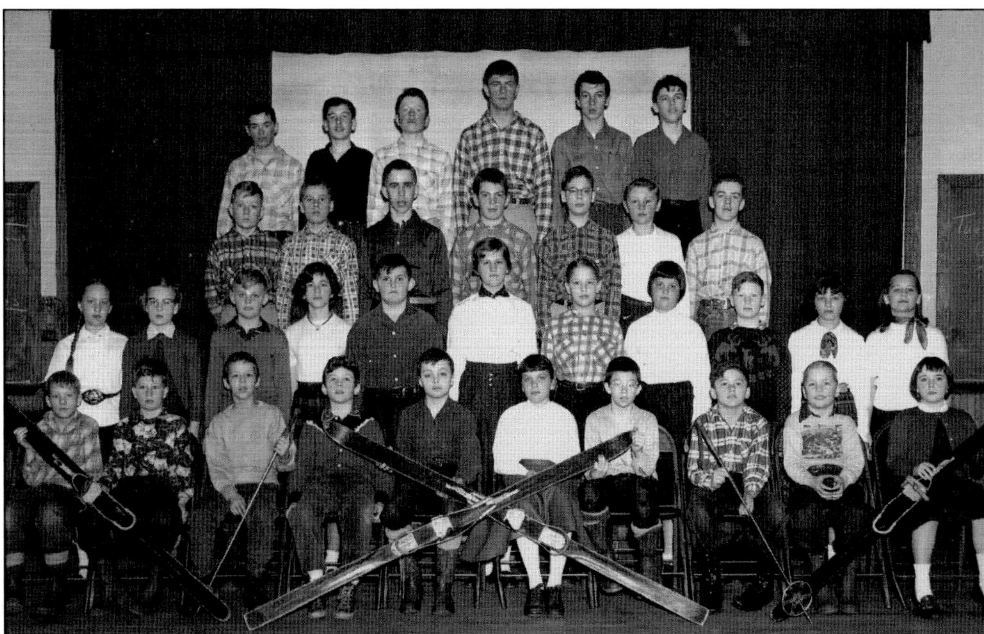

Waitsfield School Ski Club is shown here. By the 1950s, skiing had become part of the after-school activities of schools all over Vermont. Many Vermont resorts have adopted free skiing programs for fourth-graders. (Courtesy of Stephen Joslin.)